Implementing the IEEE Software Engineering Standards

SAMS

Implementing the IEEE Software Engineering Standards

Michael Schmidt

SAMS

201 West 103rd Street
Indianapolis, Indiana 46290

Trademarks

Warning and Disclaimer

Associate Publisher
Michael Stephens

Acquisitions Editor
Steve Anglin

Development Editors
Laura N. Williams
Heather Goodell

Managing Editor
Matt Purcell

Project Editor
Dawn Pearson

Copy Editor
Mary Ellen Stephenson

Indexer
Sheila Schroeder

Proofreader
Katherin Bidwell

Technical Reviewers
Charles Ashbacher
Tathagat Varma

Team Coordinator
Pamalee Nelson

Interior Designer
Karen Ruggles

Cover Designer
Alan Clements

IEEE Standards Trademarks & Disclaimers

The IEEE believes the information in this publication is accurate as of its publication date; such information is subject to change without notice. The IEEE is not responsible for any inadvertent errors.

IEEE Standards Copyright Information

The IEEE Standards referenced in this book are copyrighted by the Institute of Electrical and Electronics Engineers, Inc. All rights reserved.

IEEE Standards Information Network Endorsement Disclaimer

The IEEE Standards Information Network (IEEE-SIN) endorsement in this publication does not render this publication a consensus document. Information contained in this and other works has bee obtained from sources believed to be reliable and reviewed by credible members of IEEE Technical Societies, Standards Committees and/or Working Groups and/or relevant technical organizations. Neither the IEEE nor its authors guarantee the accuracy or completeness of any information published herein and, neither the IEEE nor its volunteers, members and authors shall be responsible for any errors, omissions or damages arising out of use of this information.

Likewise, while the IEEE and its volunteers and members believe that the information and guidance given in this work serve as an enhancement to users, all parties must rely upon their own skill and judgment when making use of it. Neither the IEEE nor its volunteers or members assume any liability to anyone for any loss or damage caused by any error or omission in the work, whether such error or omission is the result of negligence or any other cause. Any and all such liability is disclaimed.

By endorsing this publication, it should be understood that the IEEE and its volunteers and members are supplying information through this publication, not attempting to render engineering or other professional services. If such services are required, the assistance of an appropriate professional should be sought. The IEEE is not responsible for the statements and/or opinions advanced in this publication.

IEEE Review Policy

The information contained in IEEE-SIN publications, and others publications endorsed by the IEEE-SIN, is reviewed and evaluated by peer reviewers of relevant IEEE Technical Societies, Standards Committees and/or Working Groups and/or relevant technical organizations. The publisher addressed all of the reviewer's comments to the satisfaction of both the IEEE-SIN and those who served as peer reviewers for this document.

The quality of the presentation of information contained in this publication reflects not only the obvious efforts of the authors, but also the work of these peer reviewers. The IEEE-SIN acknowledges with appreciation their dedication and contribution of time and effort on behalf of the IEEE.

To order IEEE publications, call 1-800-678-IEEE or, visit our web site at www.ieee.org.

To order The IEEE Standards referenced herein, call 1-800-678-IEEE or, visit the IEEE Standards web site at www.standards.ieee.org.

 Endorsed by The IEEE Standards Information Network

Implementing the IEEE Software Engineering Standards' by Michael Schmidt is recognized by the Software Engineering Standards Committee of the IEEE Computer Society as a useful guide for software practitioners applying software engineering standards.

Dedication

To my family:

My parents, Jürgen and Hanna

My wife, Elizabeth

My children, Emily, Evan, and Erica

Acknowledgments

I would like to thank the countless IEEE members who contributed to and reviewed the standards collection over the years. Without their efforts we would have no standards.

I would also like to thank my editors, Laura Williams, for encouraging me, and putting up with me, and Heather Goodell, for her help in completing the project.

Special thanks to Jim Moore, who provided invaluable feedback on the contents of the book. I take credit for any remaining rough spots.

About the Author

Michael Schmidt was born in Cologne, Germany in 1959. His father, Jürgen Schmidt, a well-known mathematician, moved the family to the United States in 1967 on a Fulbright-Hays teaching fellowship. Mike graduated from the Kinkaid School in Houston, Texas, in 1977; received a B.A. in Mathematics from the University of California at Berkeley in 1980; and a M.A. in Mathematics from the University of Washington at Seattle in 1981. In 1980, as a student intern, Mike worked as a programmer on the cyclotron control system at Lawrence Berkeley Laboratories. After receiving his degree at UW, Mike took a position as a software engineer at Bi-M Instruments, a start-up company in Houston developing ballast control systems for offshore oil rigs. In 1981, Mike was recruited by Varian Associates in Palo Alto to work on the software for a next-generation linear accelerator for oncology care. At Varian, Mike was promoted to project engineer, leading the team for the control system software. In 1986, Mike was recruited to another start-up company, TransImage Corporation in Menlo Park, as a staff software engineer to develop a sophisticated optical-character-recognition system. In 1987, Mike joined Siemens Medical Systems, again as a project engineer to head the software team developing a next-generation control system for a linear accelerator for oncology care. Mike was promoted to manager of the software engineering department at Siemens Medical Systems, Oncology Care Systems, with responsibility for all software development in five major product areas. In 1994, Mike started Software Engineering Services, Inc., a software consulting business specializing in fixed-price projects for software in the medical device, pharmaceutical, and biotechnology industries, and other industries for which software plays a safety-critical role. SES has a long list of well-known clients in these industries, and has developed and validated software for numerous sophisticated applications. Mike also has been teaching computer science classes at University of California Berkeley Extension, and Diablo Valley College, including C++ programming, and classes on the IEEE Software Engineering Standards. In 2000, Mike joined Zeiss Humphrey Systems, a leading manufacturer of ophthalmic instruments, as the software engineering manager. Mike is an IEEE member.

About the Technical Reviewers

Charles Ashbacher has been programming for nearly 20 years, which makes him experienced and well-rounded rather than old and cynical. He is co-editor of *Journal of Recreational Mathematics* and a regular contributor to *Journal of Object-Oriented Programming*. Charles teaches computing at all levels: corporate training, college, and community education and is president and CEO of Charles Ashbacher Technologies (http://www.ashbacher.com). His background also includes stints writing commercial code and software to conduct scientific research.

Tathagat Varma received an M.Sc. Computer Science (Software) degree from J.K Institute of Applied Physics and Technology, University of Allahabad, India in 1990. He then worked with the Defence Research and Development Organization, Government of India, as a computer scientist until 1995. During this tenure, he also participated in the XIII Indian Scientific Expedition to Antarctica, where he stayed for 16 months! In August 1995, he joined Siemens Communication Software, Bangalore, where he worked in telecommunication software development for over a year. Since December 1996, he has worked with Philips Software Centre, Bangalore. Philips Software Centre is the software arm of the Royal Philips Electronics, The Netherlands. In the last three years with Philips, he has worked with Medical Systems and as SPI and QA Manager. Currently, he is managing a project that involves development of embedded software for digital set-top boxes. He is formally trained in CMM, ISO Tick-IT, and Philips Assessment Method. He is also an active reviewer for the *IEEE Software* magazine.

Table of Contents

Tell Us What You Think!

As the reader of this book, *you* are our most important critic and commentator. We value your opinion and want to know what we're doing right, what we could do better, what areas you'd like to see us publish in, and any other words of wisdom you're willing to pass our way.

As an Associate Publisher for Sams, I welcome your comments. You can fax, email, or write me directly to let me know what you did or didn't like about this book—as well as what we can do to make our books stronger.

Please note that I cannot help you with technical problems related to the topic of this book, and that because of the high volume of mail I receive, I might not be able to reply to every message.

When you write, please be sure to include this book's title and author as well as your name and phone or fax number. I will carefully review your comments and share them with the author and editors who worked on the book.

Fax: (317) 581-4770

Email: networking_sams@macmillianusa.com

Mail: *Michael Stephens*
          Sams Publishing
          201 West 103rd Street
          Indianapolis, IN 46290 USA

Introduction

Purpose

The Institute of Electrical and Electronics Engineers (IEEE) Software Engineering Standards provide a comprehensive set of standards for developing and validating software. The standards are a fantastic resource, representing countless man-years of effort. There is an ongoing program to enhance and extend the standards (approximately five new standards are developed each year). Among the most highly regarded software engineering standards available today, the IEEE standards are widely recognized in regulated industries such as the medical device industry. Proper use of the standards can help organizations improve their software development and validation process, and help implement an effective software quality system.

Unfortunately, individuals or organizations often find it difficult to get started applying the IEEE standards, for three reasons:

- The collection consists of a large number of standards.
- Each standard contains detailed and substantial information.
- The IEEE introduction and the top-level standard (IEEE/EIA 12207.0) are themselves complex and do not provide tutorial information on adopting the processes and practices in a graduated fashion.

This book is intended to help overcome these hurdles.

Implementing the IEEE Software Engineering Standards will allow individuals to learn the IEEE software engineering standards much faster and with fewer missteps. For an organization phasing in use of the standards, this book will provide an excellent road map. The intended audience includes

- Software engineering managers and engineers
- Software quality assurance managers and engineers
- Project managers

Implementing the IEEE Software Engineering Standards was written for the reader who has a working knowledge of software development and validation, at least from an informal environment. Previous experience with the IEEE Software Engineering Standards is not required to understand the material.

1

Scope

Not all the standards are discussed in the book. We will focus on the most important principles in the IEEE Software Engineering Standards collection, to show the easiest way to phase in the standards. Software process improvements should be introduced incrementally, and use of the entire IEEE standards collection cannot be realistically achieved all at once.

The standards analyzed provide the most initial benefit to the user. Core standards for such critical activities as specifying software requirements, documenting software testing, and performing software verification and validation activities are presented in detail.

Benefits resulting from use of the standards are described, to help readers motivate others in their organization. Common pitfalls that can jeopardize the successful implementation of the standards are discussed. Issues relating to harmonizing use of the standards with current industry software development practices are explored, because the standards should not be a hindrance to efficiency.

This book does not provide a comparative analysis of the IEEE Software Engineering Standards relative to other national or international standards for the same subject. Several scholarly books already serve this purpose nicely.

No attempt is made to establish a mapping between the IEEE Software Engineering Standards and specific industry regulations—such as the U.S. Quality Systems Regulations for medical device manufacturers—or to quality standards—such as the ISO-9000 standards. Application of the IEEE standards can be an extremely effective means for achieving compliance with such regulations and quality standards. But, many factors, such as the size of the organization and the inherent risks associated with the software, determine what is required for a reasonable and prudent software process model. Use of the IEEE standards to achieve compliance in specific industries should be evaluated individually for each organization.

This book does not contain a copy of any of the standards discussed. The most recent edition of the IEEE Software Engineering Standards can be purchased directly from IEEE:

IEEE Customer Service

445 Hoes Lane, PO Box 1331

Piscataway NJ 08855-1331 USA

1.800.701.4333 (in the U.S. and Canada)

1.732.981.0060 (outside of the U.S. and Canada)

`customer.service@ieee.org`

In addition, IEEE provides the Software Engineering Standards electronically via the Web through IEEE Standards On-Line Subscriptions. The Web site at http://standards.ieee.org/catalog/olis provides details on this service.

Organization of *Implementing the IEEE Software Engineering Standards*

Chapter 1, "Benefits of Software Engineering Standards," is not only intended to motivate the reader to implement the standards, but also to help the reader justify his use in his own organization. Software process improvements commonly meet resistance; overcoming it with education and other positive techniques is essential.

Chapter 2, "Guidelines for Software Process Improvements," provides recommendations based on years of the author's experience in dealing with many different organizations attempting process improvements, drawing on both successes and failures.

Chapter 3, "An Overview of the IEEE Software Engineering Standards," describes the standards as a whole, including the relationship of specific standards to each other. This chapter is intended to complement the introductory sections of the most recent edition of the IEEE standards, which contain a description of fundamental principles and a framework for the standards. Although the IEEE introduction is excellent in its generality, it is not optimized for an organization attempting its first use of the standards. This chapter provides an overview of the IEEE standards for someone looking at them for the first time.

Chapter 4, " Software Life Cycle Processes," provides a framework for the sequence of activities to be performed for software projects. This chapter describes IEEE/EIA 12207.0, which represents the top-level standard in the IEEE collection. This chapter also describes different *software life cycle models (SLCMs)*, relative to which individual projects are planned.

Chapter 5, "Work Product Standards," presents key standards for preparing important work products, such as documents and source code, during the software life cycle. Only the most important such standards, corresponding to deliverables required in *any* software project, are discussed. These standards are the easiest ones to understand, because they do not presuppose any great understanding of the software development and validation process. The impatient reader might want to proceed directly to Chapter 6 for a quick start.

Chapter 6, "Process Standards," presents fundamental standards that describe activities performed as part of the software life cycle. In some cases, these standards also describe documents, but these represent plans for conducting activities. Again, only the most important process standards, corresponding to activities expected in *any* software project, are discussed. Individuals who don't have personal experience with several substantial software projects often find process standards difficult to understand. Even then, it can be difficult to reconcile personal experience inside of your organization with the terminology of the IEEE standards. Chapter 6 attempts to make understanding the fundamental process standards as easy as possible.

Chapter 7, "Practical Lessons," finishes the book by discussing the author's experiences over the years with use of the IEEE standards in industry. This chapter discusses pitfalls as well as positive experiences, to help you get started. Industry practices are mainly oriented toward maximizing productivity, and minimizing cost and schedule. It is the author's opinion that best rapid software development practices can be reconciled with best software quality practices using the IEEE Software Engineering Standards.

CHAPTER 1

Benefits of Software Engineering Standards

Software engineering standards define the process by which software is developed and validated within an organization. Not only do the standards specify which plans, specifications, reports, and other documents shall be created during a software project, they also specify how such documents shall be evaluated and approved. The standards must span a wide range of topics, including software project management, requirements analysis, design, verification and validation, testing, configuration management, and other important aspects of software engineering.

The purpose of this chapter is twofold:

- To convince the reader that the establishment of software engineering standards provides sufficient benefits to be worth implementing

- To provide the already convinced reader with additional arguments to use for persuading the rest of his organization to adopt such standards

Benefits of implementing software engineering standards include

Increasing software quality. Use of standards helps achieve greater conformance to software requirements, reduce the number of software defects, mitigate risks associated with the software, and decrease software maintenance costs.

Reducing project cost and schedule. Use of standards provides a framework for systematic, incremental software process improvements, and helps reduce the number of defects introduced during early project phases. This reduces the cost and schedule of the testing, installation, and maintenance phases.

Achieving compliance. Use of standards helps satisfy governmental regulations and industry quality standards as they relate to software, and is essential for passing audits and achieving certification. The need to achieve compliance is a hard business reality for companies in a number of industries.

Improving manageability of software projects. Use of standards provides enhanced accuracy of project planning, detailed means of tracking projects, early measures of software quality, and improved repeatability of success stories.

Major benefits are explored in more detail later in the chapter.

Software Quality

Software engineering standards, if sufficiently comprehensive and if properly enforced, establish a *quality system*, a systematic approach to ensuring software *quality*, which is defined by IEEE Std. 610-1990 as:

(1) The degree to which a system, component, or process meets specified requirements.

(2) The degree to which a system, component, or process meets customer or user needs or expectations.

A quality system should consist of more than just testing. A modern, comprehensive approach requires a systematic process for the entire software life cycle. Quality cannot be tested into software any more effectively than quality can be inspected into finished manufactured goods. Testing of complex software systems can never be exhaustive, and a large number of software defects identified during testing, even if corrected, invariably imply that many additional software defects have not yet been discovered.

The relative importance of software quality depends on the application. However, quality is important for any software product. Improving software quality has business advantages for the following reasons:

Increased sales volume. Customer satisfaction, which can only be expected if the software meets the customers' needs and expectations, should lead directly to increased sales.

Decreased support costs. If the number of software defects can be reduced, costs associated with software installation, maintenance, service, and support can be decreased.

Reduced liability. In some applications software defects can potentially lead to injury or death, or result in damage to property or equipment. In these cases, businesses face significant liability issues. Assuring software quality becomes essential for mitigating such risks.

Software reuse. If of sufficient quality to be reused, software components can represent a significant organizational asset. Software reuse can improve the time to market for later projects, an important consideration for fast cycle time projects such as Internet applications.

Software engineering standards should not remain frozen indefinitely. They should be reevaluated periodically for possible software process improvements. Data should be collected to provide some measure of the software quality achieved in previous software projects. Metrics such as the number of defects identified during testing and the number of problem reports received from users may be used for this purpose. Such information should be carefully analyzed to identify any weaknesses in the process model and to target incremental improvements to the quality system.

Taming Project Cost and Schedule

Software projects are notorious for cost and schedule overruns. Historically, many companies with excellent track records in developing hardware products have experienced software project failures of gargantuan proportions. Software projects, if not managed properly, can simply run out of control.

Managing software development projects differs from managing hardware projects. Management techniques that worked in the past for other engineering disciplines have proven ineffective for software. A primary challenge of software engineering lies in addressing the very high complexity associated with most software. Defects can be introduced during many tasks in different phases of a software development project, through a number of intermediate documents attempting to specify the software, or in the software source code itself. Many software programs contain so many source code statements that it is essentially impossible for any one person to read through and comprehend their entirety. Although the engineering tasks are similar for hardware and software development, software engineering requires its own unique terminology, and an even greater emphasis on systematic verification and validation.

Based on many years of experience, we now know the reason why many large software projects failed: They were executed without any guiding standards whatsoever! The lack of standards reflected management inability to understand the process of software development and resulted in the setting of unreasonable goals. Without a process model, without software engineering standards, a software development project becomes a *black box*.

First, the acquirer attempts to describe the desired software functionality as best as possible to the supplier. Next, the acquirer is forced to wait for the software product to finally be delivered by the supplier. Software validation consists only of acceptance testing, to determine whether the acquirer's needs and expectations were met. If they were not, the acquirer must decide whether it is worth repeating this fallible, lengthy, and costly process. Management unfamiliar with the software development process might not be able to control a software project even within their own organization any more effectively than what was just described.

Containing project cost and schedule begins with the ability to accurately estimate them before a project starts. For this purpose, it is essential to understand what tasks must be performed, in what order, and what personnel and other resources are required for these tasks. Standardization of the process allows using actual cost and schedule information from previous projects to estimate the next project. Defining milestones helps make sure that everyone interprets the schedule in the same way.

Even when a simple software process model is already established, significant cost and schedule overruns can occur. Frequently, this happens when a more ambitious software project is attempted, and a steady stream of software defects keeps the project in the implementation and testing phases. Defects are discovered during testing, and the software is sent back for rework (revisiting the implementation phase). The corrected software is sent back for more testing, but more software defects are discovered. This cycle, even if well defined, can go on much longer than originally planned.

Experience has shown that software defects are often introduced during the requirements analysis and design phases. Defects in the deliverables of these early project phases have a greater cost and schedule impact than implementation errors if not detected prior to testing. This is because of a cascading effect: A mistake in defining the requirements might imply non-trivial redesign, in turn requiring substantial recoding of the software. In comparison, a coding error might require correction of a single software module, with no changes to the design or requirements specification.

Software testing is an inefficient mechanism for detecting defects introduced during requirements analysis and design. Other types of design controls—particularly reviews and inspections of intermediate work products, such as Software Requirements Specifications and Software Design Descriptions—help identify such defects earlier. Reviews and inspections mitigate the project cost and schedule impacts of defects more effectively than testing alone. Industry experience has shown that investment of sufficient personnel resources for effective design controls early in a project is more than offset by the associated savings during the implementation, testing, and maintenance phases. Figure 1.1 illustrates typical savings that can be achieved.

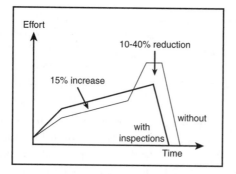

Figure 1.1 *Expected cost and schedule improvements using inspections.*

Businesses often hesitate to formalize their software development process, fearing that this would result in more busy work, and thus increase project cost and schedule. Such fears are frequently heard both from management unfamiliar with software development projects and from programming staff unaccustomed to the use of software engineering standards. Admittedly, businesses must be profitable; they cannot afford inefficient programs that increase software quality but also increase project cost and schedule significantly. An effective quality system should *reduce* both project cost and schedule, while improving the quality of the software products.

Just as software quality should be measured and analyzed for possible software process improvements, measurements should quantify the positive or negative impact of the quality system in terms of project cost and schedule. Incremental process improvements should be attempted to achieve reduced project cost and schedule, while maintaining or improving software quality.

Achieving Compliance

In certain industries, establishing effective software engineering standards is mandatory. For example, the U.S. Quality System Regulation governs medical device software. The Center for Devices and Radiological Health of the Food and Drug Administration provides guidelines for software development and validation in accordance with this regulation.

Failure to comply with governmental regulations can have disastrous business consequences, including recalls of products, closure of manufacturing facilities, and even prison sentences for executives responsible for the violations.

The ISO-9000 standards also require a systematic process for software development and validation. ISO-9000 certification is a business necessity in many cases, particularly for companies targeting the European market, and for software suppliers to ISO-9000[nd]certified companies.

These types of regulations and standards do not specify the software development and validation process to be used. Each organization can develop its own process model, as long as it satisfies general requirements imposed by the regulations. Each organization is expected to describe its own process model by means of a set of internal software engineering standards, which must be mapped to the external regulations and standards.

The IEEE Software Engineering Standards can be used in conjunction with some internal standard operating procedures to satisfy external regulations and standards. The IEEE Software Engineering Standards are specific, for example, regarding templates for creating Software Requirements Specifications—something no governmental regulations would specify in such detail. The IEEE Software Engineering Standards are widely recognized and respected, and their use can help achieve compliance in a timely and effective manner.

Achieving an effective quality system can be difficult if process compliance is the only goal. Emphasis should also be placed on improving the quality of the finished software products, and on incorporating industry best practices into the process model. Minimal process standards implemented only to satisfy external process requirements cannot be expected to yield substantive quality benefits.

Improved Manageability of Software Projects

Use of software engineering standards allows more effective management of software projects.

Project planning with software engineering standards is more accurate, because the tasks to be performed, and the order in which they are to be performed, are more clearly specified. Project personnel are more likely to understand task assignments correctly, because of the descriptions provided by the standard process model.

Project tracking with software engineering standards is more meaningful, because the life cycle model defined by the standards will specify unambiguous milestones and the means of verifying their achievement.

Software engineering standards allow evaluating software quality early in the software life cycle. Verification activities during early project phases can identify systemic quality problems, permitting corrective actions to be taken in a timely manner.

Successes with previous projects can be repeated by following the same process used before. Failures in previous projects can be analyzed, and improvements to the process model can be attempted so as not to repeat mistakes. Software engineering standards allow precise definition of a process, and thus provide the framework for process improvements.

Summary

To anyone who has worked on software projects for years, the advantages of using standards will be self-evident. Conscientious software engineers will develop personal standards in the absence of organizational standards. For larger software projects involving teams of people, and from the point of view of the organization conducting such projects, standards are essential.

Standards provide common terminology for team communication. Standards provide a well-defined reference model, relative to which management can issue assignments and track progress. Standards provide a checklist of required activities, which can be verified for quality assurance.

Standards must be followed. If an organization creates an impressive set of standards on how to develop and validate software, but fails to follow those standards in actual projects, nothing is gained. In fact, failure to follow internal standards shows a blatant disregard for quality, and is worse than not yet having established internal standards.

Standards require management commitment. It is almost impossible to effectively introduce software engineering standards into an organization whose management is not firmly committed to establishing an effective software quality system. Management support is an essential prerequisite to all attempts at software process improvements.

Standards must be maintained. They should reflect the process maturity of the organization developing and validating the software. An effective software process improvement program will periodically review its software engineering standards and target incremental improvements based on feedback from previous projects.

Software development is still a new discipline. It has been widely practiced as an unstructured, often chaotic activity, frequently resulting in software products on which no sane person would stake their life. We can compare this era to the days of unregulated pharmaceuticals in the previous century. Those times are past! Enough has been learned about software engineering, and enough effort has been invested into standards such as the IEEE Software Engineering Standards collection, that failure to establish and follow a structured process model for software development and validation is, at best, unprofessional. In certain industries, such as the medical device industry, it is illegal. We would not want our bridges built, or our airliners designed, without proper engineering techniques, and we should not expect less of the software products that have become such an integral part of our economy.

CHAPTER 2

Guidelines for Software Process Improvements

Introduction of new or revised software engineering standards into an organization represents a type of *software process improvement*. Any process change carries inherent risks. The learning curve for everyone involved can jeopardize the success of an ongoing project. Ill conceived process improvements can compromise the efficiency with which software is developed and validated. Attempting too much at once often creates problems. Disenchanted personnel might reject not only recently attempted changes, but the entire quality system. Organizations are most vulnerable to such instabilities when they are first attempting to define their process model.

This chapter provides guidelines for software process improvements, particularly for phasing in use of a subset of the IEEE Software Engineering Standards. Due to the risks mentioned previously, careful planning and proper execution is essential. These guidelines will help you effectively phase in use of the IEEE Software

Engineering Standards in your organization, while avoiding common pitfalls. More detailed information will be provided for specific standards as they are analyzed in later chapters.

This chapter presents the guidelines for process improvements as a sequence of 12 steps (or, if you prefer, a *checklist* of issues to address). These are as follows:

1. Research applicable regulations.
2. Compile data from previous projects.
3. Plan the scope of the process improvements.
4. Obtain management commitment.
5. Build ground-level support.
6. Draft Standard Operating Procedures.
7. Conduct a team review.
8. Approve and control the Standard Operating Procedures.
9. Specify the phase-in of the process improvements.
10. Train personnel in the process improvements.
11. Monitor use of the process improvements.
12. Evaluate the success of the process improvements.

Research Applicable Regulations

Before you get started with any process improvement, carefully research all applicable governmental regulations and industry quality standards that you must satisfy. If necessary, seek help in this task, because it is critical. For example, for medical device software, you will want to look at the Web site for the FDA Center for Devices and Radiological Health

www.fda.gov/cdrh/

This site contains documents such as *General Principles of Software Validation* and *Guidance for the Content of Premarket Submissions for Software Contained in Medical Devices*. These excellent guides might prove beneficial to you, even if you are not developing medical device software.

As precisely and realistically as possible, identify all discrepancies between your organization's current process, and the mandates of applicable regulations. If any such discrepancies are found, their resolution will represent your highest priority for process improvements.

This issue should be reexamined on an ongoing basis, whenever the regulations or governmental guidelines for their interpretation are updated.

Compile Data from Previous Projects

Information from previous projects can provide invaluable help in planning software process improvements. Quantitative measurements are often more helpful than anecdotal information, particularly if it is available over a statistically meaningful time period.

Even if your organization has not systematically collected software project metrics data in the past, significant information might be available from the following sources:

- **Comparisons between planned versus actual project schedules.** If available, find any schedules approved at the beginning of past projects, and measure any slippage in the actual completion of key milestones.

- **Actual project costs.** Cost information is sometimes difficult to capture. Time, material, and all applicable overhead should be accounted for, or estimated to the best of your ability. Payroll information, particularly if coded according to projects, provides a tremendous wealth of information. As for schedules, comparisons should be made between budgeted versus actual project costs.

- **Test incident reports.** Software defects identified during testing provide a measure of the software's quality. If the information is available, determine how many defects were introduced in which phase of each project.

- **Problem reports.** Software problems reported by customers or users are the most important measure of software quality. Such problems represent failures not only in the software development effort, but also in the software validation effort. If possible, categorize what software verification and validation activity might have been expected to catch the problem but failed to do so.

- **Software complexity metrics.** Use automated tools to analyze the source code from previous projects and determine the size and complexity of the software. The number of lines of code can used to measure the size of the software; taken together with the actual project cost and schedule used, the number of code lines indicates the project's relative efficiency. Excessive complexity of the source code is an excellent predictor of low software quality.

- **Existence of required documents.** Verify the existence of all required documents from previous projects, and note all discrepancies.

If a software process improvement program is already underway in your organization, you might have far more information available than suggested here. Use *all* the data at your disposal!

Analyze the statistics you have collected. Try to determine any trends. Significant problems will be readily apparent. By providing quantitative, objective information, you can more easily justify software process improvements to others.

Plan the Scope of the Process Improvements

Based on the information available to you, plan the scope of the software process improvements. As your highest priority, you should focus on correcting regulatory non-compliance and glaring problem trends from previous projects. Use of new techniques and tools to improve quality and efficiency might be next on the priority list.

You must limit the scope of the process improvements to a realistic size. You might not be able to address all the issues you have identified, perhaps not even all the high-priority items! Making your immediate process improvements succeed and laying the foundation for future process improvements are more important than defining the ultimate process model for your organization. Be pragmatic!

The key to success in planning software process improvements is to make them *incremental*. Experience has shown that modest process improvements are more successful than completely restructuring an entire process. An organization is only capable of a certain amount of change at a time.

Later parts of this book analyze specific IEEE Software Engineering Standards in detail. By reading through the standards and later chapters, you can come to your own conclusions about which of them might be appropriate for your organization. If you have no formal software standards in use, the easiest way to start is with certain *document* standards. The following IEEE standards specify the format and content of key documents, which will be produced during a software project:

Software Requirements Specifications (IEEE Std. 830). The SRS is the single most important work product developed in a software project besides the software itself. An agreement between the development group and its clients at the beginning of the project, the SRS states what the software should do. The SRS unambiguously instructs software designers during their efforts. Finally, the SRS serves as the basis for software validation and testing.

Software Test Documentation (IEEE Std. 829). Although we now recognize that software Verification and Validation (V&V) is about more than just testing, software testing remains the most basic and critical V&V activity. Testing must be documented in order to demonstrate regulatory compliance, to repeat previous tests, and to effectively manage the substantial cost and schedule associated with it.

Obtain Management Commitment

Software process improvements are doomed if management doesn't commit to making them work. The considerable overhead involved in planning and implementing the process improvements must be accounted for. There are always risks associated with any process change, and management must be properly prepared for possible temporary setbacks, so as not to overreact. The goals and expectations of the process improvements should be clearly defined so that management can draw proper conclusions as to the relative success of the improvements.

The key concepts behind your process improvement plan should be summarized for management, including:

- **Anticipated benefits.** Specify benefits of the process improvements, including better software quality, reduced project cost and schedule, regulatory compliance, and improved manageability of software projects. The benefits should be realistic and measurable.

- **Description of changes.** You must succinctly explain the current process model and proposed changes to it. Define software engineering terminology as needed for this purpose. Process diagrams can be helpful.

- **Phase-in strategy.** The anticipated cost and schedule for phasing in the proposed software process improvements must be clearly communicated. Specify clearly what resources management must provide to make the phase-in a success.

- **Evaluation program.** Define how the software process improvements will be monitored, and what quantitative measurements will be performed to evaluate their efficacy. Specify the schedule for any reports to management at the end of the phase-in period or later.

If management will not commit to the software process improvements, do not attempt them! Instead, explore the concerns voiced by management, and propose alternatives to your original process improvements based on such concerns.

Build Ground-level Support

After you've obtained preliminary management support for process improvements, you must still build consensus amongst the affected personnel. Depending on the group dynamics, it might be preferable to do this *prior* to seeking management support. In any case, you must have the support of a majority of those who will execute the process improvements.

Developing a consensus for process improvements can be an easy task, or it can seem close to impossible, depending on the personalities involved. Suggestions for process improvements should be systematically solicited, and all participants should have an opportunity to voice their opinions. A presentation can be helpful, explaining the reasons for and nature of the proposed process changes. All personnel should be reassured that they will receive sufficient training as needed and sufficient time to learn any new techniques. Process improvements should not feel like punishment to those attempting to follow them!

No discussion of this topic can be considered complete without mentioning the *cynic* who might exist in your organization, who systematically ridicules all attempts to formalize the software development process. Cynicism can serve a positive function, as a reality check, but all too often it becomes a detriment to the organization as a whole. Factionalism and decreased morale signal unproductive cynicism. Unfortunately, there are no easy answers for dealing with such cynicism, and each case must be considered individually. If your organization has a legitimate business need for the process improvements, and if an employee systematically impedes their implementation, corrective action is required. This might involve training, reassignment, or, in the worst case, dismissal of the employee. This conclusion might seem unduly harsh, but many software development groups simply can no longer afford to retain the unstructured programming methodology used in the past.

Draft Standard Operating Procedures

Standard Operating Procedures (SOPs) should be written to describe the software development and validation process. SOPs should specify terminology, the process model, documents to be created, techniques to be used, and product standards to be observed.

SOPs should be

- **Correct.** Software SOPs must accurately describe the process actually followed by your organization for software development and validation. A major discrepancy would soon become apparent in any audit, and would be unacceptable.

- **Unambiguous.** Only one interpretation of the process should be possible so that all team members understand the process in the same manner.

- **Complete.** Software SOPs should provide standards for all significant software development and validation activities in all phases of software projects. However, when first introducing SOPs, you might want to formalize only a subset of the tasks.

- **Consistent.** Software SOPs should be internally consistent, and should be consistent with SOPs from your organization's non-software processes.
- **Verifiable.** Software SOPs should be written in such a way that they can be verified by use in actual projects.

Software development and validation SOPs should serve a number of important functions for your organization:

- **Define interfaces to non-software processes.** Other parts of your organization will have their own processes, and the terminology describing them will not always map easily to software industry standards. Your SOPs should define the interfaces between the software and non-software processes in your organization, and define the translation between terminology used in software versus non-software tasks.
- **Assign responsibilities.** Responsibilities for key software development and validation activities should be assigned to departments, reflecting the organization's structure.
- **Reference specific standards.** Generally, it is better to reference standards such as individual IEEE Software Engineering Standards, rather than to duplicate information from them. Individual standards, such as IEEE Std. 830 for Software Requirements Specifications, should be explicitly referenced if they are to be followed.
- **Describe a life cycle model.** Industry standards do not specify life cycle models; rather, individual organizations should create their own models based on their size, philosophy, and other considerations. This means you must specify a standard life cycle model to be followed for software development and validation within your organization.
- **Specify tools.** Your organization might consistently use specific tools for certain activities, such as a document control system, a bug-tracking system, or CASE tools. Your SOPs should reference all such tools explicitly.
- **Provide programming standards.** Every organization is expected to maintain its own detailed guidelines for programming standards. There is no IEEE standard for this purpose.

Diagrams, forms, and other attachments can be helpful in SOPs. When new personnel enter your organization, SOPs can be an important training tool to teach responsibilities to the new team member.

How many software SOPs are needed, and how these should be formatted depends entirely on your organization. In general, it is better to separate low-level SOPs, such as programming standards, from high-level ones, such as one defining the entire software development process. When standards are separated this way, they can then be more easily updated.

The IEEE standards collection includes a top-level standard that may be useful in creating the SOPs. An international standard, ISO/IEC 12207, was adopted via IEEE/EIA 12207.0. This standard provides a top-level description of software life cycle processes, and guidance for adapting the processes. It is discussed in detail in a later section.

Conduct a Team Review

When drafts of the updated SOPs are ready, they should be reviewed by a qualified team. Representatives of all affected departments and job functions should have an opportunity to participate in the review. The review team members should have adequate time to carefully read the draft SOPs, and compile a list of concerns and questions. Conduct one or more review meetings, allotting enough time to discuss all concerns and questions.

IEEE Std. 1028, the IEEE standard for Software Reviews, is an excellent guide for conducting such reviews. Even if this standard is not being adopted by your organization, you can still follow that standard for the purpose of reviewing your SOPs. This standard is discussed in more detail later in this book.

Approve and Control the Standard Operating Procedures

SOPs should be treated as a controlled document in your organization. The level of management required for approval of SOPs should be clearly specified, and the signed, approved procedures should be archived. The manner in which such document control is performed depends on your organization. The signed paper original of the SOPs can be stored in a secure file cabinet, or your organization might have a sophisticated electronic record keeping system in place.

It is recommended that you maintain an archive of older, no-longer-effective versions of your SOPs. The historical perspective provided by your obsolete SOPs will help in planning your future software process improvements. The archive of past SOPs will demonstrate the efficacy of your software process improvement program in future audits.

One of the most critical aspects of properly controlling the SOPs is the distribution of the SOPs to the personnel who shall use them. If paper copies are used, it is important to replace all obsolete copies. If a software developer consults an obsolete SOP, the wrong process steps will be taken. If an auditor finds an obsolete SOP in use, this represents a discrepancy, and will require corrective action.

Assuming your organization has a computer network available to all affected personnel, it might be most expeditious to distribute SOPs via the network. Copying of SOPs to local drives should be discouraged, because it creates the potential problem of out-of-date SOPs as paper copies. If an intranet is available in your organization, this might represent the most effective way of publishing the SOPs for all concerned users.

Specify the Phase-in of the Process Improvements

You might want to restrict phase-in of the revised SOPs to certain pilot projects, prior to their widespread use. Even if you don't specify such pilot projects, you might want to specifically exclude certain in-progress projects. Imposing new SOPs part-way through a project will affect the costs and schedule, and the project plan will need to be revised accordingly. For some projects, the associated delays might not be acceptable, and you might decide to complete those projects using the standards in effect at their beginning.

The decisions regarding the use of revised SOPs for specific projects should be documented and approved. You might want to include this topic in your team review of the SOPs, and document these decisions in the output documents of the review.

Train Personnel in the Process Improvements

Prior to the use of new SOPs, all personnel expected to follow them should be trained in their use. At a minimum, personnel must be made aware of the new standards, given enough time to read them, and be provided an opportunity to ask questions. If an advanced technique—such as *Inspections* described in IEEE Std. 1028—is introduced, it might be appropriate to have a formal training session.

If training in the SOPs is required, you should clarify such requirements with your Human Resources department, and work with the department to ensure that all personnel, including new personnel hired at a later time, receive adequate training.

Monitor Use of the Process Improvements

Use of the new SOPs should be monitored, for these reasons:

- **Enforcement.** You must ensure that new SOPs are actually followed. Target both outright non-compliance and any misinterpretation of the new standards.
- **Measurement.** You should collect data from which you can later analyze the relative success of the process improvements. The same type of measurements you used from previous projects for planning the process improvements should be used for measuring the new projects.

At a minimum, use of the new SOPs should be verified as each project phase is completed.

Evaluate the Success of the Process Improvements

To establish an effective, ongoing process improvement program, you must evaluate the success or failure of the improvements. Feedback from the process improvement program can suggest future changes, so you can continually improve the software development and validation process.

The process improvement program can be understood as a standard closed loop control system, as shown in Figure 2.1

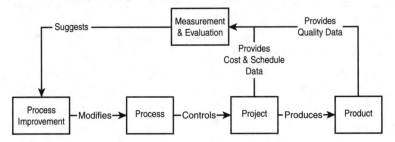

Figure 2.1 *A process improvement program diagrammed as a control loop.*

Problems encountered during attempted process improvements can be described in the language of control theory. Control theory is an advanced topic beyond the scope of this book, and accurate mathematical analysis has not yet been successfully applied to software process improvements, to the best of the author's knowledge. Conceptually, however, it is useful to make the following simple analogy: An overly ambitious process improvement program represents a control loop where the *gain* is set too high, resulting in instabilities.

For example, in a motor control loop with excess gain, the target position will be passed. As the control system continues to drive the motor, the overshoot can continue indefinitely. Analogously, if a process improvement is too large, too ambitious in scope, formalizing the software testing process can consume much of the project's resources, cost, and schedule. Management might try to overcompensate for high costs by entirely reversing the process improvement. Process decisions made under duress often exhibit such *excess gain* characteristics, and should be avoided. Many times, such actions and decisions can seem to leapfrog the organizational process capabilities in the short run, but are unsustainable in the long run.

Summary

It is essential to set realistic goals when phasing in the IEEE Software Engineering Standards. The collection taken as a whole represents a huge body of knowledge, suitable for even the largest organizations. It is completely unrealistic to expect an organization to use all of them all at once. As with any software process improvement, an *incremental* approach is required, based on the organization's level of process maturity.

Management commitment is an absolute prerequisite to any effective process improvement. Management must be willing to commit time and money, and to weather temporary setbacks, for the process improvements to succeed. Management must buy into the improvements, and accept the final responsibility for their success or failure.

Software engineers and other technical personnel must be convinced of the benefits of the process improvements. They must be given a chance to review changes to the Standard Operating Procedures. They must be trained in new techniques, and be given adequate time and support when first using the new methods on an actual project. Process improvements cannot succeed without ground-level support!

A phase-in program for the process improvements must clearly specify which projects will use the new approach first. Within the designated projects, the process improvements must be enforced, and the project carefully monitored. Data should be collected to help assess the relative success of the process improvements. Such measurements should be collected on an ongoing basis for all projects, and used to suggest future software process improvements.

The remainder of this book is dedicated to helping you identify core standards in the IEEE Software Engineering Standards collection, and to providing detailed information on these. Each of the IEEE Software Engineering Standards has the potential to provide significant benefit to your organization. You must determine what your organization is ready for.

CHAPTER 3

An Overview of the IEEE Software Engineering Standards

The IEEE Software Engineering Standards collection is so substantial that it might appear impenetrable to even experienced software professionals. It is difficult to gain an overall view of the entire collection—an issue that the collection's managers continue to address.

Older editions of the collection were published as a single volume, with the standards simply included in ascending numeric order, which unfortunately did not result in any particularly functional organization. The 1997 Edition had grown to the size of a metropolitan telephone book and with its heavier paper could certainly have inflicted bodily injury if inappropriately dropped! The *Introduction* to the 1997 Edition was so brief that it provided little more than a list of the standards; it really did not help the reader gain an overview.

The 1999 Edition was divided into four volumes organized according to a new *framework* description of the standards collection. Although well suited for systematic classification of the standards, the framework is complex and might be difficult for new readers to understand. The framework specifies the IEEE publication *Software Engineering Standards, A User's Road Map* [Moore97] as the *"Overall Guide"* for the standards collection. This excellent book further expounds on the framework model, and adds a comparative analysis of other standards outside of the IEEE collection. However, it would be more useful to an established expert on standards than to a neophyte user of the IEEE standards.

This chapter provides information complementary to the *Introduction* section of the standards collection, written for someone who is just becoming familiar with the IEEE standards. The SESC (the IEEE *Software Engineering Standards Committee*) framework model is described first, followed by a simpler organizational model of the standards. Next, interrelationships between key standards are discussed. The applicability of individual standards is then analyzed as a function of the criticality of the software application, the organization's existing process maturity, and other factors. The role of the top-level standard in the IEEE collection, IEEE/EIA 12207.0, is outlined. This standard is discussed in more detail in Chapter 4, "Software Life Cycle Processes." Finally, a brief discussion is provided on some topics not yet covered by the IEEE standards collection.

The SESC Framework

The *Introduction* section of the 1997 Edition consisted of only a brief *Historical Perspective*, followed by a *Synopses of the Standards*, with a single paragraph statement of scope and purpose for each standard. Other than mentioning IEEE Std. 730 as the historically first standard, the *Introduction* gave the reader no overview of how the different standards fit together, and no instructions on which standard a new reader should start with.

The *Introduction to the 1999 Edition* has been significantly expanded, relative to earlier versions. The *Introduction* succinctly states:

> *"The SESC collection has grown large enough that users can no longer be expected to intuitively perceive the relationships among the various component standards."*

To address this problem, the SESC created a *framework* to describe the structure of the standards collection. This framework is described in the *Introduction to the 1999 Edition*, and detailed further in *Software Engineering Standards, A User's Road Map* [Moore97].

The framework specifies six *layers* and—for the middle three layers—four *stacks*, as pictured in Figure 3.1.

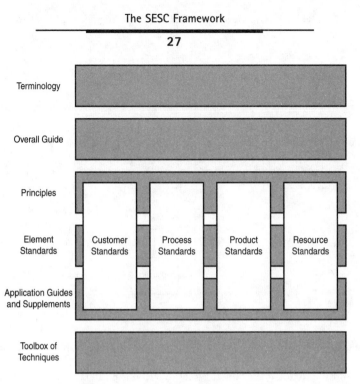

Figure 3.1 *The SESC framework model.*

The six layers are defined as follows:

1. Terminology: Documents prescribing terms and vocabulary
2. Overall Guide: One document providing overall guidance for the entire collection
3. Principles: Documents that describe principles or objectives for use of the standards in the collection
4. Element Standards: Standards that are the basis for conformity
5. Application Guides and Supplements: Guides and supplements that give advice for using the standards in various situations
6. Toolbox of Techniques: Descriptions of techniques that might be helpful in implementing the provisions of the higher-level documents

The four stacks correspond to the four *objects* in the object model of software engineering shown in Figure 3.2.

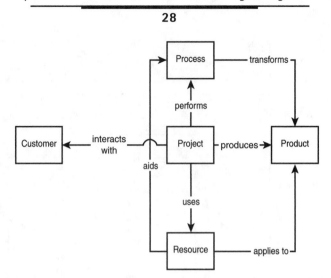

Figure 3.2 *The SESC object model of software engineering[1].*

The object model categorization of the standards might be elaborated as follows:

- Customer Standards: Standards that describe the interaction between the customer and supplier of a software engineering project
- Process Standards: Standards that describe processes spanning the life cycle of a software product or service, including acquisition, supply, development, maintenance, operations, and measurements
- Product Standards: Standards that explain the requirements for classes of software products—characteristics, measurements, evaluations, and specifications
- Resource Standards: Standards that recommend proper documentation, methods, models and tools for a well-managed software program and its related processes

Most of the standards are classified according to the framework as *Element Standards* in one of the four object categories. The four volumes are organized mostly according to the object model, with the layers not affected by this categorization distributed so as to even out the physical size of the volumes. Appendix A lists the standards contained in each of the volumes for convenience. Figure 3.3 summarizes the classification of individual standards in the SESC framework.

---

1. Figure 5 – "Objects of software engineering" from the *Introduction of the IEEE Standards, Software Engineering, 1999 Edition.*

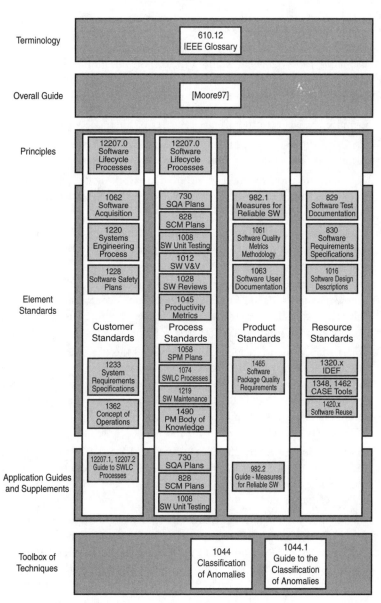

Figure 3.3 *Classification of standards in the SESC framework.*

SESC Alternative Organization of the Standards

A previous SESC classification of the standards is still listed as an alternative in the *Introduction to the 1999 Edition*. In some ways, this organization is easier to understand, which is why it is still included. The first four categories of the alternative model might be directly mapped to the framework model, as follows:

- Terminology: Maps to the *Terminology* layer of the framework model.
- Life Cycle Processes: Maps to the *Process* stack of the framework model. However, it only represents a subset of the *Process* stack.
- Tools: Maps to the *Resource* stack of the framework model. However, it only represents a subset of the *Resource* stack, corresponding to the *Tools and Environments* sub-stack.
- Reuse: Maps to the *Resource* stack of the framework model. However, it only represents a subset of the *Resource* stack, corresponding to the *Reuse Libraries* sub-stack.
- The other parts of the alternative model do not map directly onto the framework model. Each of the remaining sections contains standards from multiple parts of the framework model. The remaining parts of the alternative model are as follows:
- Project Management: Includes IEEE Std. 1058 (Software Project Management Plans) and IEEE Std. 1490 (Guide to the Project Management Body of Knowledge), classified as *Process* standards by the framework model. However, it also includes IEEE Std. 1044 (Classification for Software Anomalies), which is classified in the generic *Toolbox of Techniques* layer by the framework model.
- Plans: Includes IEEE Std. 730 (SQA Plans), IEEE Std. 828 (SCM Plans), and IEEE Std. 1012 (Software V&V) from the framework model's *Process* stack. Also includes IEEE Std. 1228 (Software Safety Plans) from the framework model's *Customer* stack.
- Documentation: Includes IEEE Std. 829 (Software Test Documentation), IEEE Std. 830 (Software Requirements Specifications), and IEEE Std. 1016 (Software Design Descriptions) from the framework model's *Resources* stack. Also includes IEEE Std. 1063 (Software User Documentation) from the framework model's *Product* stack. Also includes IEEE Std. 1233 (System Requirements Specifications) and IEEE Std. 1362 (Concept of Operations) from the framework model's *Customer* stack.
- Measurement: Includes IEEE Std. 982.1 (Measures for Reliable Software) and IEEE Std. 1061 (Software Quality Metrics Methodology) from the framework model's *Product* stack. Also contains IEEE Std. 1045 (Software Productivity Metrics) from the framework model's *Process* stack.

Problems with the SESC Models

The existing IEEE Software Engineering Standards were not developed with the SESC framework in mind. Instead, the SESC framework was developed later as an attempt to provide a systematic classification schema for a large, pre-existing set of standards. The standards don't always neatly fit into the framework model. This is evidenced by numerous standards having secondary assignments. For example, IEEE Std. 829 (Software Test Documentation) has a primary classification as a *Resource* standard, and a secondary classification as a *Process* standard. Similarly, IEEE Std. 730 (Software Quality Assurance Plans) has a primary classification as a *Process* standard, and a secondary classification as a *Product* standard. In total, there are 15 such secondary classifications of standards and guides.

The SESC alternative model suffers the same classification ambiguity problem. For example, IEEE Std. 1058 (Software Project Management Plans), is assigned to the *Project Management* category, however, being a plan, can also be in the *Plans* category. Similarly, IEEE Std. 1012 (Software Verification and Validation) is assigned to the *Plans* category, but, implicitly defining a software life cycle model, and explicitly defining the supporting verification and validation tasks for the process, can also be included in the *Life Cycle Processes* category.

A more important short-coming in both of these models is that they don't tell you how to get started. The models don't specify a phase-in strategy, and they don't specify core standards for just getting started.

For example, for your next project, do you need

- A separate *Software Project Management Plan,* according to IEEE Std. 1058?
- A separate *Software Configuration Management Plan,* according to IEEE Std. 828?
- A separate *Software Verification and Validation Plan,* according to IEEE Std. 1012?
- A separate *Software Quality Assurance Plan,* according to IEEE Std. 730?

After all, the template for a *Software Project Management Plan* includes sections for *Configuration Management, Verification and Validation,* and *Quality Assurance.* Under what conditions should you create separate plans, and when should you put all the information together into a single plan? Unfortunately, no guidelines are provided.

Admittedly, some of the individual standards provide recommendations for some questions of this type. For example, IEEE Std. 730 (SQA Plans) states that it *"applies to the development and maintenance of critical software."* It then goes on to specify the following minimum documentation:

- Software Requirements Specification
- Software Design Description
- Software Verification and Validation Plan
- Software Verification and Validation Report
- User Documentation
- Software configuration Management Plan

Thus, after you have read and understood a number of standards, you might conclude that, if you have a critical software application (*"Software whose failure would impact safety or cause large financial or social losses"*), you should follow, at a minimum, the following standards:

- IEEE Std. 730: Software Quality Assurance Plans
- IEEE Std. 828: Software Configuration Management Plans
- IEEE Std. 830: Software Requirements Specifications
- IEEE Std. 1012: Software Verification and Validation
- IEEE Std. 1016: Software Design Descriptions
- IEEE Std. 1063: Software User Documentation

Further investigation would, however, reveal that there are a number of other IEEE Software Engineering Standards, which should rightfully be considered as mandatory for critical software, including:

- IEEE Std. 829: Software Test Documentation
- IEEE Std. 1008: Software Unit Testing
- IEEE Std. 1028: Software Reviews
- IEEE Std. 1058: Software Project Management Plans
- IEEE Std. 1228: Software Safety Plans

The problem here is simply that the SESC models, and the *Overall Guide* layer[2], do not include tutorial information about which standards can be considered mandatory or appropriate for their organization or project.

---

2. Software Engineering Standards, A User's Road Map [Moore97]

It should be mentioned that IEEE/EIA 12207.0 (*Software Life Cycle Processes*) has some direct bearing on this issue. This standard specifies primary, supporting, and organizational process requirements, and guidelines for adapting these to your organization or project. This standard is discussed in detail in Chapter 4.

A Simplified Organizational Model

This section presents a simplified organizational model of the IEEE Software Engineering Standards. This model restricts itself to a subset of the standards collection, concentrating exclusively on what the author considers to be the core standards. With one exception (IEEE Std. 1042), only the *Element Standards* (those which *"are the basis for conformity"*) are considered. System engineering standards are excluded, because they pertain to a closely related but distinct field. Other standards are excluded because, although useful, they are not amongst the most essential.

We start with a simplified object model of software engineering, as shown in Figure 3.4.

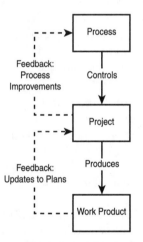

Figure 3.4 *A simplified object model of software engineering.*

The objects in this model might be described as follows:

- Process: Standards, descriptions, and other means by which an organization describes the process to be used for multiple software projects. Activities for individual projects are excluded.

- Project: A software project is a complex entity, consisting of people working together for a prolonged period of time, using tools, facilities, and other resources, to create a software product. Plans and reports of project activities are meant to be included as an element of a project, but work products, such as the software product and specifications, are excluded.

- Work Product: The software product itself, user documentation for it, and intermediate documents produced during the project to specify, describe, or document the software are all meant to be included in this object category. Examples of intermediate documents include Software Requirements Specifications and Test Case Specifications, although these will not be delivered to the end user. Documents describing project activities are *not* meant to be included in this category. Work products might be conventional documents, or they might represent electronic records, or be sections of larger documents. The *Introduction to Volume Four: Resource and Technique Standards* refers to this type of object as a *"Process Information Product"* or *"PIP"* for short, but this term is not used here because it is too cryptic.

Next, we divide software engineering activities into the following two categories, which might correspond approximately to organizational units charged with performing these activities:

- Development: Activities *"by which user needs are translated into a software product."* (IEEE Std. 610.12, definition for *Software Development Process*). These activities are meant to include *"translating user needs into software requirements, transforming the software requirements into design, implementing the design in code…"* However, activities that are intended to evaluate the development activities or their associated work products are not meant to be included here.

- Verification and Validation: Software V&V is defined by IEEE Std. 610.12 as: *"The process of determining whether the requirements for a system or component are complete and correct, the products of each development phase fulfill the requirements or conditions imposed by the previous phase, and the final system or component complies with specified requirements."* *Software Quality Assurance* activities, a broader concept, are also meant to be included, in order to include IEEE Std. 730.

This categorization of activities reflects IEEE Std. 1012 (Software Verification and Validation), which also differentiates between *Development* versus *V&V Activities* and *Outputs*. This standard defines *V&V Inputs* as the outputs of either the *Development Process* or of *V&V Activities* from previous project phases. The *V&V Activities* executed in a given project phase produce additional *V&V Outputs* for that phase.

Combining these two classifications, we can organize the most important IEEE Software Engineering Standards as shown in Figure 3.5.

	Development Standards		SQA/V&V Standards	
Process Standards	1074	Software Life Cycle Processes	1012	Software Verification & Validation
	1042	Guide to Software Configuration Management	1028	Software Reviews
	1061	Quality Metrics Methodology	1008	Software Unit Testing
	982.1	*Measures to Produce Reliable Software (Process Measures)*		
Project Documentation Standards	1058	Software Project Management Plans	730	Software Quality Assurance Plans
	828	Software Configuration Management Plans	1012	*Software Verification & Validation (Plans and Reports)*
	1228	Software Safety Plans	829	*Software Test Documentation (Plans, Logs and Reports)*
Work Product Standards	830	Software Requirements Specifications	829	Software Test Documentation (Test Specifications)
	1016	Software Design Descriptions		
	1063	Software User Documentation		
	982.1	Measures to Produce Reliable Software (Product Measures)		

Figure 3.5 *A simplified classification of the standards.*

Note that this simplified model still requires that certain standards be assigned multiple slots. However, in each case, we can clearly specify which subsections of these standards belong exclusively to which category. For example, the *Test Plan, Test Item Transmittal Report, Test Log, Test Incident Report, and Test Summary Report* sections of IEEE Std. 829 (Software Test Documentation) represent *Project Documentation* standards, whereas the *Test Case Specification* and *Test Procedure Specification* sections represent *Work Product* standards. The first set of test documents (plans and reports) describes planned and actual activities for the particular project; the second set of test documents (specifications) describes expected behavior of the software product.

The next section will explore interrelationships between the key standards listed previously, based on project information flow. The following section provides guidelines on applicability of the standards using a maturity model.

Information Flow Between Documents Specified by Core Standards

The IEEE standards call for certain documents to be produced. These might represent plans, reports, specifications, or other types of documents. These might be conventional documents, electronic records, or sections of larger documents. The information flow between these documents defines an implicit relationship between the standards governing those document types. The specifics will depend on the individual project, but consider the information flow model shown in Figure 3.6.

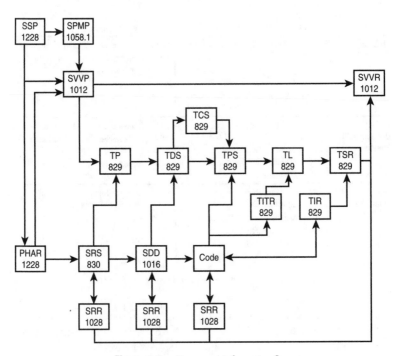

Figure 3.6 *Document information flow.*

This diagram uses the following list of acronyms:

PHAR	Preliminary Hazard Analysis Report
SDD	Software Design Description
SPMP	Software Project Management Plan
SRR	Software Review Report
SRS	Software Requirements Specification
SSP	Software Safety Plan
SVVP	Software Verification and Validation Plan
SVVR	Software Verification and Validation Report
TCS	Test Case Specification
TDS	Test Design Specification
TIR	Test Incident Report
TITR	Test Item Transmittal Report
TL	Test Log
TP	Test Plan

TPS	Test Procedure Specification
TSR	Test Summary Report

SRR is not a standard acronym, but is meant to represent a report for any of the types of software reviews specified by IEEE Std. 1028, including *Audit Reports, Inspection Reports, Management Review Reports, Technical Review Reports,* and *Walkthrough Reports.* This standard and the five types of software reviews are discussed in more detail in Chapter 6, "Process Standards."

This diagram might seem complex if your organization does not yet produce much software documentation, but at the same time it is greatly simplified relative to complex projects for critical applications. As a note, IEEE/EIA 12207.1 provides material useful in building an information model for complex projects.

It is worth mentioning that system-level documentation is not shown, but that a *System Requirements Specification* (IEEE Std. 1233) and other system level plans, specifications, and descriptions are logical inputs to the SSP, PHAR, SPMP, SRS, and other software documents. Software requirements are derived from system requirements, and, ideally, should be traced to system requirements.

User Documentation, governed by IEEE Std. 1063, is not shown on the diagram. The HAR and SRS are both logical inputs for the User Documentation, which in turn might be considered input for the TPS documents. This was omitted only to keep the diagram simple.

Software reviews can be effectively used for *any* of the software documents shown in the diagram, not only for the SRS, SDD, and code. The number and type of software reviews can be specified by the SVVP.

An SCMP (Software Configuration Management Plan, IEEE Std. 828) and an SQAP (Software Quality Assurance Plan, IEEE Std. 730) are not included in the diagram. This was done to simplify the diagram, not to imply that these are unimportant. These (and the SVVP, and even the SSP) can be written as sections of the SPMP. This would be expeditious if only one individual is responsible for maintaining the plans for all these activities.

Finally, the test documentation schema shown in Figure 3.6 follows the full set of types of test documents specified by IEEE Std. 829. The author has found this to be an excellent, modular style of documenting testing activities, but many organizations use a simplified test documentation schema. This is discussed further in a Chapter 5, "Document Standards."

Applicability of Standards

This section discusses which IEEE software engineering standards are applicable to your organization or project under which circumstances. Included in this concept is an incremental phase-in of the standards, because it is unrealistic to expect to use all of them at once. The guidelines provided here are not meant to be definitive. You must carefully analyze laws, regulations, guidelines, and other standards specific to your application domain to determine the minimum acceptable process model. Figure 3.7 provides guidelines for implementing specific standards based on the criticality of the application, the size of the project team, the existing process maturity of the organization, and any external requirements for the process.

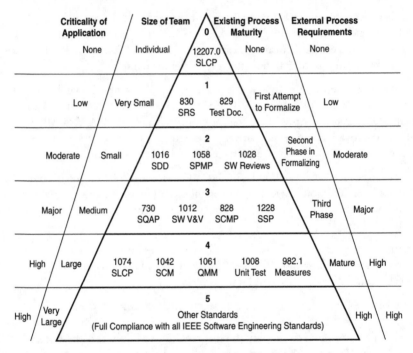

Figure 3.7 *Pyramid of applicability—a simple maturity model.*

There is an obvious and direct relationship between the number of IEEE Software Engineering Standards successfully adopted by an organization and the software process maturity of that organization. By specifying a rational and orderly adoption sequence for the standards, the *Pyramid of Applicability* in Figure 3.7 provides a simple *Maturity Model*. This can be used to assess an organization's maturity, and plan software process improvements.

As the *criticality* of the application increases, the number of standards that can be followed increases also. The criticality is a function of both the severity and probability of hazards and errors. The *Software Integrity Level* concept defined in IEEE Std. 1012 is a synonym for criticality, and that standard specifies the minimum set of V&V tasks that can be performed as a function of the software integrity levels. The terms used in the diagram are borrowed from IEEE Std. 1012, with *"None"* referring to a software integrity level 0. Figure 3.6 is not intended to recommend forgoing activities unless the stated criticality is reached. The information flow diagram is presented only to recommend full conformance with the IEEE standard for an activity if that criticality is reached. For example, *Management Reviews* should be performed even for *Low* criticality software, even if these are not yet conducted in accordance with IEEE Std. 1228 for Software Reviews.

As the size of a team grows, the more need it has for standards to manage the project activities. Conversely, if more standards are needed for other reasons, more personnel might be required, for example, to support more independent review and testing activities. Figure 3.7 is *not* meant to imply that, if you can develop the software with just a few people, you can ignore most of the software engineering standards. Management must take responsibility for the appropriateness of the software process, and provide adequate personnel and other resources to support the process.

The existing process maturity of the organization will limit what set of standards can reasonably be expected to be implemented successfully. As described in Chapter 2, "Guidelines for Software Process Improvements," changes to the process should be approached incrementally. It is unrealistic to expect to introduce more than a few of the IEEE Software Engineering Standards at once.

However, external requirements might dictate attributes of the software process, and might force an organization to make a larger change to its process. For example, the Quality System Regulation affecting medical device manufacturers in the United States provides hard requirements for the process of developing and validating medical device software. The IEEE standards collection can help make compliance more achievable, both because the IEEE standards are recognized and respected by regulatory bodies such as the FDA, and because adoption of the IEEE standards means that the substantial effort to develop such standards does not have to be performed in-house.

The following subsections briefly describe the process model at each level in the maturity model. The levels of this maturity model are distinct from the levels of the SEI CMM model, and there is no intent to imply otherwise. The reader is also referred to the summary descriptions of the standards provided in the *Introduction to the 1999 Edition*.

Level 0

Level 0 in the maturity model corresponds to adoption of high-level processes, but the absence of any formalized element standards. This level is appropriate only if there is absolutely no criticality to the software, and there are no external requirements for additional standards.

IEEE/EIA 12207.0 provides appropriate guidance at maturity level 0. This standard exists at the "principles" layer according to the SESC framework model.

IEEE/EIA 12207.0 establishes a common framework for all software life cycle processes, as follows:

- Primary processes, including acquisition, supply, development, operation, and maintenance
- Supporting processes, including documentation, configuration management, quality assurance, verification, validation, joint review, audit, and problem resolution
- Organizational processes, including management, infrastructure, improvement, and training

Adoption of IEEE/EIA 12207.0 will help clarify the tasks that should be performed, for example, during the software development process. It does not provide much specific guidance on how to perform some of these tasks. For example, it specifies that *"the developer shall establish and document software requirements"* and that these should include *"functional and capability specifications"* and *"interfaces external to the software item,"* but does not specify the format or detailed information content of a Software Requirements Specification. For this, the element standard IEEE Std. 830 (*IEEE Recommended Practice for Software Requirements Specifications*) is needed.

This level allows adopting simpler process models than lower levels. For example, the V&V processes of IEEE/EIA 12207.0 are far simpler than those of IEEE Std. 1012. One could use the V&V processes of IEEE Std. 12207.0 as a first step and later adopt the more detailed process provided by IEEE Std. 1012. As another example, even at a low level of maturity, organizations need some semblance of configuration management. The IEEE/EIA 12207.0 configuration management process is good enough until one gets to the higher level of maturity and applies IEEE Std. 828 (*IEEE Standard for Software Configuration Management Plans*).

IEEE/EIA 12207.0 is discussed in more detail in Chapter 4.

This level of process maturity is adequate for some organizations. The author has seen sophisticated, complex software applications developed despite the lack of organizational standards for documentation and processes. The high quality of the final software bore tribute to the abilities, dedication, and survival of the project team. The problem with this approach is that individuals become indispensable and project successes are not easily reproduced. For critical applications, organizational or project standards for processes and documentation are essential.

Level 1

Level 1 in the maturity model corresponds to the simplest process for a software project beyond the "black box" of Level 0. A *Software Requirements Specification* is written to document *what* the software should do, and *Test Documentation* is created to demonstrate that the software actually does this.

This level is only suitable for low criticality applications, and low external requirements for the process. This level is recommended for a first attempt to formalize the software process.

IEEE Std. 830 for Software Requirements Specifications defines a standard for developing complete and unambiguous specifications of the software's functional characteristics. The SRS is probably the single most important software document. The SRS represents an agreement between the client and development groups on the software. The SRS instructs the software engineers as to what they shall design. The SRS is an essential input document for developing tests. The SRS helps determine acceptance of the software product at the end of the development process. The author has found IEEE Std. 830 to work extremely well for a wide variety of applications, and to help inexperienced personnel learn to document software requirements quickly and effectively.

Writing a good SRS is a difficult task, which requires skill and experience. Too often, the design is described, instead of the requirements being specified. The SRS should document *what*, not *how*. This is easier said than done for many software engineers. If informal design documentation has already been created, do not be tempted to start with this to create an SRS. IEEE Std. 830 provides a flexible set of templates for creating a truly useful SRS.

IEEE Std. 829 for Software Test Documentation specifies a variety of documents and an implicit associated process model for software testing. Software testing is the single most basic and indispensable software V&V activity. If software is not tested, it can almost be guaranteed to not function correctly.

A project might specify a subset of the work products from IEEE Std. 829 in the *Test Plan*. The author has found the modular style for test documentation of this standard to be an excellent alternative to the more monolithic approach typical of proprietary techniques. At first, the large number of different types of documents appears overly complex, but over years of use the author has learned to appreciate this standard more and more. It is important to remember that conformance with this standard does not require producing all the document types for each project, and that the various documents might actually be written as sections of a single larger document if this is preferred.

At this level of process maturity, formalized software testing is probably restricted to *system-level* testing, because the lower-level software design units are not systematically specified.

The adoption of IEEE Std. 829 and IEEE Std. 830 represent a major process improvement over Level 0, and will require substantial effort to implement correctly.

Level 2

Level 2 in the maturity model formalizes several additional important parts of the software process beyond those of Level 1. Level 2 formalizes creation of a project plan, the documentation of the software design, and a systematic approach to reviewing work products.

This level of process maturity is suited to projects of moderate criticality, or moderate external requirements for the process model. It is recommended for a second phase of formalization of the software process.

The most important type of plan, the *Software Project Management Plan*, is formalized in IEEE Std. 1058. An SPMP helps ensure that a systematic process is defined for its project. In the absence of other plans, it should describe Verification and Validation, Software Quality Assurance, and Software Configuration Management activities, in Section 7 of the template defined in the standard. The author has found the SPMP template in IEEE Std. 1058 to be excellent, providing a comprehensive list of issues that, if worked out in detail and updated as the project progresses, provides all the information needed to effectively plan and manage a project.

The *Software Design Description* (IEEE Std. 1016) documents the software design, both high-level and low-level. It describes *how* the software will address its requirements, in sufficient detail to enable the implementation of the software to proceed, and to enable testing of individual modules. Availability of a SDD thus allows for software testing to be performed more effectively at the *integration* and *unit* levels.

Software Reviews represent the second most important form of V&V activity besides testing. IEEE Std. 1028 provides a concise, yet complete description of five major types of software reviews. *Technical Reviews*, *Walk-throughs*, or particularly *Inspections* are invaluable design controls during early project phases. *Management Reviews* are essential for management to assume responsibility for a project in a meaningful way, and should be part of any project. *Audits* are important as a quality assurance technique, to help enforce process compliance.

Level 2 represents a major software process improvement relative to Level 1. It is not recommended to attempt more than this combination at once.

Level 3

Level 3 in the maturity model extends Level 2 with standards for software quality assurance, verification and validation, configuration management, and software safety. Each of these standards provides templates for writing plans. These standards imply additional project activities, beyond simply creating the plans. For example, the configuration management standard requires that a systematic process be defined for requesting, evaluating, approving or disapproving, and implementing changes to a controlled work products *(Configuration Items)*. Similarly, the V&V standard specifies in detail a wide variety of V&V activities to be performed in different project phases, as a function of the *Software Integrity Level* determined near the beginning of the development process.

The level of process maturity is suited to major criticality applications, or for when major external requirements exist for the process. This level is recommended for a third phase of process formalization.

IEEE Std. 730, the first of the IEEE Software Engineering Standards, provides a template for creating Software Quality Assurance Plans. This standard applies to *critical* software, and states that a subset of the requirements might be applied to non-critical software. For critical software, it specifies minimum documentation requirements for the project, including:

- Software Requirements Specification (SRS)
- Software Design Description (SDD)
- Software Verification and Validation Plan (SVVP)
- Software Verification and Validation Report (SVVR)
- User Documentation
- Software Configuration Management Plan (SCMP)
- Other documentation, including a Software Project Management Plan (SPMP)

It is reassuring to note that, by Level 3, we have included standards for each of these types of required documents.

IEEE Std. 1012 describes *Verification and Validation* activities to be performed in a project as a function of the *Software Integrity Level*. We recall that V&V is defined by IEEE Std. 610.12 as:

> *The process of determining whether the requirements for a system or component are complete and correct, the products of each development phase fulfill the requirements or conditions imposed by the previous phase, and the final system or component complies with specified requirements.*

The software integrity level represents the criticality of the software, and a scale of 0 to 4 is defined in the standard. Minimum V&V tasks are specified for the different integrity levels, and are organized into activity groups. V&V activities are shown in a waterfall Software Life Cycle Model, but may be mapped to other models. The standard also provides templates for writing a Software Verification and Validation Plan, and a Software Verification and Validation Report. Software testing and review activities form the core of the V&V activities.

Std. 1012 is a large and complex standard, and will appear daunting at first. It lists a large number of project activities and work products, which might seem to be too much relative to your previous projects. The 1998 revision of this standard has helped this matter significantly, because it provides guidelines for tailoring the V&V activities according to the integrity level. This mechanism enables focusing limited project resources on the V&V activities that can provide the most benefit, while still maintaining conformance with the standard. V&V activities can benefit the project, in terms of quality gains, and reduced overall cost and schedule. V&V should not result in unproductive busywork!

IEEE Std. 1012 draws on IEEE Std. 829 for Software Test Documentation, and IEEE Std. 1028 for Software Reviews, because they provide more detailed instructions for performing these two fundamental V&V techniques. IEEE Std. 1012 is a higher-level standard, which allows you to plan and execute your project V&V activities in a more systematic manner. For example, even if you were performing software reviews at Level 2, at Level 3 you now have specific requirements for what reviews must be performed as a function of the software criticality.

IEEE Std. 828 for Software Configuration Management Plans specifies a formal approach to identifying and controlling changes to project work products, including the software itself. The controlled work products are referred to as *Configuration Items*. The configuration items must be identified, and changes to the items, controlled. A *Configuration Control Board* (CCB, also sometimes called a "Change Control Board") is required for the critical task of approving or disapproving changes to configuration items. This very flexible standard enables a CCB to be an individual or a group, and allows for multiple CCBs.

For many organizations, the change from an informal approach to decision making (approving or disapproving changes) to an orderly process can be profound. With an informal process, in some organizations, an autocratic manager might make all decisions, in other organizations a democratic consensus building approach might be required. The most ineffective technique, found all too often, consists of opposing factions struggling against each other in a harsh Darwinian contest to enforce their point of view. A formalized change control process helps transform critical project decision making from a disruptive, unpredictable headache to a civilized, manageable task.

IEEE Std. 1228 for Software Safety Plans is intended to improve the safety of critical software. It calls for identification and analysis of hazards, and the analysis of the software requirements, design, code, testing, and change activities relative to these hazards. The *Risk* assigned to hazards in this standard corresponds to the *Software Integrity Level* from Std. 1012. The *Criticality Analysis* specified by Std. 1228 is an important task of correlating the system risks to the software, and thus driving the scope of the V&V activities. If you have a safety critical software application, you should follow this standard.

Level 4

Level 4 in the maturity model represents conformance with all key IEEE Software Engineering Standards listed in Figure 3.5. It corresponds to a mature process, and is suited to high criticality software applications.

IEEE Std. 1074 is a standard for developing a *Software Life Cycle Process* (SCLP). The SLCP is project-specific, and must be derived from a *Software Life Cycle Model* (SLCM) to be selected by the organization. The standard does not specify any standard SLCMs, but defines a set of *Activities* organized into different *Activity Groups* that must be mapped to the SLCM. This standard is useful not only for generating the SLCP, but also for independent assessment of the adequacy of the SLCP. Use of this standard will help ensure that the project plan and other related plans are sufficiently comprehensive for their intended purpose.

IEEE Std. 1042 (*IEEE Guide to Software Configuration Management*) is classified by the *Introduction to the 1999 Edition* as an *Application Guide* rather than an *Element Standard*. It might thus be viewed as an elaboration of IEEE Std. 828 for Software Configuration Management Plans. It is the only guide to be included in the core standards group, because it provides substantial additional information beyond IEEE Std. 828. Application of IEEE Std. 828 in conjunction with the guidelines provided by IEEE Std. 1042 can reasonably be expected to yield a more substantial and mature software configuration management process than use of IEEE Std. 828 alone.

IEEE Std. 1008 provides a standard for performing *Software Unit Testing*. Unit testing is defined by IEEE Std. 610.12 as *"Testing of individual hardware or software units or groups of related units."* The term "module" is often used interchangeably with the word "unit" and might be more familiar to the reader. Unit-level testing is performed on individual software modules or groups of software modules, and is an important technique for validating critical software applications. Critical software requirements should be traced through the design to individual modules in the implementation, and unit testing should be focused on these critical software modules. IEEE Std. 1008 in no way supercedes IEEE Std. 829 for software test documentation.

IEEE Std. 1061 for a *Software Quality Metrics Methodology* describes how to institute quantifiable quality measures for software. It does not define specific metrics as IEEE Std. 982.1 does. Instead, it describes a process for establishing software quality requirements, and identifying, implementing, analyzing, and validating software quality metrics for those requirements. IEEE Std. 982.1 and IEEE Std. 1061 can be used in combination.

IEEE Std. 982.1 *(IEEE Standard Dictionary of Measures to Produce Reliable Software)* provides a catalog of both process and product measures used as indicators of reliability. *Software Reliability* as defined in this standard *("The probability that software not cause the failure of a system for a specified time under specified conditions.")* represents an effective measure of the more general concept of *Software Quality.* This standard might be used effectively in combination with IEEE Std. 1061. Some of the measures might be applied during software reviews prior to testing, for example, for *Code Inspections.*

Level 5

Level 5 in the maturity model represents conformance with the entire set of IEEE Software Engineering Standards. This corresponds to a high level of process maturity, and is suited to high criticality software applications, even for very large organizations. Because the IEEE standards are continually revised, and new standards are added, an ongoing program is required to maintain conformance with all the standards.

Level 5 is outside the scope of this book. If you are ready for this level, you don't need to be reading this book, except perhaps for your personal amusement.

Missing Standards

The IEEE Software Engineering Standards collection is a dynamic body of knowledge, which is growing at a fast pace. One of its goals is to remain sufficiently generic so that each organization can use new techniques and tools, while still maintaining conformance. Stylistic preferences are excluded from the standards collection, but, at the organizational level, must finally be decided. Several important types of standards must be provided by the organization to supplement the IEEE standards, including:

- Programming Standards. Organizations are expected to maintain standards for the development of the software source code. Their purpose is to increase software quality, by proper commenting, limiting module complexity, systematic naming conventions, and other techniques. Such standards are often dependent on the choice of programming language, and might represent stylistic preferences of the team members. It is important to an organization to standardize these conventions, to allow for more effective use of multiple software engineers.

- Design Standards. Organizations may also benefit from design standards. These can help ensure that consistent techniques are used, for example, in conjunction with object-oriented design methods. Guiding principles, such as encapsulation and information hiding, may be defined, and checklists may be developed to help with design reviews.

- Criticality Rating Standards. The risk ratings of IEEE Std. 1228 and the software integrity levels of IEEE Std. 1012 can be specified in more concrete terms for your application domain. The mapping can reflect any regulations or guidelines for your industry. For example, in the medical device industry, FDA guidelines for software development and validation are written in terms of the *Level of Concern*, which might be *Major, Moderate,* or *Minor.* To demonstrate compliance with the FDA guidelines using the IEEE standards, an appropriate mapping must be established between the FDA's level of concern and the software integrity levels of IEEE Std. 1012.

- Software Life Cycle Models. The organization might want to define a standard Software Life Cycle Model, to provide standard consistent terminology for its software development process, and to serve as a template for the Software Life Cycle for each project. The IEEE standards do not specify a SLCM, even though IEEE Std. 1074 provides guidelines for how to select and adapt one. A number of competing models have been developed, and each organization should have the flexibility of selecting or developing its own model.

Summary

The most effective way to gain a working knowledge of the IEEE Software Engineering Standards is to restrict the focus to a few standards at a time. The emphasis should be to attain a practical, usable understanding of several standards, without getting distracted by the collection as a whole. The aim of this book is to help the reader get started with the core standards in a pragmatic manner.

Several key concepts have been presented in this chapter:

The SESC framework and alternative models

A simplified organization model for the standards collection

A list of the most important standards to get started with

An information flow model showing the relationship between the core standards in terms of project activities

A simple maturity model providing guidelines for the applicability of specific standards based on the criticality of your application domain, existing process maturity of your organization, and other factors.

Chapter 4, "Software Life Cycle Processes," will provide the context for further understanding of the individual standards.

CHAPTER 4

Software Life Cycle Processes

This chapter discusses *software life cycle processes*, and how you apply them for specific projects. Software life cycle processes refer to primary processes such as software acquisition, supply, development, operation, and maintenance, as well as supporting and organizational processes.

This chapter presents the top-level standard in the IEEE collection, IEEE/EIA 12207.0. This standard provides a framework for software life cycle processes, as well as a roadmap for the other IEEE software engineering standards. It specifies a classification schema of processes, activities, and tasks covering all aspects of software engineering.

For individual projects, IEEE/EIA 12207.0 may be *tailored* and must be *mapped* onto a *Software Life Cycle Model* (SLCM). *Tailoring* means the deletion of non-applicable processes, activities, and tasks. *Mapping* means establishing a sequence of the activities specified in IEEE/EIA 12207.0 according to a selected SLCM.

A *SLCM* is a framework, selected by each organization, on which to map the activities.IEEE discourages excessive tailoring, by specifying two levels of compliance with IEEE/EIA 12207.0: *tailored* and *absolute* (Annex F). Absolute compliance requires that all mandatory processes, activities, and tasks (specified via "shall" or "will") are implemented.

IEEE Std 1074 (*IEEE Standard for Developing Software Life Cycle Processes*) is also presented. This standard describes the process by which a software process architect selects a SLCM, maps activities onto the SLCM, and combines these with *organizational process assets* to create the *Software Life Cycle Process* for an individual project. IEEE Std. 1074 also defines its own classification schema of activity groups and activities. The mapping between the schemas from IEEE/EIA Std. 12207.0 and IEEE Std. 1074 is provided in this chapter.

This chapter describes a number of SLCMs, and discusses some of the advantages and disadvantages of these. Selection of a SLCM is extremely important, because if you don't, , you are implicitly using the "Black Box Model" for your software development process. This common approach is briefly considered, but it has many disadvantages. The first useful SLCM described is the *classic waterfall model*, as this is the easiest to understand. The *spiral model* is considered next, because this is the most successful alternative to the waterfall model. Finally, modified waterfall models are presented, which address some of the deficiencies of the classic waterfall model without sacrificing its simplicity of concept.

IEEE/EIA 12207.0, the "Principles" Standard

This section presents the top-level standard in the IEEE collection, IEEE/EIA 12207.0, and several associated guides:

- IEEE/EIA 12207.0-1996, IEEE/EIA Standard, Industry Implementation of International Standard ISO/IEC 12207:1995, (ISO/IEC 12207) Standard for Information Technology-Software life cycle processes
- IEEE/EIA 12207.1-1997, IEEE/EIA Guide for Information Technology, Software life cycle processes, Life cycle data
- IEEE/EIA 12207.2-1997, IEEE/EIA Guide, Software life cycle processes, Implementation considerations

ISO/IEC 12207:1995 is reproduced within IEEE/EIA 12207.0. The other two standards, IEEE/EIA 12207.1 and IEEE/EIA 12207.2, are guides rather than element standards. However, they serve a particularly important role in mapping between IEEE/EIA 12207.0 and various other element standards in the IEEE collection.

IEEE/EIA 12207.0 is the only standard classified in the "principles" layer of the SESC framework. It plays a special role in the standards collection, as a framework for all the other standards.

By adopting a key international standard (ISO/IEC 12207:1995), the IEEE collection is largely harmonized with important international standards and regional standards. IEEE has an ongoing initiative for such harmonization.

IEEE/EIA 12207.0 describes the activities to be performed during the software life cycle into five primary, eight supporting, and four organizational *processes*. Each process is decomposed into a set of *activities*, and each activity is described in terms of specific required or recommended *tasks*.

Primary Life Cycle Processes

IEEE/EIA 12207.0 defines the following primary life cycle processes:

1. *Acquisition process. Defines the activities of the acquirer, the organization that acquires a system, software product, or software service.*

2. *Supply process. Defines the activities of the supplier, the organization that provides the system, software product, or software service to the acquirer.*

3. *Development process. Defines the activities of the developer, the organization that defines and develops the software product.*

4. *Operation process. Defines the activities of the operator, the organization that provides the service of operating a computer system in its live environment for its users.*

5. *Maintenance process. Defines the activities of the maintainer, the organization that provides the service of maintaining the software product; that is, managing modifications to the software product to keep it current and in operational fitness. This process includes the migration and retirement of the software product.*

The most complex of these processes is the development process. This is also undoubtedly the one of greatest interest to the majority of readers, so we will look at it more closely.

Development Process

The development process is described in terms of 13 *activities* by IEEE/EIA 12207.0:

1. *Process implementation*
2. *System requirements analysis*
3. *System architectural design*
4. *Software requirements analysis*
5. *Software architectural design*

6. *Software detailed design*

7. *Software coding and testing*

8. *Software integration*

9. *Software qualification testing*

10. *System integration*

11. *System qualification testing*

12. *Software installation*

13. Software acceptance support

This list of activities has a finer granularity than the development process activities defined in some of the IEEE element standards. A mapping between IEEE/EIA 12207.0 and some of the element standards is provided in Table 4.1.

During the process implementation activity, a Software Project Management Plan should be produced; see IEEE Std. 1058.

System requirements analysis, system architectual design, system integration, and system qualification testing are really system engineering rather than software engineering activities because they involve hardware as well as software requirements and design decisions. The field of system engineering is closely related to software engineering, and the inclusion of these activities in IEEE/EIA 12207.0 must be understood in this context.

During the software requirements analysis, a Software Requirements Specification should be produced; see IEEE Std. 830.

During the software architectual design, the decomposition and dependency design views of the Software Design Description should be produced; see IEEE Std. 1016.

During the software detailed design, the interface and detailed design view of the Software Design Description should be produced; see IEEE Std. 1016.

During the software coding and testing, source code should be created, and unit testing should be performed. A number of IEEE element standards apply to this activity, including:

- IEEE Std. 829, IEEE Standard for Software Test Documentation
- IEEE Std. 982.1, IEEE Standard Dictionary of Measures to Produce Reliable Software
- IEEE Std. 1008, IEEE Standard for Software Unit Testing
- IEEE Std. 1061, IEEE Standard for a Software Quality Metrics Methodology
- IEEE Std. 1465, IEEE Standard Adoption of International Standard ISO/IEC 12119:1994 (E), Information Technology, Software packages, Quality requirements and testing

IEEE Std. 829 is also applicable to other testing activities, such as software qualification testing.

Supporting Life Cycle Processes

IEEE/EIA 12207.0 defines the following supporting life cycle processes:

1. *Documentation process. Defines the activities for recording the information produced by a life cycle process.*

2. *Configuration management process. Defines the configuration management activities.*

3. *Quality assurance process. Defines the activities for objectively assuring that the software products are in conformance with their specified requirements and adhere to their established plans. Joint Reviews, Audits, Verification, and Validation may be used as techniques of Quality Assurance.*

4. *Verification process. Defines the activities (for the acquirer, the supplier, or an independent party) for verifying the software products and services in varying depths depending on the software project.*

5. *Validation process. Defines the activities (for the acquirer, the supplier, or an independent party) for validating the software products of the software project.*

6. *Joint review process. Defines the activities for evaluating the status and products of an activity. This process may be employed by any two parties, where one party (reviewing party) reviews another party (reviewed party) in a joint forum.*

7. *Audit process. Defines the activities for determining compliance with the requirements, plans, and contract. This process may be employed by any two parties, where one party (auditing party) audits the software products or activities of another party (audited party).*

8. *Problem resolution process. Defines a process for analyzing and removing the problems (including nonconformances), whatever their nature or source, that are discovered during the execution of development, operation, maintenance, or other processes.*

The verification, validation, joint review, and audit processes may be viewed as sub-processes of the Quality Assurance process. It is also common to group the verification and validation processes together, and to subsume within them the joint review and audit processes (as, for example, in IEEE Std. 1012, IEEE Standard for Verification and Validation). Audits may also be viewed as a special type of software review (as, for example, in IEEE Std. 1028, IEEE Standard for Software Reviews). The problem resolution process may also be viewed as a sub-process of the configuration management process and/or the quality assurance process.

The relative lack of independence of these supporting processes may initially be puzzling. For example, in IEEE/EIA 12207.0, separate verification plans and validation plans are specified, but IEEE Std 1012 specifies a combined Software

Verification and Validation Plan. Actually, IEEE/EIA 12207.0 doesn't specify any documents at all. It only specifies that certain data is to be recorded. The user of IEEE/EIA 12207.0 determines how to package the data into documents via the documentation process.

Organizational Life Cycle Processes

IEEE/EIA 12207.0 defines the following organizational life cycle processes:

1. *Management process. Defines the basic activities of the management, including project management, related to the execution of a life cycle process.*

2. *Infrastructure process. Defines the basic activities for establishing the underlying structure of a life cycle process.*

3. *Improvement process. Defines the basic activities that an organization (that is, acquirer, supplier, developer, operator, maintainer, or the manager of another process) performs for establishing, measuring, controlling, and improving its life cycle process.*

4. *Training process. Defines the activities for providing adequately trained personnel.*

Tailoring Process

IEEE/EIA 12207.0 defines the *tailoring process* as

> ... *a process for performing basic tailoring of this International Standard for a software project.*

In the section 1.3 of the standard, this is described as follows:

> *This International Standard contains a set of processes, activities, and tasks designed to be tailored in respect of software projects. The tailoring process is deletion of non-applicable processes, activities, and tasks.*

In Annex A of IEEE/EIA 12207.0, the following four activities are specified for the tailoring process:

1. *Identifying project environment*
2. *Soliciting input*
3. *Selecting processes, activities, and tasks*
4. *Documenting tailoring decisions and rationale*

Tailoring is discouraged. It is included only for compatibility with the international standard. Annex F of IEEE/EIA 12207.0 defines two levels of compliance, tailored and absolute. This is intended to encourage selection of complete processes, and to disallow inappropriate claims for conformance to this standard. In order to claim absolute compliance with either the entire standard, or selected processes, all mandatory activities and tasks of the processes (specified using "shall" or "will") must be followed.

Although IEEE/EIA 12207.0 describes tailoring on a project basis, this may be done on an organizational basis as well. In an SOP, the deletion of non-applicable processes, activities, and tasks may be specified just once for an organization. Further tailoring may still be specified on a project basis, for example in a Software Project Management Plan.

Not explicitly mentioned for the tailoring process by IEEE/EIA 12207.0 is that a SLCM must be selected and the activities must be mapped onto the SLCM. This process is described by IEEE Std 1074 *(IEEE Standard for Developing Software Life Cycle Processes)*. IEEE/EIA 12207.0 B.4 does mention that one must

> *Determine which life cycle model(s) are relevant and applicable for the project, such as Waterfall, evolutionary, builds, pre-planned product improvement, Spiral. All such models prescribe certain processes and activities that may be performed sequentially, repeated, and combined; in these models, the life cycle activities in this International Standard should be mapped to the selected model(s).*

Further guidance on the selection of a SLCM and mapping is provided in Annex I of IEEE/EIA 12207.2, which describes four models:

1. Waterfall Model
2. Incremental Model
3. Evolutionary Model
4. Reengineering Model

We will be considering specific SLCMs later in this chapter.

Correlating IEEE/EIA 12207.0 to Element Standards

The following two IEEE element standards also specify software life cycle processes and associated activities:

- IEEE Std. 1012, IEEE Standard for Software Verification and Validation
- IEEE Std. 1074, IEEE Standard for Developing Software Life Cycle Processes

These standards have a slightly different classification schema, as summarized in Table 4.1.

Table 4.1. **Correlation of Life Cycle Processes and Element Standards**

IEEE/EIA 12207.0	IEEE Std. 1012	IEEE Std. 1074
Acquisition process (5.1)	Acquisition process (5.2)	Software importation activities (A.2.3)
Supply process (5.2)	Supply process (5.3)	
Development process (5.3)	Development process (5.4)	Project initiation activity (A.1.1), Project planning activities (A.1.1), Pre-Development Activity Groups (A.2), Development Activity Groups (A.3), Post-Development Activity Groups (A.4), Evaluation Activities (A.5.1)
Process implementation (5.3.1)	Concept activity (5.4.1)	Project initiation activities activity (A.1.1), Project planning activities (A.1.2), Concept exploration activities (A.2.1)
System requirements analysis activity (5.3.2)	Concept activity (5.4.1)	System allocation activities (A.2.2)
System architectual design activity (5.3.3)	Concept activity (5.4.1)	System allocation activities (A.2.2)
Software requirements analysis activity (5.3.4)	Requirements activity (5.4.2)	Requirements activities (A.3.1)
Software architectual) design activity (5.3.5	Design activity (5.4.3)	Design activities (A.3.2)
Software detailed design activity (5.3.6)	Design activity (5.4.3)	Design activities (A.3.2)
Software coding and testing activity (5.3.7)	Implementation activity (5.4.4)	Implementation activities (A.3.3)
Software integration activity (5.3.8)	Test activity (5.4.5)	Implementation activities (A.3.3)
Software qualification testing activity (5.3.9)	Test Activity (5.4.5)	Evaluation activities (A.5.1)
System integration activity (5.3.10)	Test Activity (5.4.5)	Implementation activities (A.3.3)
System qualification testing activity (5.3.11)	Test Activity (5.4.5)	Evaluation activities (A.3.3)
Software installation activity (5.3.12)	Installation & checkout activity (5.4.6)	Installation activities (A.4.1)
Software acceptance support activity (5.3.13)	Installation & checkout activity (5.4.6)	Installation activities (A.4.1)
Operation process (5.4)	Operation process (5.5)	Operation and Support activities (A.4.2)

IEEE/EIA 12207.0	IEEE Std. 1012	IEEE Std. 1074
Maintenance process (5.5)	Maintenance process (5.6)	Maintenance activities (A.4.3), Retirement activities (A.4.4)
Documentation process (6.1)		Documentation development activities (A.5.3)
Configuration management process (6.2)		Software configuration management activities (A.5.2)
Quality assurance process (6.3)		Evaluation activities (A.5.1)
Verification process (6.4)		Evaluation activities (A.5.1)
Validation process (6.5)		Evaluation activities (A.5.1)
Joint review process (6.6)		Evaluation activities (A.5.1)
Audit process (6.7)		Evaluation activities (A.5.1)
Problem resolution process (6.8)		Evaluation activities (A.5.1), Software configuration management activities (A.5.2)
Management process (7.1)	Management process (5.1)	Project management activity groups (A.1)
Infrastructure process (7.2)		
Improvement process (7.3)		Evaluation activities (A.5.1)
Training process (7.4)		Training activities (A.5.4)

In addition IEEE Std. 610.12 *(IEEE Standard Glossary of Software Engineering Terminology)* also provides an opinion on decomposing the software life cycle as part of its definition of that term:

> *The software life cycle typically includes a concept phase, requirements phase, design phase, implementation phase, test phase, installation and checkout phase, operation and maintenance phase, and, sometimes, retirement phase. Note: These phases may overlap or be performed iteratively.*

Clearly, IEEE Std. 610.12 is most closely harmonized with IEEE Std. 1012 with regards to the software life cycle decomposition schema.

An information item matrix is provided in IEEE/EIA 12207.1 Table 1, which traces information items from IEEE/EIA 12207.0 to specific IEEE element standards. This table is not reproduced here; please refer to the standard.

Additionally, a mapping of IEEE/EIA 12207.0 processes to specific IEEE element standards and guides (as well as some non-IEEE standards) is provided in Annex M of IEEE/EIA 12207.2. This is summarized in Table 4.2.

Table 4.2. **Mapping Processes to Standards and Guides.**

IEEE/EIA 12207.0 Process	IEEE Element Standards and Guides
Acquisition process	982.1, 1062, 1228
Supply process	
Development process	829, 830, 1008, 1016, 1016.1, 1028, 1074, 1074.1, 1228
Operation process	
Maintenance process	1219
Documentation process	
Configuration management process	828, 1012, 1042, 1059
Quality assurance process	730, 730.1, 1061, 1298
Verification process	1012, 1028, 1059
Validation process	1012, 1028, 1059
Joint review process	1028
Audit process	1028
Problem resolution process	1044, 1044.1
Management process	1045, 1058.1
Infrastructure process	1209, 1348, 1420.1
Improvement process	
Training process	

The IEEE software engineering collection is a work-in-progress, and it can be expected that standards will be developed over the next few years to cover holes in the availability of element standards for certain IEEE/EIA 12207.0 processes.

IEEE Std 1074, Developing the Software Life Cycle Process

This section provides an overview of using IEEE Std. 1074 *(IEEE Standard for Developing Software Life Cycle Processes)* for selecting a SLCM, *mapping* the activities of the standard onto the SLCM, and applying the *operational process assets (OPAs)* to create the software life cycle process *(SLCP)* for a specific project.

There are two aspects of IEEE Std 1074: It specifies a process model for developing an SLCP, and it provides a schema of activities that are to be mapped onto the selected SLCM. The latter role of IEEE Std. 1074 overlaps with IEEE/EIA 12207.0, since that standard also provides a schema of processes, activities, and tasks. The relationship between the two schemas was shown in Table 4.1. The activity schema of IEEE Std. 1074 will not be further analyzed here. You must decide whether you want to use the schema from IEEE/EIA 12207.0 or IEEE Std. 1074, or both.

The process of developing a SLCP according to IEEE Std 1074 involves three steps:

1. Selecting an SLCM
2. Mapping onto the SLCM (Creating an SLC)
3. Establishing an SLCP

These steps are illustrated in Figure 4.1 (which is similar to Figure 1 IEEE Std. 1074).

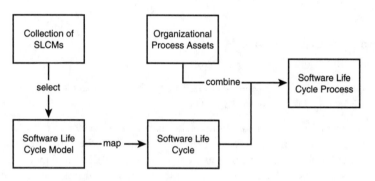

Figure 4.1 *Developing a Software Life Cycle Process.*

We will consider these three steps in more detail.

Selecting the SLCM

IEEE Std. 1074 defines SLCM as follows:

> **software life cycle model (SLCM):** *The framework, selected by each using organization, on which to map the Activities of this standard....*

The IEEE standards do not specify an SLCM for you. In particular, IEEE Std. 1074 states

> *This standard does not provide a collection of SLCMs. Providing such a collection of SLCMs is outside the scope of this standard.*

This is done to permit maximum flexibility for the development organization, which is free to select the latest process model best suited to its purpose.

Some IEEE standards give examples of specific SLCMs, however. For example, IEEE/EIA 12207.2 Annex I shows four possible SLCMs (waterfall model, incremental model, evolutionary model, and reengineering model) as figures, and IEEE Std. 1490's Figure 2-5 shows a spiral model.

Some IEEE standards appear to be written in terms of a particular SLCM. For example, IEEE Std. 1012 *(IEEE Standard for Verification and Validation) Figure 1 summarizes* verification and validation activities using a classic waterfall model. However, this does not mean that in order to conform with IEEE Std. 1012 you must use the waterfall model as your SLCM. You can map the verification and validation activities to a different SLCM, as is clear from a closer reading of this standard.

We will look at a number of possible SLCMs later in this chapter, and discuss advantages and disadvantages of different ones.

Mapping onto the SLCM

IEEE Std. 1074 defines *mapping* as follows:

> **mapping:** *Establishing a sequence of the Activities in this standard according to a selected software life cycle model (SLCM).*

As mentioned previously, the activities to be mapped could refer to those defined in IEEE Std. 1074 or those in IEEE/EIA 12207.0, or both. Because IEEE/EIA 12207.0 is a higher-level standard and a cornerstone of IEEE's strategy for harmonizing the standards collection with international standards, it might be expedient to use its activity classification schema.

By mapping, the *software life cycle* (SLC) is created. This is defined by IEEE Std. 1074 as follows:

> **software life cycle (SLC):** *The project-specific sequence of Activities that is created by mapping the Activities of this standard onto a selected software life cycle model (SLCM).*

During mapping, the activities must be placed in an executable sequence, and standard activities not used must be documented and justified. An example of mapping is provided in Annex B of IEEE Std. 1074. The mapping may be shown via a trace matrix, where standard activities are listed in the rows, and the components of the SLCM are listed in columns, as in Annex B.2 of the standard.

Establishing the SLCP

Artifacts that help define an organization's software project environment are referred to as *Organizational Process Assets* (OPAs). They consist of such items as the policies, standards, procedures, metrics, tools, methodologies, and the history of previous projects.

Once the SLC is has been developed, the available OPAs are applied to the SLC to establish the SLCP. For each activity in the SLC, its output information must be mapped to *deliverables* reconciled with the OPAs. Annex C of IEEE Std 1074 provides a template for documenting the assignment of activity outputs to deliverables.

Simplifying the SLCP Development Process

In the author's experience, many project engineers do not have the experience or available time to develop a SLCP effectively. In this case, it is recommended to simplify the SLCP development process, by incorporating predefined SLCMs into SOPs. Of course, minor tailoring of such predefined SLCMs is still needed, but this can consist merely of deleting non-applicable activities and work products.

Organizations with a high degree of process maturity will appreciate the flexibility offered by IEEE Std. 1074 in selecting SLCMs on a project-by-project basis. However, if you are attempting to implement a simple software development process for your organization, it can be expeditious to select one SLCM as a standard (as an Organizational Process Asset). This will simplify both your *Standard Operating Procedures* (which can then be written in terms of a single SLCM) and your project plans (which can reference the standard SLCM). Even if you want to allow multiple SLCMs, it is recommended that you prequalify them, describe them in your operating procedures, and consider them as part of your Organizational Process Assets. Assuming that you pick a single, standard SLCM for your organization, the Software Life Cycle Planning can be simplified relative to the general model provided by Std. 1074 (see Figure 4.2).

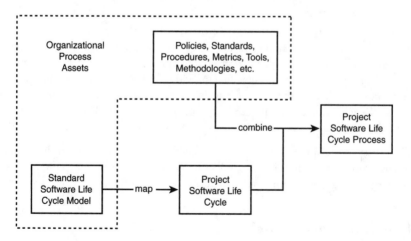

Figure 4.2 *Simplified Software Life Cycle Planning.*

According to this simplified planning process, you no longer have to select an SLCM for a project. Instead, you merely apply your organization's standard SLCM to the particular project. The SLCM is described by your organization's standard operating procedures, and your project plan can simply reference these (other standard information contained in project plans must still be included, of course). If your standard operating procedures allow and describe several SLCMs, your project plan simply specifies which SLCM is being used, referencing the standard operating procedures. This simplified approach to software life cycle planning is particularly useful if your organization executes many small software projects, rather than one or two large projects.

The Black Box Model

When no SLCM is used at all, software development can only be thought of as a *black box* relative to the system development process. This is a degenerate SLCM in its own right, pictured in Figure 4.3, sometimes also called the *Code-and-Fix* model. With this model, you are lucky to have a written specification to start with. Coding begins immediately, and bugs are fixed as they are discovered. If you are lucky, you will eventually end up with a software build suitable for release.

Figure 4.3 *Software development as a black box.*

This model offers no management control other than the decision to release the product after the volume and criticality of known bugs have been reduced acceptably. Software quality assurance is restricted to system level testing. No intermediate tasks or work products are specified, providing no framework for any other V&V activities. Clearly, this approach is unacceptable if the software has any safety risks, if there are any quality requirements, or if you must predict project cost and schedule accurately.

All software professionals know stories of failed projects conducted in this manner. Because you are reading this book, it can be assumed that you are trying improve your organization's software development process beyond this level of maturity.

The Waterfall Model

Although widely disparaged as inefficient, the *waterfall model*, the oldest, useful life cycle model for software development, still has many advantages. It is easy to understand, easy to explain, and easy to demonstrate compliance with. Use of a waterfall model expedites application of standards such as IEEE Std. 1012 (*Software Verification & Validation*), which are presented in terms of a waterfall model. For projects that lend themselves to a sequential scheduling approach, a simple waterfall model is often the most efficient. Only when the project risks are substantial enough to require more flexibility in task scheduling does the waterfall model compare unfavorably with more sophisticated models.

In the waterfall model, a project proceeds through a sequence of *phases*, from start to finish. Each phase is defined in terms of *inputs*, *tasks*, and *outputs*. At the end of each phase, a *phase review meeting* should be conducted to verify that all tasks have been performed, and that all outputs are ready for the next phase.

A representative waterfall model is provided by IEEE Std. 1012. Although this standard focuses on software verification and validation activities, its waterfall model also implicitly defines software development activities. Restricting our focus to the *Development Process* part of IEEE Std. 1012, we see a generic waterfall model, as shown in Figure 4.4.

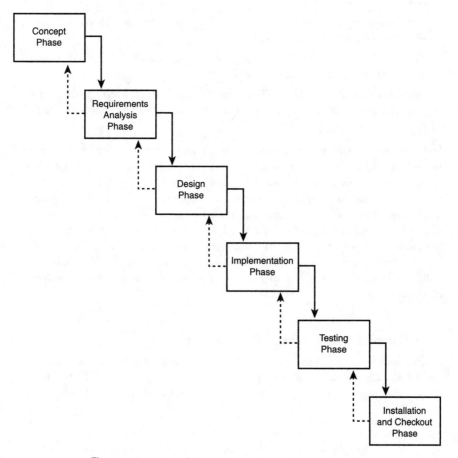

Figure 4.4 *A waterfall SLCM, according to IEEE Std. 1012.*

The phases of this specific waterfall model are described by IEEE Std. 1012 as follows:

Concept Phase. *Represents the delineation of a specific implementation solution to solve the user's problem. The system architecture is selected, and system requirements are allocated to hardware, software, and user interface components.*

Requirements Analysis Phase. *Defines the functional and performance requirements, interfaces external to the software, qualification requirements, safety and security requirements, human factors engineering, data definitions, user documentation for the software, installation and acceptance requirements, user operation and execution requirements, and user maintenance requirements.*

Design Phase. *Software requirements are transformed into an architecture and detailed design for each software component. The design includes databases and interfaces (external to the software components, between the software components, and between software units).*

Implementation Phase. *Transforms the design into code, database structures, and related machine executable representations.*

Testing Phase. *Covers software testing, software integration, software qualification testing, system integration, and system qualification testing.*

Installation and Checkout Phase. Installation of the software product in the target environment and the acquirer's acceptance review and testing of the software product.

In Figure 4.4, forward progress through the phases flows down, like cascading water. The upward arrows defy gravity, require extra energy, and are generally bad news. They show that phases sometimes need to be revisited, because of issues identified in later project phases. When software defects are identified during testing. For example, the problem might be traced back to the requirements specification, which would then need to be revised. This, in turn, would undoubtedly require the design and implementation to also be updated, causing major project delays. Clearly, a key project management goal is to minimize such delays, by providing effective reviews of intermediate work products prior to software testing, to detect such defects as early as possible.

Overlap of Phases in the Waterfall Model

A strict interpretation of the sequencing of phases in a waterfall model is almost never used. Theoretically, the next phase should not be started until the previous phase has completed. This would imply that some project resources are idle while the last tasks in the phase are being completed. This idleness is usually unacceptable in terms of project cost and schedule. In practice, some amount of overlap of project phases is assumed, and the model is best interpreted as allowing this. Even IEEE Std. 1012 shows a slight overlap in project phases in its waterfall model figure. The degree of phase overlap allowed by the model should be clearly specified. Alternative degrees of overlap can be categorized as follows:

- **No Overlap (Pure Waterfall Model).** The phases are expected to execute sequentially. A recommendation by the phase review meeting to proceed to the next phase is required. Completion of some project tasks can be deferred, but need to be clearly identified by the phase review meeting. Follow-up to such deferred tasks should be provided, and a *phase completion report* should be issued to document final completion of the phase.

- **One Phase Overlap.** Adjacent phases are allowed to execute concurrently, but a phase should not be started if its second-to-last predecessor has not yet been completed. According to this interpretation, design activities can proceed in parallel with requirements analysis, but coding should not start until authorized by a requirements analysis phase review meeting.

- **Overlapping Phases (Sashimi model).** Project phases are allowed to overlap extensively. Even the testing phase can be started prior to the completion of the concept phase. Phase review meetings should still be held, and a phase should not be completed until all predecessor phases have been completed. This degree of laxness in phase overlap changes the character of the SLCM substantially, and the Sashimi Model is often described as a *modified waterfall model* (see the section later in this chapter titled, "Modified Waterfall Models") rather than as a simple waterfall model.

Figure 4.5 pictures the waterfall model with one phase overlap and Figure 4.6 pictures the Sashimi SLCM.

In Figure 4.6, the phases are shown with an increased duration as the amount of overlap increases. This is realistic, because allocation of resources to multiple phases implies delays in finalizing earlier phases. Even with additional project resources, overlapping phases do not necessarily yield significant schedule improvements. The waterfall model with one-phase overlap provides a good compromise between structure and flexibility. The Sashimi model has many of the risks of a completely unstructured approach, because it provides few guidelines for sequencing project activities. The Sashimi model has the saving virtue of being easy to introduce into an organization with a currently unstructured process.

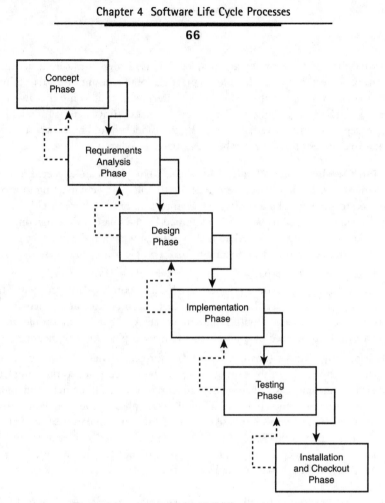

Figure 4.5 *A waterfall SLCM with one phase overlap.*

Work Product Data Flow in the Waterfall Model

The waterfall models are oriented towards *work products*. Each phase is expected to
create prespecified work products, which can be documents or the software itself.
The outputs of one phase become the inputs to the next phase. With a pure
waterfall model, all phase inputs must be available to start a phase, whereas for
waterfall models with varying degrees of phase overlap, preliminary work can start
before the inputs have been finalized.

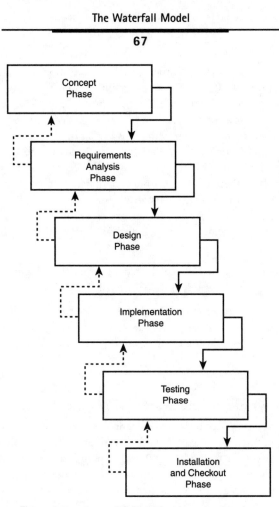

Figure 4.6 *A waterfall SLCM with overlapping phases.*

After a work product has been completed (drafted, reviewed, and reworked), it should be released as a *Configuration Item* subject to standard configuration management practices (see IEEE Std. 828 and Std. 1042). Identifications of defects in the work product during later project phases represent *Software Problem Reports, and identification of deficiencies in the original requirements specification documents that need to be incorporated later in the project represent Software Change Requests* and should be adequately documented. These should be presented to the appropriate *Configuration Control Board* for approval or disapproval. Records should be maintained both for verification of the rework, and to provide statistical data for future software process improvements.

Reviews of work products should always include verification of conformance to preceding work products. If a discrepancy is identified during the review, it might very well be the predecessor work product that must be modified. In this case, a *Software Change Request* must be issued, because the predecessor will already have been released to configuration management. Waterfall models are sometimes presented with documents such as the *Hazard Analysis Report* or the *Software Requirements Specification* listed as outputs of multiple phases. This is done to show that, in many projects, these documents must be updated later in the project to reflect results from later phases. It is simpler to list each work product as the output of only one phase, and to track any later rework as a visit back to that earlier phase. It is important to reduce such backward work flow in order to increase project efficiency.

Figure 4.7 shows the data flow of the same work products as Figure 4.6, only organized according to the waterfall model from IEEE Std. 1012.

Figure 4.7 is not meant to be exhaustive in terms of listing phase outputs. Items such as user documentation clearly need to be added for even small projects. It is interesting to see, however, how the data flow from Figure 4.6 maps to the waterfall model.

Rapid Prototyping in the Waterfall Model

One of the most effective techniques for decreasing project cost and schedule is *rapid prototyping* of software to explore and analyze project risks early in the life cycle. There are two ways to model rapid prototyping in the simple waterfall models: specifying rapid prototyping as an activity of early project phases, or starting the implementation phase early, overlapped with preceding phases.

Certain types of software prototypes are traditionally constructed during the concept and requirements analysis phases, without much concern about the propriety of such techniques. For example, user interface simulations are beneficial for analyzing software requirements, particularly when working with non-technical software customers. Algorithms and timing studies are also commonly performed during early project phases to mitigate risks. Prototypes can range from slide shows of screen layouts to interactive simulations developed using special software prototyping tools, to skeletal implementations of the software using the tools and environment of the final software. The last category requires further scrutiny, because it can be expected that the prototypes will evolve into the final software, causing quality concerns. The remaining discussion focuses exclusively on this case.

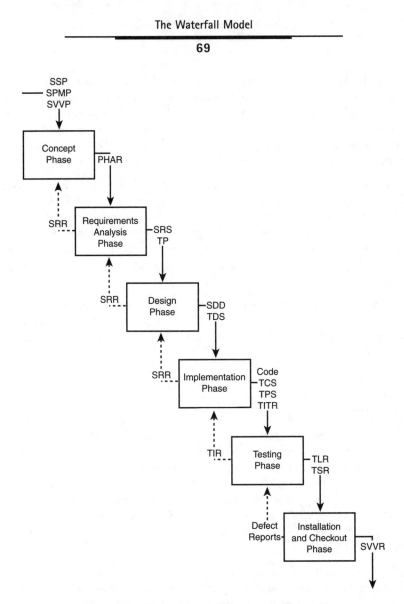

Figure 4.7 *Work product data flow in a waterfall model.*

Rapid prototyping raises quality questions. If the prototype is developed in an *ad hoc* manner, without attempting to follow standards, and is then used as the basis of the final implementation, software quality can be jeopardized. The greatest danger lies in the prototype being initially developed as a throwaway, but later being used for the product because of schedule pressure. Clearly, all personnel involved must understand that the prototype is intended to evolve into the final software *prior to* the construction of the prototype. In this case, standards must be followed during the construction of the prototype, and the prototype should be reviewed for conformance to requirements and standards.

Waterfall models with overlapping phases, particularly the Sashimi model, provide a more natural framework for rapid prototyping. Prototyping is modeled as an early activity of the implementation phase, and early software builds are used to provide feedback to the concept, analysis, and design phases. The disadvantage of the Sashimi model is that it does not guide the interactions between the concurrent phases, and threatens to allow the life cycle to degenerate into an entirely unstructured process.

Although it is possible to incorporate rapid prototyping into simple waterfall models using these techniques, more sophisticated SLCMs such as the Spiral Model and modified waterfall models are more natural for this purpose. We will look at such models in subsequent sections.

Spiral Model

The *spiral model* is a SLCM allowing for multiple iterations through similar project activities. Forward progress is represented as a spiral, starting at the center, proceeding through some number of *cycles*, and ending with the completion of the project. A *cycle review* should be conducted at the end of each cycle, similar to the phase review of a waterfall model. The different types of project activities conducted during the iterations (the *cycle activity groups*) can be represented as quadrants in the diagram, or, more generally, as slices, as of a pie. The number of iterations can be specified in advance, or can be planned dynamically, based on the results of the previous iteration.

Depending on the specifics of the iteration planning and categorization of cycle activity groups, the Spiral Model really represents a family of SLCMs. The Spiral Model is a sophisticated approach to software life cycle planning, and requires some maturity on the part of the organization using it.

The Spiral Model is widely recognized. It is described in IEEE Std. 1490-1998, *IEEE Guide, Adoption of PMI Standard, A Guide to the Project Management Body of Knowledge*. This standard contains a section on *Representative Project Life Cycles*. For software development, only a single SLCM is described, a spiral model with four cycles and four activity groups. This is shown in Figure 4.8.

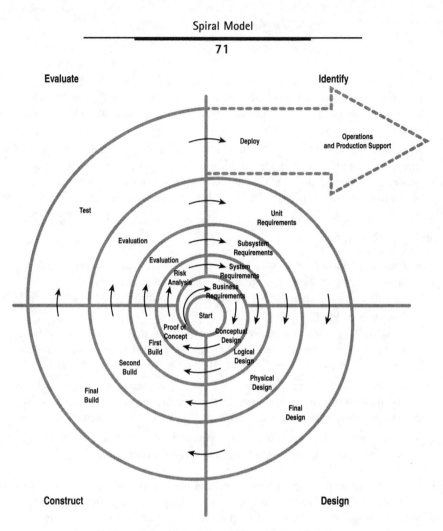

Figure 4.8 *The spiral model from IEEE Std. 1490.*

This is a simple spiral model. The quadrants (activity groups) map to the core phases of a standard waterfall model:

Identify. Similar to the *Requirements Analysis* phase of the waterfall model. Different types of requirements are analyzed depending on which cycle you're in: business requirements, system requirements, subsystem requirements, or unit requirements.

Design. Similar to the *Design* phase of the waterfall model. Different levels of design are performed depending on which cycle you're in: conceptual design, logical design, physical design, or final design.

Construct. Similar to the *Implementation* phase of the waterfall model. Different prototypes or software builds are constructed depending on which cycle you're in: proof of concept (prototype), first build, second build, or final build.

Evaluate. Similar to the *Testing* phase of the waterfall model. Different types of evaluation or testing activities are performed on the outputs of the previous quadrant, depending on which cycle you're in: risk analysis of the proof of concept, evaluation of preliminary builds, and testing of the final build.

The four cycles are specified in advance in this spiral model, and are described in IEEE Std. 1490, as follows:

- **Proof-of-concept cycle.** Capture business requirements, define goals for proof-of-concept, produce conceptual system design, design and construct the proof-of-concept, produce acceptance test plans, conduct risk analysis, and make recommendations.

- **First build cycle.** Derive system requirements, define goals for first build, produce logical system design, design and construct the first build, produce system test plans, evaluate the first build, and make recommendations.

- **Second build cycle.** Derive subsystem requirements, define goals for second build, produce physical design, construct the second build, produce system test plans, evaluate the second build, and make recommendations.

- **Final cycle.** Complete unit requirements; finalize design; construct final build; and perform unit, subsystem, system, and acceptance tests.

The terms conceptual, logical, physical, and final design in this model are not further defined in the IEEE Software Engineering Standards. They should be understood in the sense of providing sufficient design guidelines to implement the software prototype or build of the current cycle.

If you use a spiral model, it is not critical that you use exactly four cycles or four activity groups. The general spiral approach can be tailored to your specific needs.

Risk-Oriented Spiral Models

Any spiral model is clearly well suited for performing rapid prototyping. A *proof of concept* and construction of preliminary software builds are effective techniques for managing project risks. Risks can be explored and assessed prior to accrual of undue project cost and duration. Some spiral models emphasize risk reduction even further by incorporating risk analysis explicitly into the life cycle model. Risk analysis is added as an activity group, and planning of the next iteration is done dynamically, based on assessed risks. When risks have been sufficiently reduced, the last cycle unfolds analogously to a simple waterfall model, to ensure that all required project deliverables are finalized.

The details of how to represent the risk analysis and cycle planning can differ from one model to another. As an example, each cycle can consist of the following steps (activity groups):

Cycle Planning. The cycles are planned immediately prior to their execution, based on information from previous cycles. You must commit to an approach for the next cycle, and determine objectives, alternatives, and constraints.

Risk Analysis. Risks are identified, and alternatives for mitigating the risks are explored.

Development. Deliverables for the cycle are created. This can include proof of concepts, prototypes, preliminary software builds, or documents such as software requirements specifications, design descriptions, and so on.

Verification & Validation. Evaluation, reviews, testing, and other V&V activities are performed. These activities can be done concurrently with other cycle activities if appropriate.

Figure 4.9 shows the risk-oriented spiral model corresponding to the previous steps.

Risk-oriented spiral models allow for more effective risk management than traditional waterfall models—this is what they are designed for. Early cycles target risk analysis and mitigation, so any insurmountable risks are identified early, preventing project cost and schedule catastrophes. If a major change in product concept is required, it can be plotted early, without having committed too much money or time. The capability of this model to manage risks effectively comes at a price: complexity. Greater demands are placed on management when using a risk-oriented spiral model.

Work Product Data Flow in the Spiral Model

If the spiral is unwound, the spiral model looks like a waterfall model, but with more phases than usual. Each activity group in each cycle can be thought of as a phase in an equivalent waterfall model. Alternatively, each preliminary cycle could be considered one phase. The final cycle will look like the final phases of a conventional waterfall model. In the last cycle, all outstanding project work products must be finalized. This typically includes detailed design, code, and test documentation. The software requirements and high-level design will usually have been finalized in previous cycles.

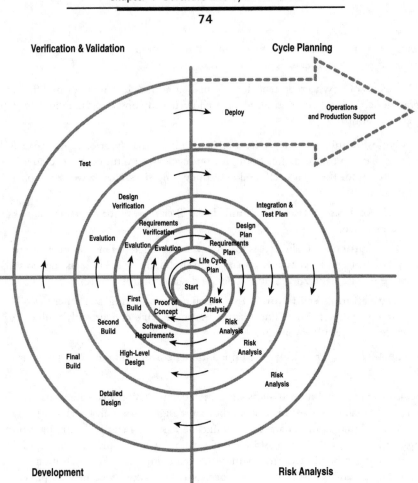

Figure 4.9 *The risk-oriented spiral model.*

For example, in the risk–oriented spiral model shown in Figure 4.9, the software requirements specification is shown as an output of the second cycle, and the high-level design description is shown as an output of the third cycle. In the fourth and final cycle, the detailed design specification, finalized code, and test documentation are all produced. Reviews are performed in multiple cycles, as work products are finalized, and such review reports are additional deliverables of each cycle. At the end of each cycle, a *cycle review* should be performed, to verify that all activities planned for the cycle have been successfully completed. The results of this review will serve as an input for planning the next cycle.

In the spiral models, preliminary builds are created in the non-final cycles. The source and executable files for these builds should be considered configuration items, because the software is expected to evolve from them. Design and code reviews should be performed, to identify any unacceptable aspects of the preliminary builds. Even if a preliminary build is adequate for the purpose of evaluating risks in the current cycle, defects in the design or implementation should be catalogued for eventual resolution in the final build. The spiral model thus places greater demands on configuration management, and should probably not be attempted without at least a rudimentary configuration management process in place.

Modified Waterfall Models

In this section, we will consider waterfall models modified for the purpose of incorporating rapid prototyping and risk-reduction. Many other modifications to the simple waterfall model are possible, but we will not try to list them exhaustively.

The perspective gained by considering spiral models will guide our efforts to extend the waterfall model. We have already noted that if a spiral is "unwound," it yields a lengthy but simple waterfall model. Because the spiral models are more difficult to manage, our goal will be to describe simpler models that still provide substantial benefit from rapid prototyping and risk reduction.

Waterfall/Spiral Hybrid Model

One of the primary benefits of the spiral model is risk reduction via rapid prototyping. The last cycle of a spiral model looks substantially like the latter phases of a simple waterfall model. In the last cycle, all unfinished work products must be completed and verified. We can make the analogy of the spiral's last cycle to the waterfall model more explicit by simply unwinding it, and modeling it as a conventional waterfall. The spiral is *only* used for risk-reduction, and the waterfall is used to complete the project (see Figure 4.10). The concept phase is replaced entirely by the spiral. The requirements analysis and design phases can be conducted as part of the spiral, or they can be deferred to the waterfall, depending on the application.

The advantage of the waterfall/spiral hybrid model is that the spiral does not need to be managed as precisely for V&V activities, because these are largely deferred to the waterfall stage.

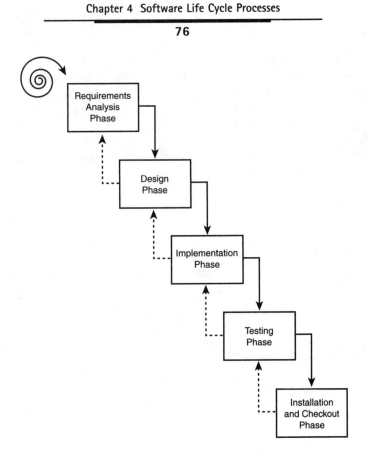

Figure 4.10 *The waterfall/spiral hybrid model.*

Study Project Model

One approach to allowing a substantial rapid prototyping effort is to split a project into two sub-projects: a study project, dedicated to construction of a prototype and its analysis, and an engineering project that uses results obtained from the study. The engineering project can be executed using a conventional waterfall model. This is pictured in Figure 4.11.

This is clearly a very simple approach. It can be viewed as a two-iteration spiral, with one initial cycle dedicated to risk analysis. However, it can be explained and managed without the complexity of the full Spiral Model.

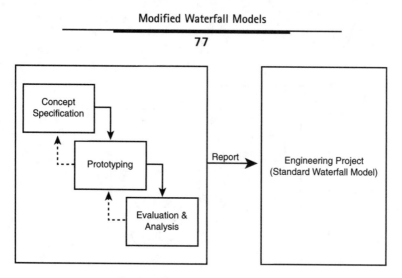

Figure 4.11   *The study project model.*

Milestone Build Model

Another effective technique for incorporating rapid prototyping into the SLCM is to allow for creation of *milestone builds,* each dedicated to addition of key functionality, usually in decreasing order of risk. Standard phases of the waterfall model are repeated for the creation of each build, allowing for systematic V&V activity. High-risk functionality is explored during early periods of the project, reducing potential impact on project cost and schedule if difficulties arise. Figure 4.12 shows the milestone build model.

The number of milestone builds should be planned at the outset of the project. The highest risk functionality should be incorporated into the earliest builds possible, to allow risks to be addressed at the earliest possible time.

For example, the first milestone build can be dedicated to constructing only the user interface. The user interface specification, design, and implementation are developed in full compliance with standard V&V activities, and are tested to provide early feedback on this high-risk portion of the software. When the user interface has been finalized, the remaining functionality of the software is then developed, again following the standard waterfall model with full V&V activities.

The milestone build model is an excellent process model for proving concepts one by one when attempting a totally new technology. In a new technology area, one does not always know if the technology will work, and milestone builds can be planned in accordance with such risks.

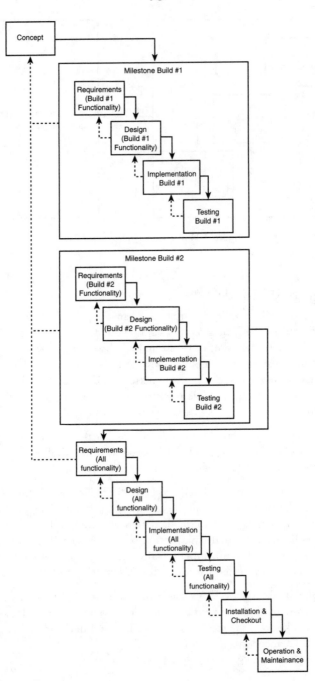

Figure 4.12   *The milestone build model.*

The milestone build model is also a natural fit for software enhancement projects, where additional functionality is added to an existing software product. Often, several unrelated enhancements are included in one project. In the milestone build model, the highest-risk enhancement is developed first. When this is completed, the next-highest-risk enhancement is developed, and so on.

The advantage of this model is that it allows for risk-reduction, similar to that in the spiral model, while avoiding the spiral model's complexity. It is as easy to use the milestone build model as to use any simple waterfall model. Standards such as IEEE Std. 1012 for Software Verification & Validation are easily mapped onto the milestone build model, and it is straightforward to explain the model to project personnel and external auditors.

Summary

For a top-down start to using the IEEE software engineering standards collection, you may want to start with IEEE/EIA Std. 12207.0. It defines processes, activities, and tasks covering everything having to do with software engineering. Processes suitable to your particular needs can be selected and implemented. If you want more detail, you can use specific IEEE element standards.

For a specific project, you must select a software life cycle model. It is recommended to start with a simple or modified waterfall model. The combination of clearly defined phase inputs, tasks, and outputs and the straightforward manner of verifying compliance via phase review meetings make waterfall models easy to use. Even a novice software engineer or an inexperienced software auditor should be able to understand a waterfall model description of a project.

Rapid prototyping of software is the most effective single technique available to mitigate the primary deficiency of the waterfall models: inefficiency. In order to minimize project cost and schedule risks, the Software Life Cycle Model should allow constructing software prototypes during early project phases. The study project model and milestone build model provide straightforward means for incorporating risk-reduction.

When an organization has sufficient process maturity, rapid prototyping can be naturally and effectively integrated into the software life cycle using the spiral model.

The IEEE Software Engineering Standards provide complete flexibility for you to select a Software Life Cycle Model appropriate to your project and organization. Selecting an optimal Software Life Cycle Model is a key step in increasing software project efficiency.

CHAPTER 5

Work Product Standards

This chapter describes *work product* standards. These are standards for user documentation, requirements specifications, design descriptions, the software itself, and test documentation. *Process* standards are described in Chapter 6.

This chapter is an excellent place to jump into if you are impatient and want to get started quickly. It is not difficult to understand the context of these standards, because they do not depend heavily on the process.

Perhaps the most difficult concept to understand relating to the work product standards is the difference between a *Software Requirements Specification (SRS)* and a *Software Design Description*. To the seasoned software veteran, distinguishing between these two might seem to be a trivial issue, but in many organizations these terms are misunderstood, particularly by management. A Software Requirements Specification documents *what* the software shall do, and a Software Design Description documents *how* the software does it. These documents have naturally different audiences. The Software Requirements Specification should be developed and reviewed jointly by the customer and supplier of the software. Consequently, non-technical personnel are often involved in developing and reviewing an SRS. Such individuals would have little chance of success in understanding the software design, and would have little or no interest in it.

A Software Design Description, on the other hand, is a technical document produced by software professionals for other software professionals. From a project management perspective, it is intuitive to first analyze *what* the software should do before too much effort is spent designing *how* it should do it. This idea is modeled by having separate requirements and design phases in the project life cycle. Thus, finishing the Software Requirements Specification represents an earlier project milestone than completing the Software Design Description. The difference in audiences and the distinct project milestones they represent are excellent reasons for carefully differentiating between these two different types of documents.

It is interesting to note that there are not many standards applicable to the software itself. The *Introduction to the 1999 Edition* has the following explanation:

> *Software engineering standards have traditionally focused on process rather than product, so it is not surprising that this section of the collection is relatively sparse.*

IEEE Std. 982.1 (*IEEE Standard Dictionary of Measures to Produce Reliable Software*), and IEEE Std. 1061 (*IEEE Standard for a Software Quality Metrics Methodology*) are the primary standards in the IEEE collection applicable directly to the software. IEEE Std. 1465 (Adoption of International Standard ISO/IEC 12119-1994(E)) is so high-level that it provides less direct benefit. IEEE Std. 1465 is not covered in this book.

In particular, *programming standards* are not provided by the IEEE Software Engineering Standards. Programming standards ought to be written, however, either for each project, or for your organization as a whole. Programming standards should establish commenting and naming conventions, and provide guidelines for limiting software complexity. IEEE Std. 982.1 helps with the latter, by providing several measures for software complexity, such as *Cyclomatic complexity.*

Each section in this chapter describes either an individual standard or several related standards on a similar topic. For each topic, the same section titles are used for easy reference. Each section consists of the following information:

- An overview
- Benefits of the standards
- Relationships of the standards to other IEEE standards
- The target audience
- Project phases affected by the standard (relative to the standard IEEE waterfall model described previously)

- A detailed description of the standard, for example, looking at the prototype outlines for documents
- Recommendations for phase-in, including practical considerations

The order of presentation of individual standards follows the model described in Section 3.4 (Applicability of Standards), following the recommended sequence of phase-in of the standards. Thus, the more fundamental standards that you might want to consider implementing first are presented first.

User Documentation Overview—IEEE Std. 1063

This section describes user documentation standards in the IEEE Software Engineering Standards collection.

The following is the IEEE *element standard* on this topic:

IEEE Std. 1063-1987 (R1993), *IEEE Standard for Software User Documentation*

The *Introduction to the 1999 Edition* summarizes IEEE Std. 1063 as

SESC's standard for traditional printed user manuals; on-line documentation is excluded from its scope.

Most software needs a manual. User documentation, assuming that it is required, constitutes a critical link for the quality of the software product. IEEE Std. 1063 provides detailed guidelines for the structure and information content of software user documentation.

The standard describes a list of user document *components*, and provides guidelines as to whether these components are mandatory or optional. Recommendations for the content, organization, and presentation of the body of the document are provided for two modes:

Instructional Mode—Intended for users who need to learn about the software

Reference Mode—Intended for users who need to refresh their memory about the software.

These modes are not mutually exclusive, because the user documentation set can have individual documents or sections of documents written in different modes.

Benefits

Use of IEEE Std. 1063 can improve the quality of software user documentation. By providing a checklist of mandatory and optional document components, including topics for the body of the document, this standard will help ensure the completeness of user manuals.

By providing guidelines for inclusion of Cautions and Warnings, the standard addresses the important task of labeling for the purpose of mitigating software risks.

Because of the tangible nature of this standard, it is straightforward to put into practice. Recommended as one of the first standards to implement, it provides a useful test case for phasing in use of the IEEE Software Engineering Standards.

Relationship to Other Standards

It is important to distinguish between software user documentation and the Software Requirements Specification as described by IEEE Std. 830 *(IEEE Recommended Practice for Software Requirements Specifications)*. These documents are developed for different purposes, and target different audiences. Software user documentation is intended to provide information to users of the software, whereas a Software Requirements Specification is written to specify functional characteristics of the software to the software developers and testers. A Software Requirements Specification often specifies details that are not of interest to users, such as software processing requirements for communication interface events. Software user documentation is principally concerned with the user interface or possibly a database structure, and is intended to *instruct about,* rather than *specify,* these topics.

Software user documentation is an important means of reducing software safety risks. It is referenced by IEEE Std. 1228 *(IEEE Standard for Software Safety Plans)* as a documentation requirement. Std. 1228 has the following specific requirement for software user documentation:

> *Information that may be significant to the safe installation, use, maintenance, and/or retirement of the system shall be prepared.*

Software reviews, as described in IEEE Std. 1028 *(IEEE Standard for Software Reviews)*, and software testing, as described in IEEE Std. 829 *(IEEE Standard for Software Test Documentation)*, are primary means for validating software user documentation.

Audience

Final user documentation is typically developed by technical writers rather than by software developers. Thus technical writers can be viewed as the primary audience of this standard. However, software developers can write an initial draft of the user documentation, and also profit from this standard. The foreword to the standard has the following to say about this:

> *This standard does not cover the actual writers and publishers of user documentation. The responsibility for ensuring that satisfactory software user documentation is produced rests with the organization that generates the software.*

Software development and software quality assurance personnel should review the final user documentation. User documentation is also important input to software testing activities, and is thus examined by software test personnel. Defects in the user documentation identified during reviews or testing, including errors of omission, should reference this standard for terminology.

Project Phases Affected

IEEE Std. 1012 *(IEEE Standard for Software Verification and Validation)* specifies user documentation as inputs to V&V inputs for the Requirements, Design, Implementation, Test, and Installation and Checkout phases. This means that the user documentation should be written and updated during these phases. A first draft of the user documentation is commonly written during the Requirements Analysis phase, and is updated during the Design and Implementation phases as more detailed information becomes available. User documentation should be viewed as one of the *test items* for the Test phase, in which it is validated.

Detailed Description

IEEE Std. 1063 defines a simple process model for identifying required software user documentation, which is done *prior* to writing the user documentation. This planning process consists of the following four steps:

1. **Identifying the Software.** The standard states: *The software, its user interfaces, and the tasks that users perform with the software, shall be identified at the start of documentation planning.*

2. **Determining the Document Audience.** The intended audience for the documents must be identified. The standard states: *The identified audience will dictate the document presentation style and level of detail.*

3. **Determining the Document Set.** The software user documentation (the *document set*) can be organized as multiple documents. The individual documents should be identified.

4. **Determining Document Usage Modes.** An *instructional* mode or *reference* mode, or both, must be selected for the individual user documents. This choice will affect the organization and content of the main body of each document.

The standard defines 12 basic components of a software user document, and provides guidelines on whether these should be considered mandatory or optional. These guidelines vary, depending on whether they apply to a single-volume document or a multi-volume document, and the document's size. The 12 components are

Title Page. This should include the document name, version, and date; it will identify software being described and the organization issuing the software and documentation.

Restrictions. Restrictions for the use or copying of the document or software should appear on the title page or immediately thereafter. Copyright, trademark, and other legal notices should appear according to accepted conventions.

Warranties. Warranties, contractual obligations, or disclaimers should be included.

Table of Contents. This is considered mandatory for documents more than eight pages in length. Several different styles are permitted, including a comprehensive table of contents for the entire document, or a simple listing of sections, with a comprehensive section table of contents preceding each section.

List of Illustrations. A list of the titles and locations of all illustrations can be included. Separate lists for figures, tables, and exhibits are permitted.

Introduction. The introduction is intended to provide the following information: audience description, applicability statement, purpose statement, document usage description, related documents, conventions, and problem reporting instructions. The last item is especially important for software quality purposes, because it facilitates user feedback and complaint reporting.

Body of Document. The content, organization, and presentation of the body of the document depend on whether an instructional or reference mode is used (modes are discussed later in this section).

Error Conditions. This should include error messages, known software problems, and associated error recovery instructions.

Appendixes. Supporting material should be attached and arranged for ease of access.

Bibliography. All publications mentioned in the document should be listed.

Glossary. Definitions of terms, acronyms, and abbreviations that might be unfamiliar to the audience should be listed alphabetically.

Index. An index is required for documents more than eight pages. This provides location references for key words and concepts.

The *body* of an *instructional* mode document can be organized according to *topics* for an *information-oriented* instructional document, or according to *tasks* for a *task-oriented* instructional document. The following contents should be included in task-oriented sections of an instructional document:

Scope. Indicates the scope of the material to be discussed in the section.

Materials. Describes any materials needed to perform user tasks covered in the section.

Preparations. Describes any actions that must be done before starting the tasks covered in the section.

Cautions and Warnings. Describe cautions and warnings that apply to the tasks. General cautions and warnings can be placed at the beginning of the section, but specific cautions and warnings should be placed on the same page and immediately before the action that requires them.

Method. Each task should be described, including what the user must do; what function, if any, is invoked; possible errors, including how to avoid them and how to resolve them; and what results to expect.

Related Information. Other useful information should be included as appropriate. This might consist of descriptions of task relationships, notes, limitations, or constraints.

The *body* of a *reference* mode document should be organized according to how a user accesses a software function, for example, by command, by menu, or by system calls. Within this organization, functions should be arranged for easy user access, for example, alphabetically. The following contents should be included for each function in a reference document:

Purpose. Describes the purpose of the function.

Materials. Describes any materials needed to use the function.

Preparations. Describes any actions that must be done before using the function.

Inputs. Identifies and describes all data required for the correct processing of the function.

Cautions and Warnings. Describes cautions and warnings that apply to the function. General cautions and warnings can be placed at the beginning of the section, but specific cautions and warnings should be placed on the same page and immediately before the action that requires them.

Invocation. Provides all information needed to use and control the function, including required parameters, optional parameters, default options, and order and syntax.

Suspension of Operations. Describes how to interrupt the function during execution and how to restart it.

Termination of Operations. Describes how to recognize function terminations, including abnormal terminations.

Outputs. Describes the results of executing the function, for example, screen display, effect on files or data, completion status values or output parameters, or outputs that trigger other actions, such as mechanical, electrical or other actions in process control applications.

Error Conditions. Describes error conditions that can occur as a result of executing the function, and how to detect that the error has occurred.

Related Information. Other useful information should be included as appropriate. This might consist of limitations and constraints, notes, and related functions.

Cautions and warnings are an especially important aspect of the user documentation, because they might be intended to mitigate safety risks. These are defined as follows by the standard:

Caution. An advisory in a software user document that performing some action might lead to consequences that are unwanted or undefined.

Warning. An advisory in a software user document that performing some action will lead to serious or dangerous consequences.

Review and testing of the user documentation should place special emphasis on the cautions and warnings, including possible omitted cautions and warnings. The wording of cautions and warnings should be as simple and clear as possible. In Section 6.1, the standard states:

...find a method to highlight selected material of special importance, especially cautions and warnings.

The wording and consistent highlighting of all cautions and warnings should be carefully reviewed.

Recommendations for Implementation

IEEE Std. 1063 is one of the easiest standards to implement. This is because it does not require any significant modifications to the software development process. This standard is the only one in the IEEE collection that can be easily and effectively introduced during the later phases of a project. Even if user documentation has already been written without the use of this standard, it can be reviewed and brought into compliance with only modest effort.

It is recommended that the organization's internal standards for software user documentation be reviewed and harmonized with IEEE Std. 1063. For new projects, the simple process model defined by the standard for identifying required user documents should be used prior to writing the software user documentation.

Summary of IEEE Std. 1063

IEEE Std. 1063 is an excellent standard with tangible benefits and straightforward usage. It is recommended as one of the first IEEE software engineering standards to implement. Because this standard does not affect the software development personnel and process to the same extent as other standards, there is little risk in its implementation, making it a suitable "test case" for software process improvements.

Requirements Specifications Overview—IEEE Std. 830

This section describes the IEEE standard for *Software Requirements Specifications:*

> IEEE Std. 830-1998, *IEEE Recommended Practice for Software Requirements Specifications*

According to IEEE Std. 830, a *Software Requirements Specification* (SRS) should address the following issues:

Functionality. What is the software supposed to do?

External interfaces. How does the software interact with people, the system's hardware, other hardware, and other software?

Performance. What is the speed, availability, response time, recovery time of various software functions, and so on?

Attributes. What are the portability, correctness, maintainability, security, and other considerations?

Design constraints imposed on an implementation. Are there any required standards in effect, implementation language, policies for database integrity, resource limits, operating environment(s) and so on?

This is what should be targeted by an SRS. There are other topics that should be excluded from an SRS, according to the standard:

> *The SRS writer(s) should avoid placing either design or project requirements in the SRS.*
>
> *(The SRS) should not describe any design or implementation details. These should be described in the design stage of the project.*
>
> *The SRS should address the software product, not the process of producing the software product.*

An SRS should not describe the software *project* or the software *design*. It should specify *what* the *software* shall do, not *how* the software shall do it, and not what the *project team* shall do. This is often a stumbling block for inexperienced SRS writers.

IEEE Std. 830 describes the following *characteristics of a good SRS*, which should be observed both when writing and reviewing an SRS:

Correct. An SRS is correct if, and only if, every requirement stated therein is one that the software shall meet.

Unambiguous. An SRS is unambiguous if, and only if, every requirement stated therein has only one interpretation.

Complete. An SRS is complete if, and only if, it includes the following elements:

a) All significant requirements, whether relating to functionality, performance, design constraints, attributes, or external interfaces.

b) Definition of the responses of the software to all realizable classes of input data in all realizable classes of situations.

c) Full labels and references to all figures, tables, and diagrams in the SRS and definition of all terms and units of measure.

Consistent. Consistency refers to internal consistency. If an SRS does not agree with some higher-level document, such as a system requirements specification, then it is not correct.

Ranked for importance and/or stability. An SRS is ranked for importance and/or stability if each requirement in it has an identifier to indicate either the importance or stability of that particular requirement.

Verifiable. An SRS is verifiable if, and only if, every requirement stated therein is verifiable. A requirement is verifiable if, and only if, there exists some finite cost-effective process with which a person or machine can check that the software product meets the requirement.

Modifiable. An SRS is modifiable if, and only if, its structure and style are such that any changes to the requirements can be made easily, completely, and consistently while retaining the structure and style.

Traceable. An SRS is traceable if the origin of each of its requirements is clear and if it facilitates the referencing of each requirement in future development or enhancement documentation.

Interfaces between separate software packages, such as communication interfaces, software interfaces, or database interfaces, are best specified in separate interface specification documents, which can then be referenced by multiple SRSs. This recommendation does not contradict the characteristic of *completeness* of a good SRS, assuming that the interface specification document itself possesses the characteristics recommended by the standard.

Software user documentation is sometimes used as a substitute when no SRS has been developed. This is typical in an unstructured software development environment. It is easy to see that even good software user documentation does not satisfy most of the characteristics of a good SRS as described previously. User documentation might be correct, consistent, verifiable, and modifiable, but it is almost never totally unambiguous, complete, and traceable.

The majority of IEEE Std. 830 is dedicated to describing the *parts of an SRS*. It provides a *prototype SRS outline*, with different alternatives provided for the section for *specific requirements*. For each section and sub-section of the prototype SRS out-line, IEEE Std. 830 provides detailed recommendations for their information content. The prototype outlines are analyzed in the "Detailed Description" section later in the chapter.

Benefits

Recall the definition of *quality* from IEEE Std. 610.12:

(1) The degree to which a system, component, or process meets specified requirements.

(2) The degree to which a system, component, or process meets customer or user needs or expectations.

A Software Requirements Specification serves a vital role for achieving software quality as the primary document intended to capture the criteria by which quality will be measured. It specifies the requirements for the software, and should reflect customer and user needs and expectations.

IEEE Std. 830 is an excellent standard. It provides templates for writing a good SRS, and detailed guidelines for the information content of each section. It is flexible, allowing a number of different outlines, to reflect different requirements analysis methodologies.

Development of a good SRS is the most important and fundamental process improvement to make (if not yet implemented). Without an SRS, it is difficult to

- Design the software, because it is not entirely clear what the software should do
- Validate the software, again because it is not clear what the software should do
- Manage the software project, because, when requirements change as they almost always do, the associated cost and schedule increases are difficult to derive and justify

Developing an SRS is required even for the most minimal software quality standards and regulations. Development of an SRS should increase software product quality, and decrease software project cost and schedule.

Relationship to Other Standards

IEEE Std. 830 references 16 other standards, saying:

This recommended practice shall be used in conjunction with (these) publications.

Here, we will explore only the most important relationships to other standards.

Software requirements analysis activities are conducted within the context of project plans as defined by other standards, such as:

- **Software Project Management Plan.** Described by IEEE Std. 1058 *(IEEE Standard for Software Management Plans)*.
- **Software Quality Assurance Plan.** Described by IEEE Std. 730 *(IEEE Standard for Software Quality Assurance Plans)*.
- **Software Verification and Validation Plan.** Described by IEEE Std. 1012 *(IEEE Standard for Software Verification and Validation)*.
- **Software Configuration Management Plan.** Described by IEEE Std. 828 *(IEEE Standard for Software Configuration Management Plans)*. This is discussed further later in the chapter.
- **Software Safety Plan.** Described by IEEE Std. 1228 *(IEEE Standard for Software Safety Plans)*. This is also discussed further later in the chapter.

An SRS is often developed for a software sub-project of a larger system project. The requirements for the entire system should be captured in a *Systems Requirements Specification*, as per IEEE Std. 1233 *(IEEE Guide for Developing System Requirements Specifications)*. The SRS should be traceable back to this document, and should be reviewed for correctness and completeness relative to this predecessor document.

The successor document to the SRS is the *Software Design Description* (SDD), as defined in IEEE Std. 1016 *(IEEE Recommended Practice for Software Design Descriptions)*. The SRS should allow the software design to be traced back to specific software requirements, and should facilitate evaluation of the SDD for correctness and completeness.

As for other important *work products*, the SRS should be verified via *software reviews*, as defined in IEEE Std. 1028 *(IEEE Standard for Software Reviews)*. *Inspections*, one of the software review techniques described in that standard, are particularly effective for evaluating an SRS.

Because the SRS is a controlling document for the software project, it is beneficial to use configuration management techniques, as described in IEEE Std. 828 *(IEEE Standard for Software Configuration Management Plans)* and IEEE Std. 1042 *(IEEE Guide to Software Configuration Management Plans)*. Desired changes in requirements should be identified, controlled, tracked, and reported using a formal process, and, if approved, should be incorporated into a revision of the SRS.

A standard not mentioned in the references for IEEE Std. 830, but one that nevertheless has an important relationship to it, is IEEE Std. 1228 *(IEEE Standard for Software Safety Plans)*. This standard defines terminology for *software safety*, specifies performing a *Preliminary Hazard Analysis,* and provides guidelines for *software safety requirements analysis.* Safety critical software requirements are clearly the most important. If an SRS is "*Ranked for Importance*," this implies that safety critical requirements should be clearly identified. The SRS should be traceable back to the *Preliminary Hazard Analysis Report*, and should be carefully reviewed for completeness and correctness in the mitigation of software hazards.

Another standard not mentioned in the references for IEEE Std. 830, but that has an important relationship to IEEE Std. 830, is IEEE Std. 829 *(IEEE Standard for Software Test Documentation).* Test planning and design, and creation of test cases and test procedures, will use the SRS as the most important input. Defects in an SRS are often discovered during test preparation and execution activities.

Audience

IEEE Std. 830 defines three categories of persons with a direct or indirect interest in the Software Requirements Specification. These definitions are as follows:

Customer: *The person, or persons, who pay for the product and usually (but not necessarily) decide the requirements.*

Supplier: *The person, or persons, who produces a product for a customer. The customer and the supplier can be members of the same organization.*

User: *The person, or persons, who operates or interacts directly with the product. The user(s) and the customer(s) are often not the same person(s).*

The standard recommends *joint preparation of the SRS* on the part of the *customer* and *supplier,* who thus together make up the primary target audience. The justification for the joint preparation is explained by the standard, as follows:

The software development process should begin with supplier and customer agreement on what the completed software must do. This agreement, in the form of an SRS, should be jointly prepared. This is important because usually neither the customer nor the supplier is qualified to write a good SRS alone.

   a) *Customers usually do not understand the software design and development process well enough to write a usable SRS.*

   b) *Suppliers usually do not understand the customer's problem and field of endeavor well enough to specify requirements for a satisfactory system.*

Therefore, the customer and the supplier should work together to produce a well-written and completely understood SRS. Joint preparation does not imply that customer and supplier must write the document jointly. Often, the customer provides descriptions of requirements via informal documents, interviews, diagrams, and other means. The supplier compiles the formal SRS, and the customer then reviews the SRS.

The requirements captured by the SRS should express both the *customer* and *user* needs and expectations. This is based on the definition of *quality* from IEEE Std. 610.12 (see the previous section). The user is only indirectly interested in the SRS, to the extent that the software developed from the SRS should, in fact, meet his needs and expectations.

Software design and test personnel use an SRS as an important *input* document for their tasks. Software quality assurance personnel can participate in reviewing an SRS, particularly for its conformance to the standard. These groups are thus secondary audiences for the standard.

Project Phases Affected

The SRS is developed during the *Requirements Analysis* phase of the project. It is the primary input to the *Design* phase, and is also an input to the *Implementation* and *Test* phases. During these later phases, the SRS usually needs to be updated. IEEE Std. 830 summarizes this as follows:

> *The SRS might need to evolve as the development of the software product progresses. It might be impossible to specify some details at the time the project is initiated (for example, it might be impossible to define all the screen formats for an interactive program during the requirements phase). Additional changes might ensue as deficiencies, shortcomings, and inaccuracies are discovered in the SRS.*

It is as important to conduct reviews for revisions of the SRS as for the original SRS completed during the Requirements Analysis phase. Revising the SRS can be viewed as a return to the Requirements Analysis phase (the upward, backward arrows in the waterfall model). It is important to use *configuration management* techniques to control changes in requirements. IEEE Std. 830 puts it this way:

> *A formal change process should be initiated to identify, control, track, and report projected changes. Approved changes in requirements should be incorporated in the SRS in such a way as to*
>
> > *Provide an accurate and complete audit trail of changes*
> >
> > Permit the review of current and superseded portions of the SRS

Uncontrolled changes in software requirements are one of the classic mistakes of software project management. The customer should be fully aware of the project cost and schedule consequences of requirements changes prior to approving them.

Detailed Description

IEEE Std. 830 provides a set of prototype SRS outlines. The organizational aspects of these outlines are not mandatory, but the informational content is. The standard states:

Although an SRS does not have to follow this outline or use the names given here for its parts, a good SRS should include all the information discussed here.

The prototype SRS outlines are all identical except for the organization of the section containing the specific requirements. The common parts of the outline are given in Figure 5.1.

```
Table of Contents
1.   Introduction
     1.1.   Purpose
     1.2.   Scope
     1.3.   Definitions, acronyms, and abbreviations
     1.4.   References
     1.5.   Overview
2.   Overall description
     2.1.   Product perspective
     2.2.   Product functions
     2.3.   User characteristics
     2.4.   Constraints
     2.5.   Assumptions and dependencies
3.   Specific requirements
Appendixes
Index
```

Figure 5.1   *Prototype SRS outline, from IEEE Std. 830.*

IEEE Std. 830 provides detailed guidelines for the information content of each of these sections, which will not be repeated here.

One common point of confusion is the difference between the *Purpose* and *Scope* sub-sections of the *Introduction*. The *Purpose* should *"delineate the purpose of the SRS"* and *"specify the intended audience for the SRS,"* whereas the *Scope* should *"identify the software by name; explain what the software will do; describe the application of the software, including benefits, objectives, and goals."* The *Purpose* pertains to the SRS as a document, whereas the *Scope* focuses on the software being specified.

Another possible point of confusion is in overlap of information content between Sections 2 and 3. For example, both of these sections might include descriptions of interfaces to, functions of, and constraints on the software. IEEE Std. 830 explains:

This section (Section 2, Overall description) does not state specific requirements. Instead, it provides a background for those requirements, which are defined in detail in Section 3 of the SRS, and makes them easier to understand.

Section 2 is an excellent place to embed diagrams, figures, and information which do not specify verifiable requirements, but assist the reader in comprehension and understanding.

An optional sub-section 2.6, not included in Figure 5.1, is allowed for *Apportioning of requirements.* The standard describes this as follows:

> *This subsection of the SRS should identify requirements that may be delayed until future versions of the system.*

Thus, Section 3 of the SRS may contain specific requirements for features that will not be included in the next planned release of the software. However, such requirements must be identified.

We will now consider the organization of the *specific requirements*, which is Section 3 of the SRS according to the prototype outline. This part of the document contains the core information—those parts that must be correct, unambiguous, complete, consistent, verifiable, and traceable. Specific requirements are usually written using the word *"shall"* to clearly identify them, particularly *functional* requirements.

IEEE Std. 830 allows for different organizations of Section 3 for specific requirements. All of these, however, are intended to include the following information items:

External interfaces. External interfaces, including both inputs to and outputs from the software, and including such interfaces as user interfaces, hardware interfaces, software interfaces, and communications interfaces, should be specified. If available and of sufficient quality, interface specification documents should be referenced. Statements of conformance to separate interface specifications should provide specific exclusions for features, aspects, and parts of the interface not supported.

Functions. *Functional requirements* specify the processing and outputs of the software for certain inputs. Specifications should be provided for validating inputs, sequencing of operations, responses to abnormal situations, and expected outputs.

Performance requirements. Both static and dynamic performance requirements should be specified. Examples of static performance requirements include the number of terminals, users, or connections supported at any one time, or the amount of data that can be stored. Examples of dynamic performance requirements include the number of transactions per unit of time, or maximum allowed response time for processing events.

Logical database requirements. Logical requirements for information stored in a database should be specified.

Design constraints. Design constraints imposed by factors such as hardware limitations should be specified.

Standards compliance. Existing standards or regulations with which the software must comply should be specified. Note that this does not refer to standards used for software development; instead, this refers to standards of the application domain.

Software system attributes. Specific attributes of the software, including reliability, availability, security, maintainability, and portability, can be specified as requirements. They should be specified so that they can be objectively verified. For example, reliability requirements can be specified as a *Mean-Time-to-Failure* (see IEEE Std. 982.1, *IEEE Standard Dictionary of Measures to Produce Reliable Software*).

It is interesting to consider the organization for the specific requirements given by an earlier version of IEEE Std. 830 from 1984. This provided four prototype outlines for SRS Section 3, all oriented to specifying functional requirements. The simplest of these is given in Figure 5.2.

```
3.  Specific Requirements
    3.1.  Functional Requirements
          3.1.1.  Functional Requirement 1
                  3.1.1.1.  Introduction
                  3.1.1.2.  Inputs
                  3.1.1.3.  Processing
                  3.1.1.4.  Outputs
          3.1.2.  Functional Requirement 2
          ...
          3.1.n.  Functional Requirement n
    3.2.  External Interface Requirements
          3.2.1.  User Interfaces
          3.2.2.  Hardware Interfaces
          3.2.3.  Software Interfaces
          3.2.4.  Communications Interfaces
    3.3.  Performance Requirements
    3.4.  Design Constraints
          3.4.1.  Standards Compliance
          3.4.2.  Hardware Limitations
          ...
    3.5.  Attributes
          3.5.1.  Security
          3.5.2.  Maintainability
          ...
    3.6.  Other Requirements
          3.6.1.  Data Base
          3.6.2.  Operations
          3.6.3.  Site Adaption
          ...
```

Figure 5.2   *Prototype Outline 1 for SRS Section 3, from IEEE Std. 830-1984.*

This organization is still useful, especially for small software applications, because of its simplicity. Although it is no longer provided as an example in IEEE Std. 830-1998, the prototype outlines are provided on an *informative* basis only, and the outline in Figure 5.2 can still be used in compliance with the standard. This organization is very straightforward to understand, because the functional requirements are simply listed sequentially. This is an effective technique if the number of functional requirements is small.

For larger software projects, it is helpful to organize functional requirements in terms of some systematic criteria. For example, a particularly effective technique is to organize functional requirements by *stimulus*, as per the following figure.

```
3.  Specific Requirements
      3.1.  External Interface Requirements
              3.1.1.  User Interfaces
              3.1.2.  Hardware Interfaces
              3.1.3.  Software Interfaces
              3.1.4.  Communications Interfaces
      3.2.  Functional Requirements
              3.2.1.  Stimulus 1
                      3.2.1.1.  Functional Requirement 1.1
                      ...
                      3.2.1.n.  Funtional Requirement 1.n
              3.2.2.  Stimulus 2
              ...
              3.1.m  Stimulus m
      3.3.  Performance Requirements
      3.4.  Design Constraints
      3.5.  Software System Attributes
      3.6.  Other Requirements
```

Figure 5.3 *Template of SRS Section 3 organized by stimulus, from IEEE Std. 830-1998.*

Organizing an SRS by stimulus is very natural for GUI software, where a large set of user actions are possible, and for software used to control devices, where hardware events must be processed.

To support object-oriented analysis methodologies, the requirements can be organized by objects or classes of objects. This is shown in Figure 5.4.

Other examples of possible organizations provided by IEEE Std. 830 include organization by system mode, user class, feature, response, functional hierarchy, and multiple organizations. There is no one right way to organize the specific requirements. The organization should aid comprehension of the requirements, and should contribute to the *maintainability* of the SRS.

```
3.  Specific Requirements
    3.1.  External Interface Requirements
          3.1.1.  User Interfaces
          3.1.2.  Hardware Interfaces
          3.1.3.  Software Interfaces
          3.1.4.  Communications Interfaces
    3.2.  Classes/Objects
          3.2.1.  Class/Object 1
                  3.2.1.1.  Attributes (direct or inherited)
                            3.2.1.1.1.  Attribute 1
                            ...
                            3.2.1.1.n  Attribute 1.n
                  3.2.1.2.  Functions (services, methods, direct or inherited)
                            3.2.1.2.1.  Functional Requirement 1.1
                            ...
                            3.2.1.2.m  Functional Requirement 1.m
                  3.2.1.3.  Messages (communications received or sent)
          3.2.2.  Class/Object 2
          ...
          3.1.p  Class/Object p
    3.3.  Performance Requirements
    3.4.  Design Constraints
    3.5.  Software System Attributes
    3.6.  Other Requirements
```

Figure 5.4 *Template of SRS Section 3 organized by object, from IEEE Std. 830-1998.*

Recommendations for Implementation

IEEE Std. 830, like other standards defining the organization and information contents of documents, appears easy to follow from a process perspective. One simply writes an SRS according to one of the prototype outlines.

In reality, writing a good SRS can be quite a challenging task. Typically, more experience is required to analyze requirements than to design or implement software. By providing detailed guidelines for the organization and information content, IEEE Std. 830 facilitates an inexperienced software engineer writing a good SRS. However, it is recommended that, if possible, an organization or person new to the task start with an SRS for a small software application. The experience gained on a small project will prevent sizeable problems for later, larger projects.

Legacy software, developed prior to the use of current standards, is an issue for many organizations. If no SRS is available for a legacy application, a decision must be made whether to reverse-engineer one. In some industries, such as the medical device industry, the decision is made for you: It is necessary to have an SRS in order to validate the software, and *retrospective validation* might be required to bring currently manufactured software into compliance with current regulations. Reverse-engineered requirements are especially challenging to write, because no design work is expected to follow, reducing motivation. It is recommended that testing be performed after a reverse-engineered SRS is developed, to validate the legacy software relative to the SRS, and to help verify the SRS itself.

For a new software application, it is recommended to use *prototyping* during the requirements phase of the project. This is specifically allowed by IEEE Std. 830, which states:

> *Prototypes are useful for the following reasons:*
>
> a) *The customer may be more likely to view the prototype and react to it than to read the SRS and react to it. Thus, the prototype provides quick feedback.*
>
> b) *The prototype displays unanticipated aspects of the system behavior. Thus, it produces not only answers but also new questions. This helps reach closure on the SRS.*
>
> c) *An SRS based on a prototype tends to undergo less change during development, thus shortening development time.*
>
> *A prototype should be used as a way to elicit software requirements. Some characteristics such as screen or report formats can be extracted directly from the prototype. Other requirements can be inferred by running experiments with the prototype.*

The creation of prototypes during the requirements analysis phase is one of the most effective techniques available for increasing confidence in the SRS, and for reducing overall project cost and schedule.

Another useful technique for analyzing and reviewing software requirements is to compare the general requirements with specific *Use Cases* or *Scenarios*, in which software behavior is characterized for specific inputs and event sequences. By considering a number of scenarios, it is possible to evaluate general requirements to determine if the general rule implies the desired specific behavior. It is not recommended, however, to specify requirements only via use cases or scenarios, because this almost always fails to meet the criterion of *completeness*.

Summary for IEEE Std. 830

Creation of good Software Requirements Specifications represents the single most important process improvement, relative to an unstructured software development approach. Only when the software requirements have been correctly, unambiguously, and completely specified is the scope of the software project properly defined, and only then is it possible to effectively validate the software.

Use of IEEE Std. 830 substantially facilitates creation of a good SRS. The document contents the standard calls for can be thought of as a checklist of important information which needs to be written down; when you are finished "filling in the blanks," you will have an excellent document. The organization of the specific requirements can be tailored to fit the requirements analysis methodology of your choice. Whether you use a structured analysis, object-oriented analysis, or other analysis techniques, you will be able to communicate the results effectively while being in compliance with this standard.

Test Documentation Overview—IEEE Std. 829

This section describes test documentation standards in the IEEE Software Engineering Standards collection.

The following is the IEEE *element standard* on this topic:

IEEE Std. 829-1998, *IEEE Standard for Software Test Documentation*

IEEE Std. 829 defines the following types of test documents:

Test Plan: A document describing the scope, approach, resources, and schedule of intended testing activities. It identifies test items, the features to be tested, the testing tasks, who do each task, and any risks requiring contingency planning.

Test Design Specification: A document specifying the details of the test approach for a software feature or combination of software features and identifying the associated tests.

Test Case Specification: A document specifying inputs, predicted results, and a set of execution conditions for a test item.

Test Procedure Specification: A document specifying a sequence of actions for the execution of a test.

Test Item Transmittal Report: A document identifying test items. It contains current status and location information.

Test Log: A chronological record of relevant details about the execution of tests.

Test Incident Report: A document reporting on any event that occurs during the testing process which requires investigation.

Test Summary Report: A document summarizing testing activities and results. It also contains an evaluation of the corresponding test items.

The relationship between these different types of documents to each other, and to the testing process, is summarized in Figure 5.5.

Depending on the size of the project, or the nature of the testing activities, not every one of these documents must necessarily be produced. For example, for a small project, it might not be necessary to write a *Test Design Specification;* it might be sufficient to go directly from writing the *Test Plan* to creating *Test Case Specifications* and *Test Procedure Specifications*.

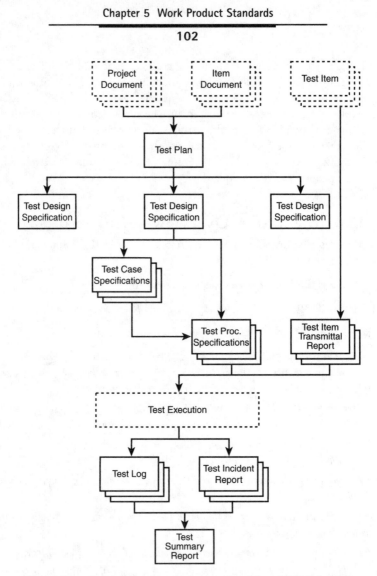

Figure 5.5 *Relationship of test documents, adapted from IEEE Std. 829.*

Software testing can be performed at different levels, for individual software *units*, sets of *units*, the software application as a whole executing in a simulation environment, or the software application integrated into the target system. IEEE Std. 829 does not define these levels of testing, but can be used to document software testing at each level. It is important to understand these different levels of testing in order to understand the context of IEEE Std. 830, and we will briefly explore this.

IEEE Std. 610.12 *(IEEE Standard Glossary of Software Engineering Terminology)* defines the following different levels of testing:

Unit Testing: *Testing of individual hardware or software units or groups of related units.*

Integration Testing: *Testing in which software components, hardware components, or both are combined and tested to evaluate the interaction between them.*

System Testing: *Testing conducted on a complete, integrated system to evaluate the system's compliance with its specified requirements.*

Other types of testing, such as *Interface Testing* are also defined by IEEE Std. 610.12, but the above three are most commonly used to categorize software testing. For example, IEEE Std. 1012 *(IEEE Standard for Software Verification and Validation)* calls for software testing at these three levels, except that it uses the term *"component testing"* instead of *"unit testing"*. Preference is given to the term *"unit testing"* because it is used by IEEE Std. 1008 *(IEEE Standard for Software Unit Testing)*, which is dedicated to this topic. IEEE Std. 1012 also defines the term *"acceptance testing"* which represents a type of system testing performed by or for the *customer* to determine whether the software meets the requirements and needs of the *user*.

System testing should always be performed. Clearly more effort is required to perform testing on all three levels. IEEE Std. 1012 provides guidelines for the required levels of testing as a function of the *software integrity level*. For a software integrity level 1, corresponding to *low criticality*, only system testing is required. For higher software integrity levels, corresponding to more critical software, unit and integration testing are also required. IEEE Std. 1012 describes *low criticality* as follows:

Selected function has noticeable effect on system performance but only creates inconvenience to the user if the function does not perform in accordance with requirements.

If the failure of certain software functionality leads to more than inconvenience to the user, unit and integration testing should be performed for that functionality.

The term *"unit"* does not have a completely standardized interpretation in the software industry; it is a synonym for *"module"* and *"component,"* which also have multiple interpretations. IEEE Std. 610.12 defines this as follows:

Unit: *(1) A separately testable element specified in the design of a computer software component.*

(2) A logically separable part of a computer program.

(3) A software component that is not subdivided into other components.

(4) (A) test unit (as defined by IEEE Std. 1008).

The last part of this definition is intended to harmonize terminology with IEEE Std. 1008 *(IEEE Standard for Software Unit Testing),* which provides the following definition:

> **Test Unit:** *A set of one or more computer program modules together with associated control data, ... usage procedures, and operating procedures that satisfy the following conditions:*
>
> *All modules are from a single computer program,*
>
> *At least one of the new or changed modules in the set has not completed the unit test,*
>
> *The set of modules together with its associated data and procedures are the sole object of a testing process.*

This definition almost raises more questions than it answers! Examples of software units based on concepts from current common programming languages include the following items:

- **Function, Procedure, Routine, or Subroutine.** These primarily encapsulate software *control flow*, and are associated with *procedural* programming and design methods. Each represents a *callable* software component.

- **Module or Compilation Unit.** These encapsulate both *data* and *control flow,* and correspond to *modular* programming and design methods. A module typically consists of data and multiple functions, procedures, and so on, all related in some manner. A module normally consists of an *interface* and an *implementation.*

- **Class.** A term used in *object-oriented* programming and design methods, and is also used to encapsulate both *data* and *control flow.* An *object* is an *instance* of a class, which represents an abstract set of objects. One of the primary differences between classes and modules is that classes can be *derived* from each other, and thus can *inherit* attributes and *methods.*

The purpose of the previous examples is not to provide a definitive or exhaustive analysis of different types of software units, but simply to provide a context for interpreting the terms "unit testing" and "integration testing." It is clear from the previous examples that the specific meaning of the term *unit* will depend on the particular design and programming method(s) used for the software. Because many different methods are in widespread use in industry today, and because we do not want to preclude new, innovative methods from being introduced, these terms remain necessarily difficult to define. However, for a given project, the *Software Design Description* should resolve any ambiguity by specifying units according to whatever method(s) used for the project. The test approach and documentation for unit and integration testing should reflect the software design.

Benefits

IEEE Std. 829 defines a standardized approach for documenting software testing, and encourages software testing to be performed more systematically. It provides the following fundamental benefits:

- **More Effective Testing.** By specifying that *test plans, test designs, test cases,* and *test procedures* be developed during earlier project phases, testing activities conducted during the *Test Phase* of the software life cycle will typically achieve better test coverage and be more effective at identifying software defects. This results in higher quality of the software product.

- **More Effective Follow-Up.** By specifying that *test incident reports* be written after tests have been performed, software defects identified during testing can be tracked more easily, to ensure proper rework of the software. By specifying that *test summary reports* be written at the end of the testing activities, proper evaluation is made as to the readiness of the software for installation, and valuable information is provided for future software process improvements.

- **Reuse of Test Cases and Test Procedures.** By documenting test cases and test procedures, these can be reused by other personnel and for later projects. If test cases and test procedures are undocumented, individual testers become indispensable, and represent resource bottlenecks.

- **Proof of Testing.** Only when software testing is documented is it possible to demonstrate later that it was performed. This might be necessary during an audit, or to provide evidence of regulatory compliance. There is a saying: "If you didn't document it, you didn't do it."

IEEE Std. 829 takes a modular approach to software test documentation, specifying numerous small documents that can be produced in different phases of the software life cycle. This approach is more flexible and efficient than the monolithic test documentation typical of many organizations. The modular approach of IEEE Std. 829 can decrease the cost and schedule associated with software testing, and can facilitate reuse of test cases and test procedures in later projects.

Relationship to Other Standards

Software testing activities are conducted within the context of broader project plans as defined by other standards, specifically:

- **Software Project Management Plan.** Described by IEEE Std. 1058 *(IEEE Standard for Software Management Plans)*.

- **Software Quality Assurance Plan.** Described by IEEE Std. 730 *(IEEE Standard for Software Quality Assurance Plans)*.

- **Software Verification and Validation Plan.** Described by IEEE Std. 1012 *(IEEE Standard for Software Verification and Validation)*.
- **Software Configuration Management Plan.** Described by IEEE Std. 828 *(IEEE Standard for Software Configuration Management Plans)*.
- **Software Safety Plan.** Described by IEEE Std. 1228 *(IEEE Standard for Software Safety Plans)*.

IEEE Std. 1012 is especially important because it provides detailed guidelines for the level of testing to be performed as a function of the *software integrity level* (see the previous discussion).

Planning, designing, and specifying testing requires certain *input* documents normally produced in accordance with other standards:

Preliminary Hazard Analysis Report. Specified by IEEE Std. 1228 *(IEEE Standard for Software Safety Plans)*. This identifies *software hazards* and associated *risks*. This is an important input for all levels of testing because testing activities should be most focused on *system safety*.

Software Requirements Specification. Described by IEEE Std. 830 *(IEEE Recommended Practice for Software Requirements Specifications)*. This defines the functional requirements of the software, and is necessary for system and integration testing.

Software Design Description. Described by IEEE Std. 1016 *(IEEE Recommended Practice for Software Design Descriptions)*. This defines the software unit decomposition and the functional specifications of the software units. It is necessary for unit and integration testing.

Specific guidelines for conducting software *unit testing* are provided by IEEE Std. 1008 *(IEEE Standard for Software Unit Testing)*, which thus complements IEEE Std. 829.

Test documents should be verified. This can be done via *software reviews* as described in IEEE Std. 1028 *(IEEE Standard for Software Reviews)*.

Audience

This standard is primarily intended for software test personnel. Software development and quality assurance personnel might be involved in reviewing test documentation, and represent a secondary audience. Software configuration management personnel can be involved in processing *Test Incident Reports* and thus also represent a secondary audience.

Both the *supplier* and *customer* can perform software testing, in some cases involving the *user* (see the previous section "Audience" for IEEE Std. 830 for a definition of these terms).

Project Phases Affected

IEEE Std. 1012 *(IEEE Standard for Software Verification and Validation)* specifies testing activities according to the following software life cycle phases.

Requirements Analysis Phase

- Test Plan Generation
- Acceptance Test Plan Generation

Design Phase

- Component Test Plan Generation
- Integration Test Plan Generation
- Test Design Generation (Component, Integration, System, and Acceptance)

Implementation Phase

- Test Case Generation (Component, Integration, System, and Acceptance)
- Test Procedures Generation (Component, Integration, and System)
- Component Test Execution

Test Phase

- Acceptance Test Procedure Generation
- Integration Test Execution
- System Test Execution
- Acceptance Test Execution

Generation of each test document should be followed by appropriate verification step such as a *software review*. Test *execution* implicitly includes generation of a *Test Log*, as many *Test Incident Reports* as needed, and a *Test Summary Report*.

Detailed Description

For the convenience of the reader, we will list the sections specified for each of the test documents by IEEE Std. 829. The standard provides detailed recommendations for what to include in each of these sections. This information is not repeated here.

Test Plan Outline

a) Test plan identifier

b) Introduction

c) Test items

d) Features to be tested

e) Features not to be tested

f) Approach

g) Item pass/fail criteria

h) Suspension criteria and resumption requirements

i) Test deliverables

j) Testing tasks

k) Environmental needs

l) Responsibilities

m) Staffing and training needs

n) Schedule

o) Risks and contingencies

p) Approvals

Test Design Specification Outline

a) Test design specification identifier

b) Features to be tested

c) Approach refinements

d) Test identification

e) Feature pass/fail criteria

Test Case Specification Outline

a) Test case specification identifier

b) Test items

c) Input specifications

d) Output specifications

e) Environmental needs

f) Special procedural requirements

g) Intercase dependencies

Test Procedure Specification Outline

a) Test procedure specification identifier

b) Purpose

c) Special requirements

d) Procedure steps

Test Item Transmittal Report Outline

a) Transmittal report identifier

b) Transmitted items

c) Location

d) Status

e) Approvals

Test Log Outline

a) Test log identifier

b) Description

c) Activity and event entries

Test Incident Report Outline

a) Test incident report identifier

b) Summary

c) Incident description

d) Impact

Test Summary Report Outline

a) Test summary report identifier

b) Summary

c) Variances

d) Comprehensiveness assessment

e) Summary of results

f) Evaluation

g) Summary of activities

h) Approvals

IEEE Std. 829 provides examples of each type of test document in an informative annex. Most of the examples are straightforward. The mechanism for logging test execution specified by IEEE Std. 829 differs from the technique used by many organizations. It is common in industry to use a copy of a test procedure, and to check off procedure steps as they are executed, sometimes filling in measured values in blanks provided for this purpose. A *test log* in the IEEE format is a document entirely separate from a *test procedure specification*. In some ways it provides more abbreviated documentation, but also allows for specifying more detail when problems are encountered. It is worth examining the first part of Section 2, and the first two days of testing in Section 3 of the standard, as shown in Figure 5.6.

---

2. Description

...

This log records the execution of the data conversion test procedure (AP08-0101).

3. Activities and event entries

June 10, 19xx   Incidents

    2:00 PM–Dick J. started testing.
    2:15 PM–Began to generate the old database.
    3:30 PM–Discovered a possible bug in the test database.   AP11-14
    6:00 PM–Completed the old test database generation. It is located on
    6:15 PM–Dick J. stopped testing.

June 11, 19xx   Incidents

    9:45 AM–Dick J. started testing.
    10:00 AM–Began to create the random number file.
    10:45 AM–Generated a sorted random number file.
    11:30 AM–Selected and printed a random subset of records from the
    12:30 PM–Dick J. stopped testing.
    12:45 PM–Jane K. started testing.
    1:00 PM–Ran the conversion program against the old test database.   AP11-15
    3:30 PM–Ran the database auditor against the new database. The   AP11-16
    4:00 PM–Jane K. stopped testing.

...

Figure 5.6 *Sample parts of a test log, adapted from IEEE Std. 829.*

Note that the *test procedure specification* AP08-0101 was referenced, but its step-by-step execution was not logged. However, when test incidents were observed, these were logged, and the corresponding *test incident reports* were referenced for traceability.

This example also shows that a test log can be shared by multiple testers, more than multiple days. A test log can also apply to multiple *test procedure specifications*, in which case the start and stop of executing a particular test procedure should be recorded in the *Activities and Event Entries* section.

Recommendations for Implementation

As with all the IEEE standards, it is prudent to implement IEEE Std. 829 with a smaller and less critical project in order to gain experience with it. One possible strategy is to convert existing test case and test procedures from a previous project to the IEEE format, in preparation for a future maintenance release of that software product.

The various documents called for by IEEE Std. 829 can be implemented as separate documents, or as sections of one or more larger documents. The latter approach might seem more familiar to many organizations, although the more modular approach is usually the most effective.

Some mention should be made of the analogy between *Test Case Specifications* and requirements analysis concepts such as *Use Cases* and *Scenarios*. The latter are used to define software requirements for specific inputs and event sequences, as opposed to general requirements intended to define software behavior for arbitrary cases. Software hazards are also often characterized with specific inputs and event sequences. If software hazards, use cases, scenarios, or similar specific cases were documented during the *Requirements Analysis Phase,* these should be translated into, or simply used as, *Test Case Specifications.*

Test Incident Reports are best stored as electronic records. This can be done using a number of different tools or techniques:

- In a database application used for software bug tracking
- In a spreadsheet, or even a text file, as a simplistic solution
- Via an intranet, for easy access by the entire project team

In any case, *Test Incident Reports* can be viewed as, or lead directly to, *Software Change Requests,* as defined in standard *Software Configuration Management* practices. See IEEE Std. 828 *(IEEE Standard for Software Configuration Management Plans)* and IEEE Std. 1042 *(IEEE Guide to Software Configuration Management).*

Test Summary Reports should be collected for the purpose of planning *software process improvements. Process measures,* such as the *Error Distribution(s)* measure—as defined by IEEE Std. 982.1 *(IEEE Standard Dictionary of Measures to Produce Reliable Software)*—should be applied to analyze test incidents for the purpose of planning process improvements.

Summary of IEEE Std. 829

Software testing is the most traditional and indispensable software V&V activity. No software product should be released without undergoing some testing. By providing a systematic approach and a standardized format for documenting software testing, IEEE Std. 829 is one of the most important of the IEEE Software Engineering Standards to implement. Taken together with IEEE Std. 830 *(IEEE Standard for Software Requirements Specifications)*, it provides a basic but effective software quality system.

The modular approach to software test documentation provided by IEEE Std. 829 might seem complex at first, but it has proven itself to be flexible and effective. It allows for different test documents to be developed during different phases of the software life cycle, and it encourages reuse of test cases and test procedures.

Design Descriptions Overview—IEEE Std. 1016

This section describes the IEEE standard for *Software Design Descriptions:*

IEEE Std. 1016-1998, *IEEE Recommended Practice for Software Design Descriptions*

IEEE Std. 1016 provides an excellent overview in its *Scope* section:

This is a recommended practice for describing software designs. It specifies the necessary information content, and recommended organization for a Software Design Description (SDD). An SDD is a representation of a software system that is used as a medium for communicating software design information.

The software design must be based on the software requirements, and it must provide the necessary information to allow the software implementation to follow. This is described in the standard's section *Purpose of an SDD:*

The SDD shows how the software system will be structured to satisfy requirements identified in the software requirements specification. It is a translation of requirements into a description of the software structure, software components, interfaces, and data necessary for the implementation phase. In essence, the SDD becomes a detailed blueprint for the implementation activity. In a complete SDD, each requirement must be traceable to one or more design entities.

The term *design entity* must be understood properly when implementing Std. 1016. The standard provides the following definition:

Design entity: *An element (component) of a design that is structurally and functionally distinct from other elements and that is separately named and referenced.*

This definition is unfortunately circular and, hence, ambiguous. Clarification is provided in the *Design Entities* section of the standard:

Entities can exist as a system, subsystems, data stores, modules, programs, and processes...

IEEE Std. 610.12 *(IEEE Standard Glossary of Software Engineering Terminology)* provides definitions for most of the "*entities* " mentioned previously:

System: *A collection of components organized to accomplish a specific function or set of functions.*

Subsystem: *A secondary or subordinate system with a larger system.*

Module: *(1) A program unit that is discrete and identifiable with respect to compiling, combining with other units, and loading; for example, the input to, or output from, an assembler, compiler, linkage editor, or executive routine.(2) A logically separable part of a program.*

(Computer) Program: A combination of computer instructions and data definitions that enable computer hardware to perform computational or control functions.

Process: (2) An executable unit managed by an operating system scheduler.

No definition is provided by IEEE Std. 610.12 for *data store,* but we can assume that this refers to either a software module consisting entirely of data definitions, or a long-term data store, such as defined by a file format or database.

Clearly, the *units* (synonym of *module* and *component*) as discussed in the prior section on software testing are one type of design entity. Recall that these can correspond to such items as *functions, procedures, routines, subroutines, compilation unit, modules,* or *classes.* There is not much standardization for *design entities* yet, which partially reflects the multitude of design methodologies available.

The following is a simplified classification of *design entities,* in which preference is given to the generic term *"unit"* for harmonization with other standards such as IEEE Std. 1008 *(IEEE Standard for Software Unit Testing). A design entity* can be one of the following:

- **Unit.** Synonym: module or component. This is some type of software source code component, consisting of data and/or control flow constructs. It is intended to map to an atomic unit of encapsulation at the software source code level.

- **Process.** As per the definition listed previously, this represents an entirely different type of design entity from a unit, one that is an operating system specific concept. Units such as subroutines, class methods, and so on can execute in the context of distinct processes, demonstrating the independence of the concepts.

- **Database.** This can be viewed either as an external entity to which the software must interface, or as a different type of design entity to be described in the SDD. A database can be accessed by multiple units and processes, demonstrating the orthogonality of these concepts.

- **Set of Lower-Level Design Entities.** This can be a *system, subsystem,* or *program* given as examples of *design entities* by the standard. The common technique of describing *hierarchies* of design entities implies that we might want to describe a set of design entities as a design entity in its own right. A set of lower-level design entities might consist of units, processes, databases, or lower-level sets.

It is unfortunate that this fundamental topic of defining the term *design entity* is so complex. This is a very important issue, however, because the purpose of an SDD is to describe design entities, and the choice of design entities will help determine the scope of *unit* and *integration testing.*

Benefits

IEEE Std. 1016 provides guidelines for creating *Software Design Descriptions* (SDD). Documenting the design of a software application in a standardized way has a number of fundamental benefits, described here:

- **Ensures adequacy of design activities.** By providing a standard for the information content of a *Software Design Description*, the standard helps ensure that sufficient effort is invested during the *Design Phase* of the software life cycle. Without a standard, it might be tempting to draw a few diagrams and proceed to implementation, without having worked out enough detail.

- **Facilitates design verification.** A *Software Design Description* in a standard format is more easily verified via software reviews. Without a standard, it is difficult to assess the adequacy of design documentation prior to committing to the final implementation of the software.

- **Simplifies software implementation.** A *Software Design Description* in a standard format provides a critical input to the software implementation phase of the software life cycle. With the software design described down to the unit level, software implementation becomes an easier task, which can be assigned to less experienced development personnel.

- **Allows for software unit and integration testing.** Software unit and integration testing require that software *units* be specified (see the previous section on software testing for discussion of *units, modules,* and *components*). Software unit and integration testing must be performed, according to IEEE Std. 1012 *(IEEE Standard for Software Verification and Validation),* if the software *risk level* is *moderate* or higher.

- **Improves software maintainability.** By describing the design more effectively than what is possible in source code comments, a *Software Design Description* facilitates new development personnel enhancing the software for maintenance purposes.

The standard provides a summary of the reason to create a SDD:

> *For both new software systems and existing systems under maintenance, it is important to ensure that the design and implementation used for a software system satisfy the requirements driving that system. The minimum documentation required to do this is defined in IEEE Std. 730-1998. The SDD is one of these required products.*

Relationship to Other Standards

Software design activities are conducted within the context of project plans as defined by other standards, such as:

- **Software Project Management Plan.** Described by IEEE Std. 1058 *(IEEE Standard for Software Management Plans)*.

- **Software Quality Assurance Plan.** Described by IEEE Std. 730 *(IEEE Standard for Software Quality Assurance Plans)*.

- **Software Verification and Validation Plan.** Described by IEEE Std. 1012 *(IEEE Standard for Software Verification and Validation)*.

- **Software Configuration Management Plan.** Described by IEEE Std. 828 *(IEEE Standard for Software Configuration Management Plans)*.

- **Software Safety Plan.** Described by IEEE Std. 1228 *(IEEE Standard for Software Safety Plans)*.

The SDD is developed using the *Software Requirements Specification* as an input. This is described by IEEE Std. 830 *(IEEE Recommended Practice for Software Requirements Specifications)*.

The *Preliminary Hazard Analysis Report* (PHAR), specified by IEEE Std. 1228 *(IEEE Standard for Software Safety Plans)*, is also an important input to the SDD. Any *software hazards* should be addressed by the design, and the SDD should be *traceable* to the PHAR to demonstrate *software safety*.

The SDD should be verified. This can be done via *software reviews*, as described in IEEE Std. 1028 *(IEEE Standard for Software Reviews)*.

Audience

The primary audience for IEEE Std. 1016 consists of software designers, who will document their work using this standard. Personnel involved in analyzing software requirements will represent a secondary audience, because they might be involved in verification of the SDD. Software implementers, who will use the SDD as an input document, will also be part of the secondary audience. Software test personnel will also use the SDD as an input document, for creating *unit* and *integration testing* documents such as *test design specifications*, *test case specifications*, and *test procedure specifications*.

Project Phases Affected

The SDD is the primary output of the *Design Phase* of the software life cycle. This is summarized in the standard as follows:

> *(The SDD) records the results of the design processes that are carried out during the design phase.*

The primary input used to create the SDD is the *Software Requirements Specification* created during the *Requirements Analysis Phase*, and the SDD should be reviewed relative to this document for correctness, completeness, and traceability. The SDD is the primary input for the *Implementation Phase*. It is also in important input for testing activities carried out during the *Test Phase,* because *unit* and *integration testing* depend on the specification of *design entities* from the SDD.

Detailed Description

IEEE Std. 1016 requires certain *information content* of, but only recommends an *organization* for an SDD. A sample table of contents for an SDD is provided in Annex A of the standard, but this is only intended to be informative (not required for compliance). The standards provide the following disclaimer for the sample outline:

> *The example of a table of contents shows only one of many possible ways to organize and format the design views and associated information presented in Clause 6 of this standard.*

First, we will examine the information content considered necessary by the standard. As has already been discussed, the document provides information on *design entities* that might have different interpretations. The information for a design entity is referred to as the *design entity attributes* by the standard. The standard specifies the following documentation requirements:

> *All attributes shall be specified for each entity. Attribute descriptions should include references and design considerations such as tradeoffs and assumptions when appropriate. In some cases, attribute descriptions may have the value none.*

For each entity, the standard requires the following attributes:

Identification

Type

Purpose

Function

Subordinates

Dependencies

Interface

Resources

Processing

Data

The standard recommends organizing the *design entity attributes* according to *design views*. This is defined by the standard as follows:

Design view: *A subset of design entity attribute information that is specifically suited to the needs of a software project activity.*

This definition is further explained in Section 6.2 of the standard as follows:

Each design view represents a separate concern about a software system. Together, these views provide a comprehensive description of the design in a concise and usable form that simplifies information access and assimilation.

The standard recommends design views consisting of *decomposition, dependency, interface,* and *detail descriptions.* This is summarized in Figure 5.7, taken from the standard.

Design view	Scope	Entity attributes	Example representations
Decomposition description	Partition of the system into design entities	Identification, type, purpose, function, subordinates	Hierarchical decomposition diagram, natural language
Decomposition description	Description of the relationships among entities and system resources	Identification, type, purpose, dependencies, resources	Structure charts, data flow diagrams, transaction diagrams
Interface description	List of everything a designer, programmer, or tester needs to know to use the design entities that make up the system	Identification, function, interfaces	Interface files, parameter tables
Detailed description	Description of the internal design details of an entity	Identification, processing, data	Flowcharts, N-S charts, PDL

Figure 5.7 *Recommended design views, from IEEE Std. 1016.*

The *decomposition description* and *dependency description* describe the global structure of the software, by defining the division of the software system into design entities, and by specifying the relationships among entities. The *interface description* documents all design entities from a usage point of view; it provides a "black box" description of the design entities. The *detailed description* provides the internal design of each entity, such as algorithms; this corresponds to a "white box" view of the design entity, with enough information to enable implementation of the entity to proceed.

These four views can be developed sequentially, each one providing an additional layer of information. Thus, the *Design Phase* can be decomposed into four *subphases,* each one with a verifiable milestone. *Software reviews* can be performed on each successive design view. This approach is especially useful in a large project.

This recommended organization can be translated into an SDD outline similar to the sample provided by the standard. The exact organization depends on the choice of design entities. For example, for a *modular design methodology* for a multi-tasking software application, the SDD outline shown in Figure 5.8 might be appropriate.

```
1.   Introduction
     1.1.   Purpose
     1.2.   Scope
     1.3.   Definitions and acronyms
     1.4.   References
     1.5.   Overview
2.   Decomposition Description
     2.1.   Module Decomposition
            2.1.1.   Module 1 Description
            2.1.2.   Module 2 Description
            ...
            2.1.m   Module m Description
     2.2.   Task Decomposition
            2.2.1.   Task 1 Description
            2.2.2.   Task 2 Description
            ...
            2.2.n   Task n Description
3.   Dependency Description
     3.1.   Module Dependency Description
     3.2.   Task Dependency Description
4.   Interface Description
     4.1.   Module Interface Description
            4.1.1.   Module 1 Interface Description
            4.1.2.   Module 2 Interface Description
            ...
            4.1.m   Module m Interface Description
     4.2.   Task Interface Description
            4.2.1.   Task 1 Interface Description
            4.2.2.   Task 2 Interface Description
            ...
            4.2.n   Task n Interface Description
5.   Detailed Design Description
     5.1.   Module Detailed Description
            5.1.1.   Module 1 Detailed Description
            5.1.2.   Module 2 Detailed Description
            ...
            5.1.m   Module m Detailed Description
     5.2.   Task Detailed Description
            5.2.1.   Task 1 Detailed Description
            5.2.2.   Task 2 Detailed Description
            ...
            5.1.n   Task n Detailed Description
```

Figure 5.8 *An SDD outline for modular design of multitasking software.*

For a software application not using multiple threads, tasks, or processes, based on an *object-oriented design methodology,* the following SDD outline shown in figure 5.9 can be used.

```
1.   Introduction
     1.1.   Purpose
     1.2.   Scope
     1.3.   Definitions and acronyms
     1.4.   References
     1.5.   Overview
2.   Decomposition Description
     2.1.   Class 1 Description
     2.2.   Class 2 Description
     ...
     2.n    Class n Description
3.   Dependency Description
     3.1.   Object Interaction Description
     3.2.   Aggregation Description
     3.3.   Inheritance Description
4.   Interface Description
     4.1.   Class 1 Interface Description
     4.2.   Class 2 Interface Description
     ...
     4.n    Class n Interface Description
5.   Detailed Design Description
     5.1.   Class 1 Detailed Description
     5.2.   Class 2 Detailed Description
     ...
     5.n    Class n Detailed Description
```

Figure 5.9   *An SDD outline for object-oriented design.*

This sample outline in Figure 5.9 shows how the *Dependency Description* view can be decomposed according to different types of *relationships* between classes and objects, as per the particular object-oriented design methodology actually used.

The standard does not require organizing the document according to the recommended design views. As long as you provide the necessary information content, you can organize the SDD as you want and still maintain compliance with the standard.

Recommendations for Implementation

As for other standards, it is recommended to first use this standard on a smaller project in order to gain experience with it. One effective strategy is to reformat and enhance the design documentation for an existing software package according to this standard. This will also help bring such legacy software into compliance with the new standards.

A key step in creating an SDD is to decide on the type of *design entities* that will be described. As was discussed previously, this choice will depend on the design methodology used. For example, a *procedural design* methodology will result in descriptions of *procedures;* a *modular design* methodology will result in descriptions of *modules;* and an *object-oriented* methodology will result in descriptions of *classes.* If a multithreading, multitasking, or multiprocessing software application is being developed, the *threads, tasks,* or *processes* will need to be described as design entities. The type of design entities to be described in the SDD should be determined at the beginning of the design phase.

In large, complex software applications, a single SDD can grow to an unmanageable size. Design planning should anticipate this issue, and specify a *hierarchy* of SDD documents, to enable individual designers or teams of designers to work on separate documents. If a hierarchical approach is used, the lower-level SDDs will correspond to individual software *subsystems,* and the higher-level SDDs will describe the decomposition of the software *system* into *subsystems.* The higher-level SDD is sometimes called a *High-Level Design Description,* and the lower-level SDDs are then called *Low-Level Design Descriptions.*

There are many design tools available, and, to the extent that these can be used to help create the SDD, they should be used. For example, diagrams created using CASE tools can be embedded in an SDD document. There are dangers, however, in relying on CASE tools so much that you do not create a conventional document. If the design is stored only in an online design database created via the CASE tool, access to the design is restricted according to the CASE tool licenses and the proper operation of the development computer systems and network. This makes configuration management of the design difficult.

Programming standards often require detailed design information to be embedded in the source files as comment blocks. If this is done, the SDD can become obsolete, if it is not also updated. Reviews should be performed to mitigate this risk. It can also be expedient to automate the extraction of detailed design information from the source code to help create the SDD.

Summary of IEEE Std. 1016

The value of *Software Design Descriptions* is widely recognized by software developers. Source code, even when extensively commented, does not effectively communicate the software design. Ironically, this is especially true with object-oriented programming languages, whose complex syntax is generally more difficult to reverse-engineer. *Software Design Descriptions* have a significant advantage over source code comments, in that they can contain pictures, diagrams, tables, and other auxiliary information. An undocumented design greatly complicates software maintenance, and provides no basis for performing software unit and integration testing; both require module specifications.

By providing a standard for Software Design Descriptions, IEEE Std. 1016 ensures that software designs are documented systematically and comprehensively. Implementing this standard is a basic step towards improving your organization's software development process.

Metrics and Measures Overview—IEEE Std. 982.1 and IEEE Std. 1061

This section describes IEEE standards for metrics and measures.

The following are the *element standards* on this topic:

> IEEE Std. 982.1-1988, *IEEE Standard Dictionary of Measures to Produce Reliable Software*
>
> IEEE Std. 1061-1998, *IEEE Standard for a Software Quality Metrics Methodology*

Additionally, the following standard at the *Guides and Supplements* layer of the *SESC Framework* model applies to this topic:

> IEEE Std. 982.2-1988, *IEEE Guide for the Use of IEEE Standard Dictionary of Measures to Produce Reliable Software*

IEEE Std. 982.2 is not analyzed in detail.

These standards can be used to evaluate the software itself, or the software development process. Some metrics and measures are applied to the software source code to analyze static characteristics such as complexity. Other metrics and measures are used to assess the dynamic characteristics of the executable software, for example, the frequency of failures. Still other metrics and measures are used for monitoring or improving the development process, for example, measuring the distribution of errors as a function of the development phases in which they were introduced.

IEEE Std. 982.1 specifies a number of software *measures*. A measure is defined by the standard as

> *A quantitative assessment of the degree to which a software product or process possesses a given attribute.*

Some of the measures can be used to assess software products, whereas others are useful for evaluating the software development process. For example, the *Cyclomatic complexity* measure is an excellent measure for software source code, with high complexity statistically correlated to an increased incidence of software defects. The *Error distribution* measure, as another example, is useful for analyzing the efficacy of the software development process, providing valuable information for planning future software process improvements.

Std. 982.1 explicitly targets software *reliability*, which it defines as follows:

> *The probability that software will not cause the failure of a system for a specified time under specified conditions.*

A *failure* is defined as

> *(1) The termination of the capability of a functional unit to perform its required function.*
>
> *(2) An event in which a system or system component does not perform a required function within specified limits.*

The emphasis on reliability by this standard is natural, because the correlation between the computed values of the measures and the existence of yet undiscovered software defects is inherently probabilistic in nature. However, the measures in Std. 982.1 have proven useful for improving software quality in a broader sense. Recall that *quality* is defined by IEEE Std. 610.12 as

> *(1) The degree to which a system, component, or process meets specified requirements.*
>
> *(2) The degree to which a system, component, or process meets customer or user needs or expectations.*

Software quality cannot usually be directly demonstrated via software measures; however, measures can be used as part of a quality system to provide increased confidence of software quality. Positive results from software measures do not by themselves imply high software quality; however, negative results from software measures usually imply low software quality.

IEEE Std. 982.1 should not be interpreted as requiring use of all its measures for compliance. Indeed, use of additional measures not listed in Std. 982.1 is entirely within the spirit of this standard.

IEEE Std. 982.2 is not an element standard in the SESC Framework Model; it is an application guide intended to supplement Std. 982.1. IEEE Stds. 982.2 and 982.1 can be considered at the same time, because they are closely harmonized. In particular, the Appendices of Std. 982.2 provide excellent detailed, practical information for each of the measures listed in Std. 982.1. If you are considering using a measure from Std. 982.1, you should definitely read through the corresponding appendix in Std. 982.2. If we refer to "Std. 982," we are referring to both of these standards considered as one.

IEEE Std. 1061 describes a process model for establishing software quality requirements and identifying, implementing, analyzing, and validating *software quality metrics*. These are defined by the standard as

> *A function whose inputs are software data and whose output is a single numerical value that can be interpreted as the degree to which software possesses a given attribute that affects its quality.*

Although the terms "measure" from IEEE Std. 982 and "metric" from IEEE Std. 1061 appear almost interchangeable, it is useful to distinguish between them. The measures from IEEE Std. 982 are general in nature and are defined a priori; they have a statistical correlation to software quality. The metrics discussed in IEEE Std. 1061 are specific to a software product, reflecting its particular quality requirements; they ideally represent an absolute measure of software quality. Unlike IEEE Std. 982, IEEE Std. 1061 does not provide a collection of metrics. Instead it describes the process by which you develop specific metrics for your project.

Benefits

The use of metrics and measures can increase software product *reliability* and *quality*, provide inputs for planning software process improvements, and help monitor the software development process. These standards thus provide important software quality assurance benefits.

Metrics and measures can also increase the effectiveness of software review and testing activities. By identifying software modules with a high probability of defects because of excess complexity, metrics and measures are useful for planning code inspections and unit testing. By providing an objective, quantitative means of evaluating source code, metrics and measures can improve the effectiveness of code inspections. Metrics and measures enable a more systematic approach to be used for test planning and test summary reporting, particularly via test coverage and test accuracy measures. In particular, unit test case planning is aided by the *Minimal Unit Test Case Determination* measure in IEEE Std. 982.

Because metrics and measures provide a quantitative means of evaluating software reliability and quality, they can provide more objective, tangible, and neutral goals for project personnel. The Foreword to IEEE Std. 982.1 states the following two intended benefits, expressed as goals of this standard:

1. *The process goal is to provide measures that may be applicable throughout the life cycle and may provide the means for continual self-assessment and reliability improvement.*

2. *The product goal is to increase the reliability of the software in its actual use environment* during the operations and support phases.

IEEE Std. 1061 states the following with regards to benefits of the use of quality metrics:

> *The use of software metrics reduces subjectivity in the assessment and control of software quality by providing a quantitative basis for making decisions about software quality.... The use of software metrics within an organization or project is expected to have a beneficial effect by making software quality more visible.*

IEEE Std. 1061 goes on to list the following more specific beneficial ways to use quality metrics:

- *Assess achievement of quality goals*
- *Establish quality requirements for a system at its outset*
- *Establish acceptance criteria and standards*
- *Evaluate the level of quality achieved against the established requirements*
- *Detect anomalies or point to potential problems in the system*
- *Predict the level of quality that will be achieved in the future*
- *Monitor changes in quality when software is modified*
- *Assess the ease of change to the system during product evolution*
- *Validate a metrics set*

Relationship to Other Standards

The standards for metrics and measures are particularly effective if used in conjunction with IEEE Std. 1028 *(IEEE Standard for Software Reviews)*. The interaction between these standards occurs in two important ways:

1. The metrics and measures provide a quantitative means of evaluating the work products and process during software reviews.

2. The metrics and measures can be used to identify parts or aspects of a work product or process that should be targeted for review.

Product metrics and measures are naturally used in combination with *technical reviews, inspections,* and *walk-throughs* (as defined in IEEE Std. 1028). *Process* measures and metrics are more natural for use with *management reviews* and *audits.* For example, the *Cyclomatic Complexity* measure can be considered during a *code inspection,* or it can be used to trigger code inspections of modules with unusually high complexity. As another example, the measure of *Manhours per Major Defect Detected* can be used during a *management review* to evaluate the efficiency of the design and code inspection processes.

The standards for metrics and measures are closely related to standards for testing, including IEEE Std. 829 *(IEEE Standard for Software Test Documentation)* and IEEE Std. 1008 *(IEEE Standard for Software Unit Testing).* These standards interact for several reasons:

Measures such as *Functional Test Coverage* and *Test Coverage* can be used for test planning and design, to create a *Test Plan* or *Test Design Specification.*

Product quality metrics should be used to generate specific test cases and procedures *(Test Case Specifications* and *Test Procedure Specifications).*

Measures such as *Test Accuracy* can be used to estimate the percentage of faults remaining, and thus produce valuable quantitative data for a *Test Summary Report.*

Complexity measures (such as the *Cyclomatic Complexity* measure) can be used to identify software modules that should be unit-tested, because modules with high complexity are more likely to have defects associated with them.

The *Minimal Unit Test Case Determination* measure can be used to plan unit test cases for a given software module.

IEEE Std. 730.1 *(Quality Assurance Planning)*, provides a general context for the use of metrics and measures as part of the quality assurance efforts for a project. In particular, the *Software Quality Assurance Plan* can call for a *Software Metrics Plan* (Section 3.4.4.8 of Std. 730.1) and use of *Metrics* (Section 3.5.2.7 of Std. 730.1).

Software *product* reliability and quality requirements should be specified in a *Software Requirements Specification*, as per IEEE Std. 830 *(IEEE Recommended Practice for Software Requirements Specifications).* Such requirements can be expressed in terms of specific product measures or metrics. On the other hand, project requirements such as quality assurance activities, should *not* be included in the *Software Requirements Specification.* Consequently, *process* measures and metrics are not normally referenced in an SRS. In IEEE Std. 1061, the first step in the methodology, namely establishing software quality requirements, can usually only be partially documented via an SRS.

Audience

The foreword to IEEE Std. 982.1 states:

This standard is intended to be of interest to design, development, evaluation (for example, auditors, procuring agency) and maintenance personnel; software quality and software reliability personnel; and to operations and acquisition support managers.

Section 1.2 of IEEE Std. 1061 states:

> *This standard is intended for those associated with the acquisition, development, use, support, maintenance, and audit of software. This standard can be used by the following: an acquisition/project manager…, a system developer…, a quality assurance/control/audit organization…, a system maintainer…, a user.…*

These standards clearly have a broad target audience. This is because there are many different types of metrics and measures that can be applied in a variety of contexts.

Project Phases Affected

Different measures from IEEE Std. 982 are applicable to different project phases. For example, the *Cyclomatic complexity* measure should be applied to the software source code during the *Implementation Phase,* whereas the *Error distribution(s)* measure should be applied during the entire software life cycle, to track *errors* as a function of the life cycle phases. The correspondence of the measures from IEEE Std. 982.1 is explored by IEEE Std. 982.2. This information is summarized in Figure 5.10

IEEE Std. 982.2 also provides columns for the *Operation & Maintenance Phase* and the *Retirement Phase,* which were intentionally left out of our discussion of *software life cycle phases.* Every measure is applicable during the *Operation & Maintenance Phase,* because the latter is a "catchall," during which the project activities normally associated with the *Concept Phase* through *Installation & Checkout Phase* are performed for software enhancements too small to warrant project status.

The *software quality metrics methodology* described in IEEE Std. 1061 represents a process that is executed during almost the entire *software life cycle.* The correspondence of the steps of the methodology to standard software life cycle phases depends on the type of quality metrics being targeted. For example, if the quality metrics target the software *product,* the correspondence might be as follows:

1. *Establishing software quality requirements* (the first step of the methodology) can be done during the *Requirements Analysis Phase.*
2. *Identifying software quality metrics* can be done during the *Design Phase.*
3. *Implementing the software quality metrics* can be done during the *Implementation Phase.* The last activity of this step, *collecting the data and computing the metric values,* can also be done during the *Test Phase* and later phases, depending on the specific quality metrics used.
4. *Analyzing the software metrics results* can be done during the *Implementation Phase, Test Phase,* and later phases, after the metric values have been computed.

5. *Validating the software quality metrics* (the last step of the methodology) is possible when sufficient direct quality data is available for analyzing, calibrating, and validating the metrics. This is useful for applying the validated metrics to later project phases, or to future projects.

	Concept	Requirements	Design	Implementation	Test	Installation & Checkout
1. Fault density	X	X	X	X	X	X
2. Defect density	X	X	X	X	X	X
3. Cumulative failure profile	X	X	X	X	X	X
4. Fault - days number	*	X	X	X	X	X
5. Functional test coverage					X	X
6. Cause and effect graphing		X	X	X	X	
7. Requirements traceability		X	X			
8. Defect indices	*	X	X	X	X	X
9. Error distribution(s)	?	X	X	X	X	X
10. Software maturity index	X	X	X			X
11. Man hours per major defect detected		X	X	X	X	X
12. Number of conflicting requirements		X				
13. Number of entries/exits per module			X	X		
14. Software science measures				X		
15. Graph-theoretic complexity for architecture		X	X			
16. Cyclomatic complexity				X	X	
17. Minimal unit test case determination				X	X	
18. Run reliability					X	X
19. Design structure			X			
20. Mean time to discover the next K faults					X	X
21. Software purity level					X	X
22. Estimated number of faults remaining (seeding)					X	X
23. Requirements compliance		X				
24. Test coverage		X	X		X	X
25. Data or information flow complexity			X	X		
26. Reliability growth function					X	X
27. Residual fault count					X	X
28. Failure analysis using elapsed time					X	X
29. Testing sufficiency					X	*
30. Mean-time-to-failure					X	X
31. Failure rate					X	X
32. Software documentation & source listings				X	X	X
33. RELY (Required Software Reliability)	X	X	X	X	X	X
34. Software release readiness					X	X
35. Completeness		X	X		X	
36. Test accuracy					X	
37. System performance reliability		X	X	X	X	X
38. Independent process reliability						X
39. Combined HW/SW system operational availability					X	X

Figure 5.10 *Applicability of measures to Software Life Cycle Phases, compiled from IEEE Std. 982.2.*

If the quality metrics are intended to measure the development process, or earlier work products such as a *Software Requirements Specification,* the steps of the methodology must be shifted to earlier project phases. If a *Software Quality Metrics Plan* is created, as per IEEE Std. 730.1 *(IEEE Standard for Software Quality Assurance Plans),* this could be written during the *Concept Phase,* and used to plan use of the software quality metrics methodology during later software life cycle phases.

IEEE Std. 1061 makes the following comment on the *life cycle:*

> *When it is possible to measure quality factor values at the desired point in the life cycle, direct metrics shall be used to evaluate software metrics. At some points in the life cycle, certain quality factor values (e.g., reliability) are not available. They are obtained after delivery or late in the project. In these cases, validated metrics shall be used early in a project to predict quality factor values.*

Thus, the standard differentiates between direct metrics, which can be used to measure absolute quality factor values, and predictive metrics used to estimate future absolute quality factor values. The latter category of metrics would ideally already have been validated via the last step of a previous application of the methodology.

Detailed Description

IEEE Std. 982.1 defines 39 distinct measures, including both *product* and *process* measures. The standard categorizes the measures according to the following schema:

> **Product Measures.** *The product measures address cause and effect of the static and dynamic aspects of both projected reliability prior to operation, and operational reliability. The following six product measure subcategories address these dimensions of reliability:*
>
> 1. *Errors; Faults; Failures—Count of defects with respect to human cause, program bugs, observed system malfunctions.*
>
> 2. *Mean-Time-to-Failure; Failure Rate—Derivative measures of defect occurrence and time.*
>
> 3. *Reliability Growth and Projection—The assessment of change in failure-freeness of the product under testing and in operation.*
>
> 4. *Remaining Product Faults—The assessment of fault-freeness of the product in development, test, or maintenance.*
>
> 5. *Completeness and Consistency—The assessment of the presence and agreement of all necessary software system parts.*
>
> 6. *Complexity– The assessment of complicating factors in a system.*

Process Measures. The three process measure subcategories are directly related to process management:

1. *Management Control—The assessment of guidance of the development and maintenance processes.*

2. *Coverage—The assessment of the presence of all necessary activities to develop or maintain the software product.*

3. *Risk; Benefit; Cost Evaluation—The assessment of the process tradeoffs of cost, schedule, and performance.*

Individual measures can be classified as both product and process measures, and can be included in multiple subcategories. The classification of measures according to these categories, shown in Figure 5.11, can be used to select measures for different purposes.

	PRODUCT MEASURES						PROCESS MEASURES		
	Errors; Faults; Failures	MTTF; Failure Rate	Reliability Growth & Projection	Remaining Product Faults	Completeness & Consistency	Complexity	Management Control	Coverage	Risk Benefit; Cost Evaluation
1. Fault density	X								
2. Defect density	X								
3. Cumulative failure profile	X								
4. Fault - days number	X						X		
5. Functional test coverage					X			X	X
6. Cause and effect graphing					X			X	
7. Requirements traceability	X				X			X	
8. Defect indices	X						X		
9. Error distribution(s)							X		
10. Software maturity index		X							X
11. Man hours per major defect detected	X				X		X		X
12. Number of conflicting requirements	X				X			X	
13. Number of entries/exits per module						X			
14. Software science measures				X		X			
15. Graph-theoretic complexity for architecture						X			
16. Cyclomatic complexity					X	X			
17. Minimal unit test case determination					X	X			
18. Run reliability				X					X
19. Design structure						X			X
20. Mean time to discover the next K faults							X		X
21. Software purity level			X						X
22. Estimated number of faults remaining (seeding)				X					
23. Requirements compliance	X				X			X	
24. Test coverage					X			X	
25. Data or information flow complexity						X			
26. Reliability growth function			X						
27. Residual fault count				X					X
28. Failure analysis using elapsed time			X	X					
29. Testing sufficiency				X				X	
30. Mean-time-to-failure		X	X						
31. Failure rate		X							X
32. Software documentation & source listings					X			X	
33. RELY (Required Software Reliability)								X	X
34. Software release readiness									X
35. Completeness					X			X	
36. Test accuracy				X	X			X	
37. System performance reliability			X						
38. Independent process reliability			X						
39. Combined HW/SW system operational availability			X						

Figure 5.11   *A measure classification matrix, from IEEE Std. 982.1.*

Between the specifications of the individual measures provided in IEEE Std. 982.1 and the additional information on each measure provided by the Appendix to IEEE Std. 982.2, it would be redundant to present detailed information and examples of each measure here. Instead, we will identify certain measures of particular merit when first starting to use this standard:

Measure #2, Defect Density. This is substantially similar to *Measure #1, Fault Density*, differing only in terminology. The distinction between *defects* and *faults* is artificial, and these two measures should be merged, and used for both *software reviews* and *testing* activities. Traditional, the measurement of *Defect Density* is oriented towards *software reviews*, particularly *design* and *code inspections*. If the *Defect Density* is sufficiently high, it can indicate that follow-up inspections are required, or that other corrective action is needed.

Measure #9, Error Distribution(s). This is an excellent process measure. By categorizing software faults according to severity and the phase in which each was introduced, the measure enables managing the software life cycle, and planning future software process improvements. It can be beneficial to add *cost* and *schedule* impacts of the errors to the information recorded. As an example, if this measure shows that a large percentage of errors can be traced back to the *Requirements Phase,* then more effort should be put into this phase in the future, including possibly allocating more personnel and time for *software reviews* of the *Software Requirements Specification.*

Measure #16, Cyclomatic Complexity. This is a standard complexity measure that can be used to evaluate the software source code to predict reliability. Tools to implement this measure are commercially available for a variety of programming languages.

Measure #1, Minimal Unit Test Case Determination. This measure is useful for planning, designing, and verifying unit testing. This measure is useful for creating *Test Case Specifications*, as per IEEE Std. 829 *(IEEE Standard for Software Test Documentation).*

Measure #24, Test Coverage. This measure is useful for assessing the completeness of testing processes, including planning, designing, and evaluating testing activities. This measure is useful for creating *Test Summary Reports,* as per IEEE Std. 829 *(IEEE Standard for Software Test Documentation).*

Measure #30, Mean–Time–to–Failure. This is a direct measure of software reliability, and can be used as a *direct quality metric,* as per IEEE Std. 1061.

The previous list is not meant to imply that these measures are inherently superior to the other measures. Rather, it is intended only to recommend certain measures when first implementing the standard. The measures listed previously are relatively easy to understand, do not overlap substantially with each other, and will provide tangible benefits.

IEEE Std. 982.2 provides a *Reliability Measurement Process* model, consisting of eight *stages*. Although this is a useful process model, summarized nicely via a process flow-chart, it is substantially similar to the process model defined by IEEE Std. 1061, which we will focus on instead.

IEEE Std. 1061 defines a *software quality metrics methodology*. This is a five-step process model for specifying quality requirements and quality metrics to be used for evaluating them. It does not specify specific metrics, although the measures from IEEE Std. 982.1 can be used, or product-specific quality measures can be defined.

The five steps of the methodology are specified by *activities* to be performed as part of each step. The correlation to the *software life cycle* was previously discussed. Here is a summary of the methodology, including the major activities for each step:

1. **Establish software quality requirements.** The purpose of this step is to produce a list of quality requirements. The activities in this step are to

    1.) Identify a list of possible quality requirements.

    2.) Determine the (final) list of quality requirements, resolving conflicts between requirements (such as between quality requirements and cost, schedule, or system functionality), and obtaining agreement by all involved parties.

    3.) Quantify each *quality factor*. A *quality factor* is defined as a *"management-oriented attribute of software that contributes to its quality."* For each quality factor, one or more *direct metrics* and corresponding *direct metric values* must be assigned. A *direct metric* is defined as *"a metric that does not depend upon a measure of any other attribute"* and can be contrasted to a *predictive metric*. A *direct metric value* is defined as *"a numerical target for a quality factor to be met in the final product."* For example, *Mean-time-to-failure* (measure #30 from IEEE Std. 982.1), is a direct metric, and a specific maximum value for this for the system would represent a direct metric value.

2. **Identify software quality metrics.** The purpose of this step is to specify and approve a metrics set. *Quality subfactors,* defined as *"a decomposition of a quality factor or quality subfactor to its technical components,"* should be defined as needed for the quality factors. They can be associated with multiple quality factors, or with higher-level subfactors. Metrics should be defined for the subfactors. The standard specifies that only *direct metrics* or *validated* metrics should be used (see Step 5 of the methodology). *Predictive* metrics not yet validated should not be used as quality metrics, even though they can be useful for other purposes. For example, *low module complexity* represents a quality subfactor that can be associated with the *reliability* quality factor, and can be measured via the *Cyclomatic complexity* metric (measure #16 from

IEEE Std. 982.1). To specify the metric set, the standard requires that certain information be documented for each metric, including such items as the metric name, numerical value of the metric that is to be achieved, associated quality factors, tools that are to be used, costs and benefits of using the metrics, and so on

3. **Implement the software quality metrics.** The purpose of this step is collect the data and compute the metric values. First, the data items that will later be collected are planned and documented, including such information as the data item name, associated metrics, procedures used to collect the data, and so on If appropriate, the measurement process is prototyped, to improve the metric and data item descriptions. Finally, the data is collected, and the metric values are computed.

4. **Analyze the software metrics results.** The purpose of this step is to analyze the metric values computed during the previous step, and to use this information to improve software quality, possibly by changing the organization or development process. The results are interpreted, and quality metric values that are outside the allowed values are identified. Validated metrics are used to make predictions of direct metric values, and direct metric values are used to ensure compliance with quality requirements during system and acceptance testing.

5. **Validate the software quality metrics.** This step validates predictive metrics, for making predictions of quality factor values in subsequent applications of the methodology. This is not required for *direct metrics*. The validity criteria to be used to validate a given metric for a given application are *correlation, tracking, consistency, predictability, discriminatory power,* and *reliability.* These are defined in detail by the standard. Thresholds must be designated for these factors, and a metric might be valid with respect to some of, but not all, the criteria.

The validation of *predictive metrics* as the last step in the quality metrics methodology is awkward, in the sense that only direct metrics can be used during the first use of the methodology. If possible, it would be desirable to use existing application data to validate predictive metrics prior to use of the methodology for a new project.

Recommendations for Implementation

Use of specific software work product measures, such as the *Cyclomatic complexity* measure, is greatly facilitated by the use of automated tools that are commercially available to compute the measures, taking the software source files for specific programming languages as inputs. The choice of specific measures can be governed in part by the tools available for the programming language(s) used for the software.

Application of such automated tools should not simply consist of computing the values and generating a summary report. Limits to allowed values should be determined according to the *software quality metrics methodology*, as specified in IEEE Std. 1061—for example, to limit maximum allowed complexity of software modules during the implementation phase.

Direct benefit from work product measures can be obtained even without such absolute limits, by focusing software V&V activities, such as *software reviews* and *unit testing*, on those software modules which score more poorly on work product reliability measures, particularly complexity measures.

All *defects* identified during any software V&V activities should be analyzed to determine corresponding *error* information, including the *severity, phase introduced,* and *discovery mechanism*, as defined for the *Error Distribution(s)* measure. This information will prove invaluable for planning future software process improvements.

Additional metrics and measures should be implemented through thoughtful quality assurance planning, based on the nature of the organization, application domain, existing process maturity, and so on.

Summary of IEEE Std. 982

Metrics and measures are an important software quality assurance tool. They can benefit both the software product, and the software development process. Specific measures defined by IEEE Std. 982, such as *Cyclomatic complexity* and *Error distribution(s)*, are easy to introduce, and quickly provide tangible benefits. The *quality metrics methodology* of IEEE Std. 1061 enables using metrics for a systematic evaluation of software product quality. By providing quantitative information, metrics and measures provide a more objective mechanism for evaluating software reliability and quality.

CHAPTER 6

Process Standards

This chapter analyzes selected *process* standards from the IEEE collection in detail. Some of these standards specify *plans*, which, although representing *work products*, describe the software development process rather than the software *product*. Process-oriented standards, whether they specify a plan or not, are discussed in this chapter.

Process standards are in some ways more difficult to implement than work product standards. This is partly, because process standards are less tangible; work product standards describe specific documents or aspects of the software itself, and thus do not require a substantial conceptual framework. Also, process standards are more difficult to implement because they presuppose implementation of some of the work product standards. For example, software requirements specifications, software design descriptions, and software test documentation are all prerequisites for compliance with software quality assurance and software verification and validation standards. This is why the work product standards were presented first.

The sections in this chapter are organized according to the same format used in Chapter 5, "Document Standards." The order of presentation of the process standards matches the recommendations for order of implementation of standards according to the simple maturity model from Chapter 3, "An Overview of the IEEE Software Engineering Standards." This order of presentation is a "bottom-up" approach, in which the lower-level standards are presented first. For example, IEEE Std. 730 *(IEEE Standard for Software Quality Assurance Plans)* is presented after IEEE Std. 1028 *(IEEE Standard for Software Reviews)* because the *former* calls for *reviews* and *audits*. In this way, by the time the high-level standards are examined, the lower-level terms have been explained.

The first standard considered deals with project management, and will be immediately useful to any software project.

Project Management

This section describes project management standards in the IEEE Software Engineering Standards collection.

The following is the IEEE *element standard* on this topic:

IEEE Std. 1058-1998, IEEE Standard for Software Project Management Plans

The following is an IEEE standard at the *Guides and Supplements* layer of the *SESC Framework* model, on the same topic:

IEEE Std. 1490-1998, IEEE Guide to the Project Management Body of Knowledge (Adoption of a PMI Standard)

IEEE Std. 1490 is not analyzed in detail.

Overview—IEEE Std. 1058

A *Software Project Management Plan* (SPMP) is described by IEEE Std. 1058 as

the controlling document for managing a software project; it defines the technical and managerial processes necessary to develop software work products that satisfy the product requirements.

The standard is suited for all software projects:

Not all software projects are concerned with development of "a new software product." Some software projects consist of a feasibility study and definition of product requirements. Other software projects terminate upon completion of product design, and some projects are concerned with major modifications to existing software products. This standard is applicable to all types of software projects; applicability is not limited to projects that develop source code for new products.

Project size or type of software product does not limit application of this standard. Small projects might require less formality in planning than large projects, but all components of the standard should be addressed by every software project.

Software projects are sometimes component parts of larger projects. In these cases, the SPMP can be a separate component of a larger plan or it can be merged into a system-level or business-level project management plan.

Use of this standard is not restricted by the size, complexity, or criticality of the software product.

Although IEEE Std. 1058 specifies the information content and format of an SPMP, it does not specify a *Software Life Cycle Model*, work products to be created, and so on. Other IEEE standards complement IEEE Std. 1058 in this regard, providing guidelines for such topics.

A compliant SPMP is comprehensive. It consists of more than just staffing information, project cost, and schedule estimates. The information content and format of an SPMP is analyzed further under the section "Detailed Description" later in this chapter. The outline defined by the standard *can* be thought of as a checklist of topics, which must be analyzed, and for which decisions must be made at the start of the project. You must also monitor these areas during the course of the project. This encourages a more systematic approach to project planning and management.

IEEE Std. 1042 complements IEEE Std. 1058 by providing an informative guide to software project management practices. The industry body of knowledge regarding software project management is growing steadily. Current books and journals should also be consulted, for advice on using new techniques and tools for possible software process improvements.

Benefits

By providing a systematic and comprehensive approach to project planning, IEEE Std. 1058 can decrease project cost and schedule, and increase software product quality.

By specifying a suitable level of detail regarding project schedules, milestones, deliverables, risks, and so on, IEEE Std. 1058 allows projects to be managed more effectively during the course of the *software life cycle*. *Management reviews* and *audits* can be conducted to establish compliance with the project plan, and to consider corrective action as required.

Of the different types of plans that can be created for a software project, the *project plan* is in many ways the most fundamental. Other types of plans—such as the *quality assurance plan*, the *verification and validation plan*, or the *configuration management plan*—can be specified as sections of the project plan. Thus, IEEE Std. 1058 provides an important benefit when first introducing the IEEE standards: It provides a convenient starting point for creating a compliant plan.

Relationship to Other Standards

IEEE Std. 1058 specifies project plans that are the controlling document for the entire software project. Plans for supporting processes are contained in the following other IEEE standards:

- IEEE Std. 730 (*IEEE Standard for Software Quality Assurance Plans*)
- IEEE Std. 828 (*IEEE Standard for Software Configuration Management Plans*)
- IEEE Std. 1012 (*IEEE Standard for Software Verification and Validation*)
- IEEE Std. 1228 (*IEEE Standard for Software Safety Plans*)

Plans created according to these other standards can be referenced in the SPMP, or these other standards can be used as guides for developing certain clauses of the SPMP.

Because the SPMP documents the Software Life Cycle Model, standards related to planning of the software life cycle should be consulted for development of the information content of the SPMP. These standards include the following:

- IEEE Std. 1012 (*IEEE Standard for Software Verification and Validation*)
- IEEE Std. 1074 (*IEEE Standard for Developing Software Life Cycle Processes*)
- IEEE Std. 12207.0 (*IEEE/EIA Standard for Industry Implementation of International Standard ISO/IEC 12207, Standard for Information Technology – Software life cycle processes*)

Relationships of specific clauses of the SPMP to other standards are described in the "Detailed Description" section later in the chapter.

The SPMP should receive a *management review*, as described by IEEE Std. 1028 (*IEEE Standard for Software Reviews*). Project conformance to the SPMP should be assessed through periodic *management reviews* and *audits*, as per IEEE Std. 1028. Guidelines for minimum required reviews and audits are provided by IEEE Std. 730 (*IEEE Standard for Software Quality Assurance Plans*), IEEE Std. 1012 (*IEEE Standard for Software Verification and Validation*), and ISO/IEC 12207 (*Standard for Information Technology—Software Life Cycle Processes*).

Audience

The introduction to IEEE Std. 1058 states:

> *This standard is intended for use by software project managers and other personnel who prepare and update project plans and monitor adherence to those plans.*

Personnel who review and implement project plans should also be familiar with this standard.

Project Phases Affected

IEEE Std. 1058 states:

> This standard can be applied to any, or all, phases of a software product life cycle.

A software project might, however, be restricted to a subset of the affected software product's life cycle. The SPMP might be restricted to only specific phases of the software product life cycle.

The SPMP should be created at the outset of the software project, prior to the *development process*, as per the terminology from IEEE Std. 1012 *(IEEE Standard for Software Verification and Validation)*.

The SPMP should be used to direct and monitor the project until its completion. The SPMP should be updated as needed throughout the project.

Detailed Description

The format of a SPMP is defined by IEEE Std 1058 (see Figure 6.1).

The standard defines two types of compliance:

> *format compliance, in which the exact format and contents of this standard are followed in a project plan; and*

> *content compliance, in which the contents of this standard are rearranged in a project plan. In the case of content compliance, a mapping should be provided to map the content-compliant project plan into the various clauses and subclauses of this standard.*

The standard has several other rules relating to compliance:

> *All compliant project plans must be titled "Software Project Management Plan."*

> *Project plans based on this standard might incorporate additional elements by appending additional clauses or subclauses.*

> *The various clauses and subclauses of an SPMP conformant to this standard might be included in the plan by direct incorporation or by reference to other plans. Access to plans incorporated by reference shall be provided for all project stakeholders.*

To summarize the compliance issues, all the information contents of the standard SPMP outline must be included, although the format can be remapped, and additional document sections can be added. Other plans, such as a *Software Quality Assurance Plan*, can be referenced.

Some of the parts of the standard outline for an SPMP are self-explanatory. Clauses 4 through 8, however, are worth examining in more detail.

Title Page
Signature Page
Change History
Preface
Table of contents
List of figures
List of tables
1. Overview
    1.1 Project summary
    1.2. Evolution of the plan
2. References
3. Definitions
4. Project organization
    4.1 External interfaces
    4.2. Internal structure
    4.3. Roles and responsibilities
5. Managerial process plans
    5.1. Start-up plan
        5.1.1. Estimation plan
        5.1.2. Schedule allocation
        5.1.3. Resource acquisition plan
        5.1.4. Project staff training plan
    5.2. Work plan
        5.2.1 Work activities
        5.2.2. Schedule allocation
        5.2.3. Resource allocation
        5.2.4 Budget allocation
    5.3. Control plan
        5.3.1 Requirements control plan
        5.3.2 Schedule control plan
        5.3.3 Budget control plan
        5.3.4 Quality control plan
        5.3.5 Reporting plan
        5.3.6. Metrics collection plan
    5.4. Risk management plan
    5.5. Closeout plan
6. Technical process plans
    6.1. Process model
    6.2. Methods, tools, and techniques
    6.3. Infrastructure plan
    6.4. Product acceptance plan
7. Supporting process plans
    7.1. Configuration management plan
    7.2. Verification and validation plan
    7.3. Documentation plan
    7.4. Quality assurance plan
    7.5. Reviews and audits
    7.6. Problem resolution plan
    7.7. Subcontractor management plan
    7.8. Process improvement plan
8. Additional plans
Annexes
Index

Figure 6.1 *The format of a Software Project Management Plan, from IEEE Std. 1058-1998.*

Clause 4 describes interfaces to organizational entities external to the project (subclause 4.1), the project's internal organizational structure (subclause 4.2), and the responsibilities of the internal organizational elements for major work activities (subclause 4.3).

The managerial processes for the project are described in clause 5. This is of particular interest to management personnel. This clause is used to describe such things as staffing, scheduling, and budgeting for the project.

Subclause 5.1 (project start-up plan) describes how to get the project started. This includes estimation of the project cost and schedule, staffing and staff training plans, and resource acquisition (for such items as computer hardware and software, facilities, support services, and so on).

Work activities and the schedule, resources, and budget allocated to each such activity are defined in subclause 5.2. A *work breakdown structure* must be used to describe the work activities and their relationships. Work activities should be described to a sufficient level of detail to enable effective assessment of project risks, and accurate estimation of resource requirements and schedule. Project scheduling software tools are useful for maintaining and reporting this type of information; diagrams, tables, and other reports from such tools can be embedded into this subclause of the SPMP.

Subclause 5.3 (control plan) specifies the metrics, reporting mechanisms, and control procedures to manage the project. Aspects of the project to be controlled include changes to the product requirements, project schedule and budget, and quality of both processes and work products.

Configuration management as described by IEEE Std. 828 *(IEEE Standard for Software Configuration Management Plans)* and IEEE Std. 1042 *(IEEE Guide to Software Configuration Management)* should be used to control changes to the product requirements. Subclause 5.3.1 of the SPMP must specify *change control procedures* and a *change control board* for this purpose.

Use of project management software is useful for tracking and reporting on project schedule, cost, and resources. Information provided by such software tools is only useful if it is analyzed, especially with regards to risks. *Management reviews*, as described in IEEE Std. 1028 *(IEEE Standard for Software Reviews)*, should be conducted periodically for the purpose of analyzing project schedule, budget, and resources.

The quality control plan (subclause 5.3.4 of the SPMP) can reference supporting process plans such as subclause 7.2 (verification and validation plan), subclause 7.4 (quality assurance plan), and clause 7.5 (reviews and audits). In subclause 5.3.4, a high-level overview of these quality control mechanisms should be provided to enable tracking and risk assessment at a project management level.

Subclause 5.4 (risk management plan) describes how to manage *project risks*. It is important to differentiate here between risks to the project (conditions, events, results, and so on, which can jeopardize the successful completion of the project) and risks as related to software safety, as defined by IEEE Std. 1228 *(IEEE Standard for Software Safety Plans)*. Unmitigated safety risks do represent project risks, but project risks can include such diverse items as inability to hire sufficient qualified staff, project schedule overruns, algorithmic unfeasibility, and so on.

Risk management is an important topic in the SPMP. Risks should be identified, analyzed, prioritized, and tracked. Contingency plans, or at least procedures for creating them, should be specified. Some risks will be clear at the beginning of the project, but a process should be defined for identifying additional risks throughout the project. *Management reviews* and *technical reviews*, as described in IEEE Std. 1028 *(IEEE Standard for Software Reviews)*, are appropriate tools for identifying, analyzing, prioritizing, and tracking project risks, and for contingency planning. Use of a *Software Life Cycle Model* particularly oriented towards risk reduction, such as the *spiral model* described in Chapter 4, "A Simple Software Life Cycle Model," is recommended for projects with substantial risk.

The activities one does to close out a project—for example, archiving of project materials—are described in subclause 5.5.

Of particular interest to technical personnel is clause 6 (technical process plans), which describes the technical processes for the project. This clause defines work products, including those that are not to be delivered to the acquirer, and the processes, methods, tools, and techniques to create them.

Subclause 6.1 (process model) should be used to define the *Software Life Cycle Model*. This should include definitions of major work activities to be performed, work products to be created, reviews to be conducted, milestones to be achieved for the project, and the timing and other relationships between these. The process can be described using a standard *Software Life Cycle Model*, such as a *waterfall model* or *spiral model*. Sufficient detail must be provided to identify project-specific work activities, work products, and so on. IEEE Std. 1012 *(IEEE Standard for Software Verification and Validation)*, IEEE Std. 1074 *(IEEE Standard for Developing Software Life Cycle Processes)*, and ISO/IEC Std. 12207 *(Standard for Information Technology – Software life cycle processes)* can be used to develop the process model. See also Chapter 4.

Software development methods are specified in subclause 6.2. For example, the subclause describes the Fusion object-oriented development method, programming languages (such as the C++ programming language), tools (such as the GNU C++ compiler), and techniques (such as software testing in a simulation environment). Methods, tools, and techniques should be described for all work products created during the project, and not just for project deliverables. This section can (indeed must) reference technical standards, policies, or procedures related to these topics.

Subclause 6.3 (infrastructure plan) describes how to establish and maintain the project development environment, including such aspects as workstations, networks, software tools, test equipment, office facilities, and support personnel such as for security, secretarial, and janitorial services.

Subclause 6.4 (product acceptance plan) specifies the process and criteria for the *acquirer* (in other standards, also referred to as the *customer*) to accept the project deliverables. The standard states:

> *Any technical processes, methods, or tools required for product acceptance shall be specified in the product acceptance plan. Methods such as testing, demonstration, analysis, and inspection should be specified in this plan.*

The product acceptance plan can be specified outside of the SPMP, for example, in a *Project Agreement*. In this case, the SPMP should reference the document, which defines the acceptance criteria, possibly providing additional detail needed for clarification.

Clause 7 of the SPMP (supporting process plans) contains plans for supporting processes (such as configuration management) *"that span the duration of the software project."* For some of the most important of these—subclause 7.1 (configuration management plan), subclause 7.2 (verification and validation plan), and subclause 7.4 (quality assurance plan)—, the IEEE Software Engineering Standards collection provides other standards for such plans. These are IEEE Std. 828 *(IEEE Standard for Software Configuration Management Plans)*, IEEE Std. 1012 *(IEEE Standard for Software Verification and Validation)*, and IEEE Std. 730 *(IEEE Standard for Software Quality Assurance Plans)*, respectively. If separate supporting process plans are developed, such plans can simply be referenced in the corresponding subclause. Alternatively, the corresponding IEEE standards for the supporting process can be used as *guides* (not targeting full compliance) for writing abbreviated plans directly in the subclauses of the SPMP.

To define the work products to be created during the software project as a function of the *software integrity level*, one should turn to subclause 7.3 of the SPMP (documentation plan) which draws on IEEE Std. 1012 *(IEEE Standard for Software Verification and Validation)*.

Subclause 7.5 of the SPMP (reviews and audits plan) can reference IEEE Std. 1028 *(IEEE Standard for Software Reviews)* to define the *methods* and *procedures* used for this purpose. It can also draw on IEEE Std. 730 *(IEEE Standard for Software Quality Assurance Plans)* and IEEE Std. 1012 *(IEEE Standard for Software Verification and Validation)* to define the specific reviews and audits to be performed during the course of the project. This subject is further explored in section 6.2 on *Software Reviews*.

Subclause 7.6 of the SPMP (problem resolution plan) is intended to *"specify the resources, methods, tools, techniques, and procedures to be used in reporting, analyzing, prioritizing, and processing software problem reports generated during the project."* Examples of such problem reports include *Test Incident Reports* as defined by IEEE Std. 829 *(IEEE Standard for Software Test Documentation)* and *anomalies* listed in *Software Review Reports* as per IEEE Std. 1028 *(IEEE Standard for Software Reviews)*. The *problem reports* are primarily oriented toward the *software product*, rather than other *work products*. This topic is primarily one of *configuration management*, which defines the process to be used for requesting changes, evaluating proposed changes, approving or disapproving changes, and implementing changes to a *control item* such as the *software source code*. The configuration management process involves development, verification, and validation, as well as configuration management personnel. Configuration management is described by IEEE Std. 828 *(IEEE Standard for Software Configuration Management Plans)* and IEEE Std. 1042 *(IEEE Guide to Software Configuration Management)*; it is discussed further in Section 6.5.

The subcontractor management plan is found in subclause 7.7 of the SPMP and can be created using IEEE Std. 1062 *(IEEE Recommended Practice for Software Acquisition)*. This standard addresses *commercial off-the-shelf* software (COTS), *modified off-the-shelf* software (MOTS), and *fully developed* software products provided by subcontractors. For the SPMP, only MOTS and fully developed, subcontracted software products need to be considered for this section. In fact, these types are what IEEE Std. 1062 is primarily oriented to. IEEE Std. 1062 defines a nine-step *software acquisition process* that can be referenced in the SPMP.

Subclause 7.8 of the SPMP (process improvement plan) can be addressed via appropriate *management reviews*, as defined by IEEE Std. 1028 *(IEEE Standard for Software Reviews)*. These are intended to *"evaluate the effectiveness of management approaches"* and to *"generate a list of action items, emphasizing risks"*. Management reviews can be used to initiate process improvements as corrective actions taken during the course of a project. *Audits*, also defined by IEEE Std. 1028, are also useful for this purpose, providing information regarding compliance of the audited organization to standards, procedures, regulations, and so on. Audits provide information to management that can be used to initiate process improvements during the project. General guidelines for process improvements are provided in Chapter 2, "Guidelines for Software Process Improvements,"; software reviews are discussed further in Section 6.2.

Warning

One noticeable omission in Clause 7 of the SPMP is a subclause for a *Software Safety Plan*. This is clearly important for any *safety-critical software*, and can be included as subclause 7.9 of a SPMP. The format and information contents of a *Software Safety Plan* is provided in IEEE Std. 1228 *(IEEE Standard for Software Safety Plans)*.

Clause 8 of the SPMP (additional plans) is intended to *"contain additional plans required to satisfy product requirements and contractual terms."* This is separated from clause 7 because these plans might play other than a supporting role for the software life cycle, or might not span the duration of the software project. One of the examples provided by the standard is a *product support plan*. No specific plans are mandated by the standard for this clause; the information content of this clause is inherently project specific.

IEEE Std. 1490 *(IEEE Guide to the Project Management Body of Knowledge)* will not be discussed in detail here. It provides information that might be useful for project management, including descriptions of specific techniques that have proven useful in industry.

Recommendations for Implementation

It is recommended to target *format compliance* with this standard, to avoid the mapping requirement for merely *content compliant* plans. This standard can also be useful as a guide for creating non-compliant plans.

It is recommended to create an SPMP template, to facilitate creating plans for specific projects. The standard itself comments on this:

> Some organizations may have generic project plans based on this standard, so that development of a particular project plan will involve tailoring of the generic plan in areas such as the process mode, supporting processes, and infrastructure, and adding project-unique elements such as schedule, budget, work activities, and risk management plan.

Use of commercial project scheduling tools is beneficial. Schedule charts, resource tables, and other resources created via such tools can be embedded into the project plan.

A SPMP is a complex document, and, as the primary control mechanism for a software project, carries significant risk. Consequently, it is recommended to perform a *management review* of the plan, as per IEEE Std. 1028 *(IEEE Standard for Software Reviews)*. It is also recommended to control changes to the SPMP in accordance with IEEE Std. 828 *(IEEE Standard for Software Configuration Management Plans)* and IEEE Std. 1042 *(IEEE Guide to Software Configuration Management)*.

Due to the relatively large spectrum of personnel who might be involved in creating, reviewing, approving, implementing, and auditing project plans, training is an important issue for introducing IEEE Std. 1058 to an organization. A presentation of the standard SPMP outline, including an explanation of the information contents intended for each section, will be beneficial when using the standard for specific projects.

Summary of IEEE Std. 1058

Implementation of IEEE Std. 1058 is easier than most other *process* standards, because it is primarily oriented to defining the information content and format of a single document. It is not categorized as a *work product* standard because this document, the *Software Project Management Plan*, is used to control the *software life cycle*. This standard, however, does not itself define any particular aspects of the software life cycle; it is merely a standardized mechanism for documenting it.

IEEE Std. 1058 can be thought of as providing a checklist of topics that should be analyzed, and for which decisions should be made, at the outset of a software project. The project should be monitored during the entire software life cycle relative to the plan, and changes in management strategy should be devised to correct problems identified. The information provided in a compliant SPMP goes well beyond the staffing, cost, and schedule estimates typically provided by informal project plans. By encouraging more systematic project planning, this standard can provide substantial benefits, such as reducing project cost and schedule and increasing software product quality.

IEEE Std. 1490 provides supplemental information regarding project management techniques. It is a guide, rather than a standard intended for compliance.

Software Reviews

This section describes standards in the IEEE Software Engineering Standards collection for conducting *software reviews*. This term includes such concepts as *reviews*, *inspections*, and *audits*.

The following IEEE *element standard* addresses this topic:

IEEE Std. 1028-1997, IEEE Standard for Software Reviews

Overview—IEEE Std. 1028

IEEE Std. 1028 states its purpose as follows:

> *The purpose of this standard is to define systematic reviews applicable to software acquisition, supply, development, operation, and maintenance. This standard describes how to carry out a review.*

The primary purpose of such reviews is to identify *anomalies* in the review item, so that these can be corrected. This term is defined by the standard as follows:

> **Anomaly:** *Any condition that deviates from expectations based on requirements specifications, design documents, user documents, standards, and so on or from someone's perceptions or experiences. Anomalies may be found during, but not limited to, the review, test, analysis, compilation, or use of software products or applicable documentation.*

The terms *defect, error, fault,* and *bug* are sometimes used instead of *anomaly*.

To define its scope, the standard defines *systematic* as follows:

> *This standard provides minimum acceptable requirements for systematic software reviews, where "systematic" includes the following attributes:*
>
> a) *Team participation,*
> b) *Documented results of the review,*
> c) *Documented procedures for conducting the review.*

The standard does not pertain to more informal reviews, which it calls *nonsystematic:*

> *Reviews that do meet the requirements of this standard are considered to be nonsystematic reviews. This standard is not meant to discourage or prohibit the use of nonsystematic reviews.*

An important aspect of the standard is that informal reviews can continue to be used without jeopardizing conformance to the standard. Systematic reviews can be implemented for specific purposes, and nonsystematic reviews used for other purposes. The standard does *not* specify what items shall be reviewed or for what purposes.

Software reviews might correspond to conventional meetings, or use the latest telecommunication technology.

The standard defines five different types of *software reviews,* as follows:

> **Management Review:** *A systematic evaluation of a software acquisition, supply, development, operation, or maintenance process performed by or on behalf of management that monitors progress, determines the status of plans and schedules, confirms requirements and their system allocation, or evaluates the effectiveness of management approaches used to achieve fitness for purpose.*

> **Technical Review:** *A systematic evaluation of a software product by a team of qualified personnel that examines the suitability of the software product for its intended use and identifies discrepancies from specifications and standards. Technical reviews may also provide recommendations of alternatives and examination of various alternatives.*

> **Inspection:** *A visual examination of a software product to detect and identify software anomalies, including errors and deviations from standards and specifications. Inspections are peer examinations led by impartial facilitators who are trained in inspection techniques. Determination of remedial or investigative action for an anomaly is a mandatory element of a software inspection, although the solution should not be determined in the inspection meeting.*

Walk-through: *A static analysis technique in which a designer or programmer leads members of the development team and other interested parties through a software product, and the participants ask questions and make comments about possible errors, violation of development standards, and other problems.*

Audit: *An independent examination of a software product, software process, or set of software processes to assess compliance with specifications, standards, contractual agreements, or other criteria.*

The definition provided by the standard for *Inspection* should not contain the word "visual," because this is superfluous and too restrictive. Sight-impaired personnel can participate effectively in inspections.

The Figure 6.2 provides selected comparative information on these review types.

Characteristic	Management Review	Technical Review	Inspection	Walk-through	Audit
Objective	Ensure progress: recommend corrective action: ensure proper allocation of resources	Evaluate conformance to specifications and plans; ensure change integrity	Find anomalies; verify resolution; verify product quality	Find anomalies; examine alternatives; improve product; form for learning	Independently evaluate compliance with objective standards and regulations
Decision-making	Management team charts course of action; decisions made at the meeting or as a result of recommendations	Review team requests management or technical leadership to act on recommendations	Review team chooses predefined product dispositions; defects must be removed	The team agrees on changes to be made by the author	Audited organization, initiator, acquirer, customer, or user

Figure 6.2 *A comparison of the five review types, from IEEE Std. 1028 Annex B.*

The five review types are further described in the "Detailed Description" section later in the chapter.

For each of the review types, the standard specifies that a *Review Report* be generated, which is referred to as a *Management Review Report, Technical Review Report, Inspection Report, Walk-through Report,* or *Audit Report.* It is interesting to note that these reports themselves can be systematically reviewed.

The review items are referred to as *software products* by the standard, which defines this term more loosely than IEEE Std. 610.12 *(IEEE Standard Glossary of Software Engineering Terminology):*

Software product: *(A) A complete set of computer programs, procedures, and associated documentation and data. (B) One or more of the individual items in (A).*

These somewhat confusing definitions are given additional clarification later in the standard:

The term "software product" is used in this standard in a very broad sense. Examples of software products include, but are not limited to, the following:

a) *Anomaly reports*

b) *Audit reports*

c) *Back up and recovery plans*

d) *Build procedures*

e) *Contingency plans*

f) *Contracts*

g) *Customer or user representative complaints*

h) *Disaster plans*

i) *Hardware performance plans*

j) *Inspection reports*

k) *Installation plans*

l) *Installation procedures*

m) *Maintenance manuals*

n) *Maintenance plans*

o) *Management review reports*

p) *Operations and user manuals*

q) *Procurement and contracting methods*

r) *Progress reports*

s) *Release notes*

t) *Reports and data (for example, review, audit, project status, anomaly reports, test data)*

u) *Request for proposal*

v) *Risk management plans*

w) *Software configuration management plans*

x) *Software design descriptions*

y) *Software project management plans*

z) *Software quality assurance plans*

aa) *Software requirements specifications*

bb) *Software safety plans*

cc) *Software test documentation*

dd) *Software user documentation*

ee) *Software verification and validation plans*

ff) *Source code*

gg) *Standards, regulations, guidelines, and procedures*

hh) *System build procedures*

ii) *Technical review reports*

jj) *Vendor documents*

kk) *Walk-through reports*

The standard recommends using each of the five review types for different types of documents (on an informative basis). These recommendations are summarized in Figure 6.3.

Several software products recommended for specific review types are not listed in the generic examples of software products by the standard, and several generic examples of software products are not recommended for any specific review type. Also, a number of software products can effectively be evaluated via additional review types other than those recommended by the standard. These issues are all addressed in Figure 6.3.

Benefits

Software reviews are the most important software V&V activity besides *software testing.* By evaluating various *work products* early in the *software life cycle*, any *anomalies* in the work products, such as missing or incorrect requirements, can be identified and corrected earlier than with testing alone. This helps to reduce project cost and schedule.

Thorough and comprehensive software reviews might not only identify defects earlier; in some cases, they can reveal defects that would have been difficult to expose via testing. By complementing software testing, software reviews can increase the quality of the final software product.

Software reviews specify formalized meetings. Meetings are held as a matter of course by all organizations. By improving the efficiency of meetings, and guiding them for a specific purpose and outcome, this standard can improve the cost and schedule of software projects. Bad meetings are a common complaint in the workforce, and by attacking this common problem, the standard can help improve an organization's morale.

Software Product	Management Review	Technical Review	Inspection	Walk-through	Audit
a) Anomaly reports	X				*
b) Audit reports	X				*
c) Back up and recovery plans	X				X
d) Build procedures		*	*	*	*
e) Contingency plans	X				X
f) Contracts	*	*			X
g) Customer or user representative complaints	X	*			X
h) Deliverable media		*	*	*	X
i) Disaster plans	X				X
j) Hardware performance plans	X				X
k) Inspection reports	*	*			*
l) Installation plans	X				X
m) Installation procedures		X	X	X	X
n) Maintenance manuals		X	X	X	*
o) Maintenance	X				X
p) Management review reports	*		*		X
q) Operations and user manuals		*		*	X
r) Procurement and contracting methods	X				X
s) Progress reports	X		X		*
t) Release notes		X	*	X	*
u) Reports and data	*	*	*	*	X
v) Request for proposal	*				X
w) Risk management plans	X				X
x) Software configuration management plans	X				X
y) Software design descriptions		X	X	X	X
z) Software project management plans	X				X
aa) Software quality assurance plans	X				X
bb) Software Product Analyses	X	*			*
cc) Software requirements specifications		X	X	X	X
dd) Software safety plans	X				X
ee) Software test documentation		X	X	X	X
ff) Software user documentation		X	X	X	X
gg) Software verification and validation plans	X				X
hh) Source code			X	X	X
ii) Standards, regulations, guidelines, and procedures					X
jj) System build procedures		X		X	X
kk) Technical review reports	X		X		X
ll) Unit development folders		*			X
mm) Vendor documents	*	*	*	*	X
nn) Verification and validation reports	X				*
oo) Walk-through reports	*	*			X

X – recommended for review type by standard

* – possibly should have been recommended for review type

Figure 6.3 *Use of the five review types according to product type, from IEEE Std. 1028.*

Software reviews are easy to document, and thus provide objective evidence of *design controls*, as required for compliance with regulations such as the FDA Quality Systems Regulations for medical device manufacturers.

Relationship to Other Standards

Application of IEEE Std. 1028 to specific software quality assurance and V&V activities should be planned in the context of the overall software life cycle, as specified by the following other standards:

- IEEE Std. 730, *IEEE Standard for Software Quality Assurance Plans*
- IEEE Std. 1012, *IEEE Standard for Software Verification and Validation*
- IEEE Std. 1058, *IEEE Standard for Software Project Management Plans*
- IEEE Std. 1074, *IEEE Standard for Developing Software Life Cycle Processes*
- IEEE Std. 1228, *IEEE Standard for Software Safety Plans*
- ISO/IEC 12207, *Standard for Information Technology—Software Life Cycle Processes*

Software reviews, as described by IEEE Std. 1028, identify *anomalies* in *software products*, providing an *input* to the *configuration management* process. This is described by the following standard:

- IEEE Std. 828, IEEE Standard for Software Configuration Management Plans

IEEE Std. 1028 can be used to review *work products* relative to standards for such work products, as discussed in Chapter 5, "Document Standards," including

- IEEE Std. 829, *IEEE Standard for Software Test Documentation*
- IEEE Std. 830, *IEEE Standard for Software Requirements Specifications*
- IEEE Std. 982.1, *IEEE Standard Dictionary of Measures to Produce Reliable Software*
- IEEE Std. 1016, *IEEE Standard for Software Design Descriptions*
- IEEE Std. 1061, *IEEE Standard for a Software Quality Metrics Methodology*
- IEEE Std. 1063, *IEEE Standard for Software User Documentation*

IEEE Std. 1028 can be used to review plans and processes relative to corresponding standards, including:

- IEEE Std. 730, *IEEE Standard for Software Quality Assurance Plans*
- IEEE Std. 828, *IEEE Standard for Software Configuration Management Plans*
- IEEE Std. 1008, *IEEE Standard for Software Unit Testing*
- IEEE Std. 1012, *IEEE Standard for Software Verification and Validation*
- IEEE Std. 1058, *IEEE Standard for Software Project Management Plans*
- IEEE Std. 1074, *IEEE Standard for Developing Software Life Cycle Processes*
- IEEE Std. 1228, *IEEE Standard for Software Safety Plans*

IEEE Std. 1028 can be used to evaluate work products or processes relative to standards, regulations, and so on outside of the IEEE Software Engineering Standards collection as well. For example, a *Code Inspection* could focus on compliance with project *Programming Standards*.

Audience

This standard is intended for use in a wide variety of circumstances. It is useful for both management and technical teams, for development, testing, and quality assurance personnel. Both the *customer* and *supplier*, and even the *user*, as discussed for IEEE Std. 830 *(IEEE Standard for Software Requirements Specifications)*, can be involved in software reviews.

Guidelines for personnel roles for the different types of software reviews are shown in Figure 6.4.

Characteristic	Management Review	Technical Review	Inspection	Walk-through	Audit
Group attendance	Management, technical leadership and peer mix	Technical leadership and peer mix	Peers	Technical leadership and peer mix.	Auditors, audited organization, management and technical personnel
Group leadership	Usually the responsible manager	Usually the lead engineer	Trained facilitator	Facilitator or author	Lead auditor
Presenter	Project representative	Development team representative	A reader	Author	Auditors collect and examine information by audited organization

Figure 6.4 *Personnel roles for the five review types, from IEEE Std. 1028 Annex B.*

Project Phases Affected

Software reviews can be conducted during all project phases.

Annex A of the standard *(Relationship of this standard to the life cycle processes of other standards)* provides a possible mapping of the five review types to the following standards:

- IEEE Std. 730, *IEEE Standard for Software Quality Assurance Plans*
- IEEE Std. 1012, *IEEE Standard for Software Verification and Validation*
- IEEE Std. 1074, *IEEE Standard for Developing Software Life Cycle Processes*
- ISO/IEC 12207, *Standard for Information Technology—Software Life Cycle Processes*

The mapping described for IEEE Std. 730 and IEEE Std. 1012, updated for the 1998 versions of these standards, is shown in Figure 6.5.

Other V&V tasks specified by IEEE Std. 1012 for various phases, such as *Criticality Analysis*, *Traceability Analysis*, *Hazard Analysis*, *Risk Analysis*, and *Interface Analysis* can also be performed via software reviews, specifically *Technical Reviews*, *Inspections*, or *Walk-throughs*.

The specific reviews referenced in Figure 6.5 are described further in the sections on the corresponding standards.

Detailed Description

IEEE Std. 1028 specifies the following information for each of the five review types:

- **Introduction:** The purpose of the review type, an overview of the review procedures, and examples of software products suitable for this type of review. This section does not specify mandatory actions, recommendations, or alternative methods as related to conformance to the standard.
- **Responsibilities:** The roles and responsibilities of the participants.
- **Input:** The inputs needed for the review.
- **Entry Criteria:** Conditions required for starting the review, including authorization and initiating event.
- **Procedures:** The steps for the review including management preparation, planning, overview meeting, preparation, examination, and rework activities.
- **Exit Criteria:** Conditions required for completing the review.
- **Output:** The minimum set of deliverables from the review. This represents one of the *Review Reports* previously mentioned.

Standard	Clause	Review title	Corresponding IEEE Std. 1028-1997 review type
IEEE Std. 730-1998	3.6.2.1	Software Requirements Review	Technical Review
	3.6.2.2	Preliminary Design Review	Technical Review
	3.6.2.3	Critical Design Review	Technical Review
	3.6.2.4	Software V&V Plan Review	Management Review
	3.6.2.5	Functional Audit	Audit
	3.6.2.6	Physical Audit	Audit
	3.6.2.7	In-Process Audits	Audit
	3.6.2.8	Managerial Reviews	Management Review
	3.6.2.9	Software Configuration Management Plan Review	Management Review
	3.6.2.10	Post-mortem Review	Management Review, Technical Review
	3.6.3.1	User Documentation Review	Technical Review, Inspection, Walk-through
	3.6.3.2	Quality Assurance Audit	Audit
IEEE Std. 1012-1998	5.1.1	Management Review of V&V	Management Review
	5.2.1	System Requirements Review	Technical Review
	5.3.1	Contract Verification	Management Review, Technical Review
	5.4.1	Concept Documentation Evaluation	Technical Review
	5.4.2	Software Requirements Evaluation	Technical Review, Inspection, Walk-through
	5.4.3	Software Design Evaluation	Technical Review, Inspection, Walk-through
	5.4.4	Source Code and Source Code Documentation Evaluation	Technical Review, Inspection, Walk-through
	5.4.6	Installation Configuration Audit	Audit
	5.5.1	Operating Procedures Evaluation	Technical Review, Inspection, Walk-through

Figure 6.5 *Possible mapping to the five review types, adapted from IEEE Std. 1028.*

The five review types are described in the following sections. The concise specifications of the review types by the standard are not repeated verbatim here. Instead, the roles of the participants are described, a process diagram is provided to complement the standard, and the contents of the *review report* and the decision-making process are analyzed.

Management Reviews

The roles of the participants in a *Management Review* are as follows:

1. **Decision Maker:** Determines if the review objectives have been met,
2. **Review Leader:** Plans and conducts the review, and issues the *Management Review Report.*

3. **Recorder:** Documents anomalies, action items, decisions, and recommendations made during the review examination, and provides this to the review leader.

4. **Management Staff:** Participate in the review.

5. **Technical Staff:** Provide information for the review.

6. **Customer or User Representative:** Optionally invited by the reviewer leader, to participate in the review, provide information for the review, or for other purposes.

The standard provides the following curious description of the *Decision Maker:*

> *The decision maker is the person for whom the management review is conducted.*

This should not be understood as requiring an autocrat for whose sole benefit the review is conducted. (The review is conducted to benefit the organization and the project.) Rather, this must be understood in the context of the entry criteria specified by the standard, in particular

> *A statement of objectives for the review is established by the management personnel for whom the review is being carried out.*

In other words, the responsibility for evaluating the successful achievement of the review goals is entrusted to the management personnel who initially specified those objectives.

The management review process is summarized in Figure 6.6.

The overview session is optional, to be requested by the review leader. The standard allows conducting this during the beginning of the (first) review meeting. In this case, it will occur after the participants have prepared for the review meeting, thus decreasing its utility. It is recommended that, if an overview session is required, it be held prior to the preparation step.

The *management preparation* description for management reviews contains steps both prior to the review, and following the review. The standard does not list the crucial step of management personnel creating a statement of objectives for the review, although this is required as a precondition for the review. Usually, the statement of objectives is specified prior to review, via a *Software Project Management Plan* or other plan. However, if a management review is to be conducted whose purpose is not specified by a plan, the statement of objectives should be created by management prior to other process steps.

One of the examination goals of a management review is to *"Generate a list of action items, emphasizing risks."*

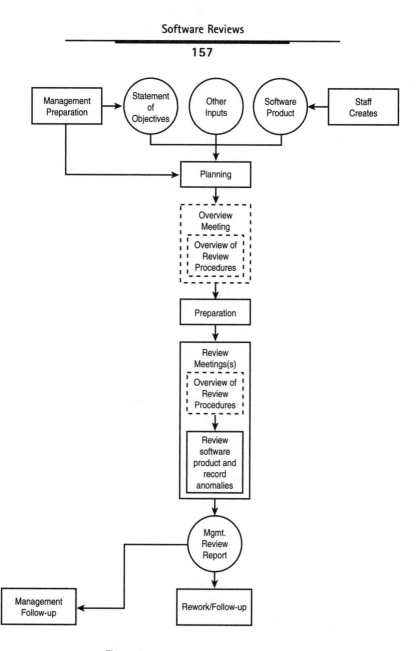

Figure 6.6 *The management review process.*

Identifying anomalies is not listed as an examination goal for a management review, although reviewing anomalies identified prior to the review meeting is. This is appropriate, given that both the primary participants as well as the target audience are management personnel.

A *Management Review Report* must be issued by the review leader, and must contain the following information according to the standard:

a) *The project being reviewed*

b) *The review team members*

c) *Review objectives*

d) *Software product reviewed*

e) *Specific inputs to the review*

f) *Action item status (open, closed), ownership and target date (if open) or completion date (if closed)*

g) *A list of anomalies identified by the review team that must be addressed for the project to meet its goals*

The decision-making process for a *management review* differs from a *technical review* in that decisions, rather than merely recommendations, can be made during the review. *Management reviews* can be compared to *inspections* in this regard, because inspections also are intended to allow decisions to be made during the review. In the case of inspections, the scope of such decisions is restricted to technical issues involving *work products*. For management reviews, such decisions are focused on management issues usually involving *software life cycle processes*.

Technical Reviews

The roles of the participants of a *Technical Review* are the same as for a *Management Review*, except for redefined tasks for technical versus management personnel:

Management Staff can participate in the review for the purpose of identifying issues that require management resolution.

Technical Staff participate in the review and evaluate the software product.

The technical review process is summarized in Figure 6.7.

As in a *management review*, one of the examination goals of a technical review is to generate a list of action items, emphasizing risks. Unlike in a management review, identification of anomalies is another examination goal. This is appropriate, given that technical personnel are the primary participants, but the information provided by a technical review is intended for management personnel.

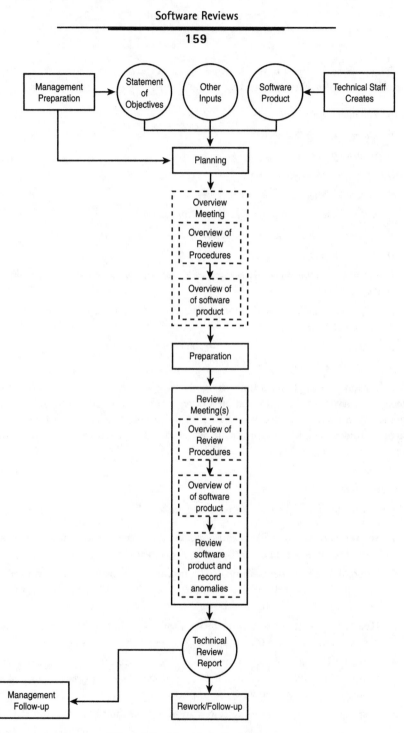

Figure 6.7 *The technical review process.*

A *Technical Review Report* must be issued by the review leader, and must contain the following information according to the standard:

a) *The project being reviewed*

b) *The review team members*

c) *Software product reviewed*

d) *Specific inputs to the review*

e) *Review objectives and whether they were met*

f) *A list of resolved and unresolved product anomalies*

g) *A list of unresolved system or hardware anomalies or specification action items*

h) *A list of management issues*

i) *Action item status (open, closed), ownership, and target date (if open) or completion date (if closed)*

j) *Any recommendations made by the review team on how to dispose of unresolved issues and anomalies*

k) *Whether the software product meets the applicable regulations, standards, guidelines, plans, and procedures without deviations*

The decision-making process for a *technical review* is more restricted than that for a *management review* in that information and recommendations are provided to management, who will make decisions based on this input. For reviews involving active participation by technical personnel, in which decisions regarding the review item are to be made, *inspections* should be used instead.

Inspections

The roles of the participants of an *inspection* are as follows:

1. **Inspection Leader:** Plans and conducts the review, ensures that the inspection objectives are met, and issues the *Inspection Report*.

2. **Recorder:** Documents anomalies, action items, decisions, and recommendations made during the review examination, and provides this to the inspection leader (who can fulfill this role if necessary).

3. **Reader:** Leads the inspection through the software product, for example, paraphrasing several lines, functions, paragraphs, or sections.

4. **Author:** Prepares the software product for the inspection, provides information on the software product during the inspection, and reworks the software product as needed following the inspection meeting.

5. **Inspector:** Identifies and describes anomalies in the software product.

For successful inspections, it is important to restrict the role of the *author* during the inspection meeting to providing information regarding the work product, and in particular to not become engaged in defending the work product. At the same time, it is important to restrict the role of the *inspectors* to identification and description of objective defects in the work product, and to disallow subjective evaluation of the entire work product that might cause a defensive reaction on the part of the author. The responsibility for guiding the participants to fulfill their assigned roles lies exclusively with the *inspection leader*.

The inspection team is intended to exclude management personnel, according to the standard:

> *Individuals holding management positions over any member of the inspection team shall not participate in the inspection.*

This stipulation is intended to encourage open exchange of ideas during the inspection.

The *inspection* process is summarized in Figure 6.8.

The *inspection meeting* is more structured than a *management review* or *technical review* meeting. This is because of the challenge of covering significant amounts of technical information within time constraints, while avoiding problems related to the review team dynamics.

Unlike management or technical reviews, inspections are primarily focused on the identification of anomalies. Generating a list of action items emphasizing risks is not specified as a primary goal of inspections by the standards. This is appropriate, because inspections are conducted by technical personnel, and provide information to technical personnel.

An *Inspection Report* must be issued by the inspection leader, and must contain the following information according to the standard:

a) *The project being inspected*

b) *The inspection team members*

c) *The inspection meeting duration*

d) *The software product inspected*

e) *The size of the materials inspected (for example, the number of text pages)*

f) *Specific inputs to the inspection*

g) *Inspection objectives and whether they were met*

h) *The anomaly list, containing each anomaly's location, description, and classification*

i) *The inspection anomaly summary listing the number of anomalies identified by each anomaly category*

j) *The disposition of the software product*

k) *An estimate of the rework effort and rework completion date*

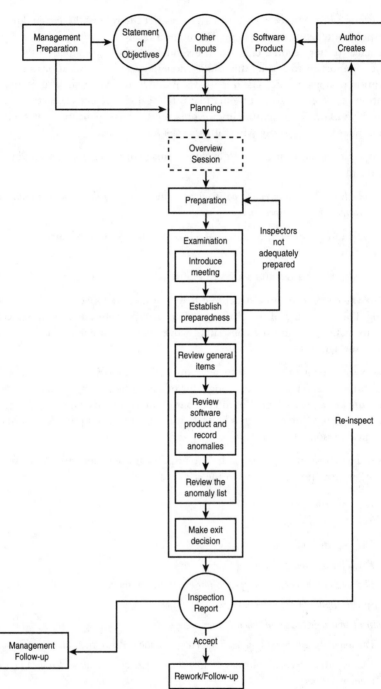

Figure 6.8 *The inspection process.*

The *software product disposition* must be one of the following choices:

a) *Accept with no or minor rework. The software product is accepted as is or with only minor rework (for example, that would require no further verification).*

b) *Accept with rework verification. The software product is to be accepted after the inspection leader or a designated member of the inspection team (other than the author) verifies rework.*

c) *Re-inspect. Schedule a re-inspection to verify rework. At a minimum, a re-inspection shall examine the software product areas changed to resolve anomalies identified in the last inspection, as well as side effects of those changes.*

The disposition of the software product should be based on the number and severity of the anomalies identified, and the estimated rework effort. If the required rework is sufficiently restricted in scope, well-specified, and without potential side effects, so as to allow it to be efficiently verified by the inspection leader or a designated inspector, then a re-inspection is not necessary. A re-inspection should be performed if the scope of the rework is substantial, the rework cannot be clearly specified, or side effects of the rework are possible.

The standard states that software anomalies can be categorized according to IEEE Std. 1044 *(IEEE Standard Classification for Software Anomalies)*. Categories considered mandatory by IEEE Std. 1044 are as follows:

1. *Actual Cause: What caused the anomaly to occur?*

2. *Disposition: What happened to close the anomaly?*

3. *Project Activity: What were you doing when the anomaly occurred?*

4. *Project Cost: Relative effect on the project budget to fix.*

5. *Project Phase: In which life cycle phase is the product?*

6. *Project Schedule: Relative effect on the product schedule to fix.*

7. *Resolution: What action to take to resolve the anomaly.*

8. *Severity: How bad was the anomaly in more objective engineering terms?*

9. *Source: Where was the origin of the anomaly?*

10. *Symptom: How did the anomaly manifest itself?*

11. *Type: What type of anomaly/enhancement is at the code level?*

It is not necessary to comply with IEEE Std. 1044 for the purpose of conforming to IEEE Std. 1028, however. The primary purpose of the classification of anomalies in the *inspection report* is to provide data for planning software process improvements. You can tailor the classification according to your software process improvement program. For anomalies identified by inspections, knowing the *project phase* (both during which the anomaly was detected, and during which the anomaly was first introduced), the *project cost* and *schedule* impacts, and the *severity* is particularly useful. It can also be useful to estimate the project cost and schedule impact if the anomaly had not been identified during the inspection, assuming that it would have been discovered during software testing.

As a non-mandatory aspect of data collection during inspections, the standard suggests the following *anomaly ranking*, which could be documented under h) from the *Inspection Report:*

> *Anomalies may be ranked by potential impact on the software product, for example, as*

> a) *Major. Anomalies that would result in failure of the software product or an observable departure from specification.*

> b) *Minor. Anomalies that deviate from relevant specifications but will not cause failure of the software product or an observable departure in performance.*

In any case, anomalies should be evaluated for *risk* according to the *Software Safety Plan*, as described by IEEE Std. 1228 *(IEEE Standard for Software Safety Plans)*. Even if the risk is not used for classification of anomalies, it should be used to disposition the software product.

The decision-making process for an *inspection* differs from a *technical review* in that the inspection is authorized to make decisions regarding required rework of the software product. In this regard, it is a more powerful tool, intended to delegate decision-making responsibility to technical personnel.

Walk-Throughs

The roles of the participants of a *walk-through* are as follows:

1. **Walk-Through Leader:** Plans and conducts the walk-through, defines the objectives of the walk-through and ensures that these are met, and issues the *Walk-Through Report.*

2. **Recorder:** Documents decisions and identified actions during the walk-through meeting.

3. **Author:** Presents the software product in the walk-through.

4. **Team Member:** Participates in the walk-through.

The author is not as restricted in a walk-through as in an inspection. The standard enables the author to function as the *walk-through leader* and/or as the *recorder*. Only one other team member is required besides the author to conduct a walk-through, making the cost and schedule of walk-throughs lower and shorter, respectively, than those of inspections. Walk-throughs are also easier to implement from the point of view of managing the review team dynamics, because there is less chance of putting the author in a defensive position (or the other reviewers in an attacking position). However, walk-throughs are not as effective, generally speaking, as well-conducted inspections in identifying anomalies, for the very reasons that they are easier to implement.

As in an *inspection*, management personnel is specifically excluded from a *walk-through* team:

> *Individuals holding management positions over any member of the walk-through team shall not participate in the walk-through.*

The *walk-through* process is summarized in Figure 6.9.

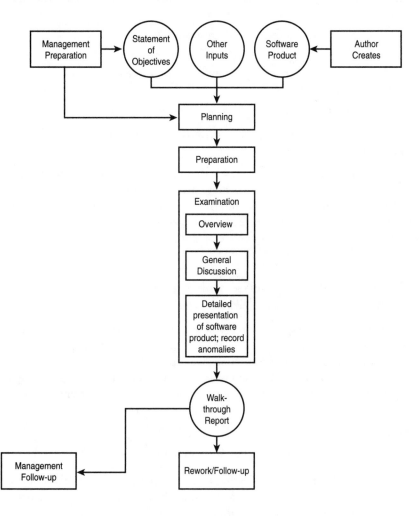

Figure 6.9 *The walk-through process.*

Like *inspections*, walk-throughs are primarily focused on the identification of anomalies. This is because, like inspections, walk-throughs are conducted by technical personnel, and provide information to technical personnel.

A *Walk-Through Report* must be issued by the walk-through leader, and must contain the following information according to the standard:

a) *The walk-through team members*

b) *The software product being examined*

c) *The statement of objectives that were to be accomplished during this walk-through meeting and whether they were met*

d) *A list of the recommendations made regarding each anomaly*

e) *A list of actions, due dates, and responsible people*

f) *Any recommendations made by the walk-through team on how to dispose of deficiencies and unresolved anomalies*

g) *Any proposals made by the walk-through team for follow-up walk-throughs.*

The classification of anomalies can be performed in the same manner as in inspections.

The decision-making process for a walk-through is more restricted than for an inspection, in that a walk-through is more oriented toward providing information, and less oriented to reworking of anomalies. An inspection cannot be completed until the software has been accepted and anomalies have been resolved, whereas the exit criteria for a walk-through are only the following:

a) *The entire software product has been examined.*

b) *Recommendations and required actions have been recorded.*

c) *The walk-through output has been completed.*

In an inspection, a re-inspection might be mandated, whereas in a walk-through, it would only be proposed. In a sense, one can think of a walk-through as an "Inspection Lite," useful to organizations that do not have the personnel resources or process maturity for conducting inspections, or that are not willing to delegate as much decision-making to technical personnel as is required for inspections.

Audits

The roles of the participants in an *audit* are as follows:

1. **Lead Auditor:** Must be free from bias and influence, and is responsible for planning and conducting the audit, ensuring that the audit meets its objectives, and issuing the *Audit Report*.

2. **Recorder:** Documents anomalies, action items, decisions, and recommendations made during the audit, providing this to the lead auditor.

3. **Auditor:** Examines products, documents the participants' observations, and recommends corrective actions.

4. **Initiator:** Decides upon the need for an audit, its purpose and scope, the evaluation criteria, and the audit team, reviews the *Audit Report*, and determines the follow-up actions required.

5. **Audited Organization:** Provides a *liaison* to the auditors, provides all information requested by the auditors, and implements corrective actions and recommendations from the audit.

The *audit* process is summarized in Figure 6.10.

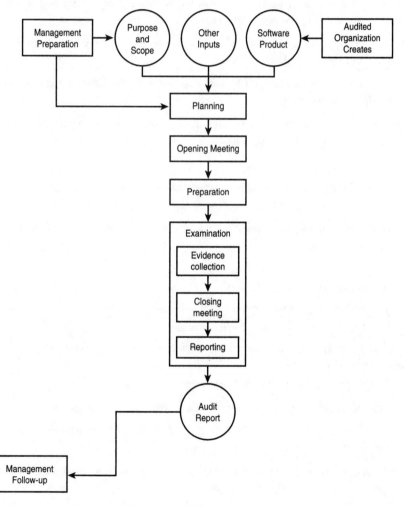

Figure 6.10   *The audit process.*

A primary examination goal of audits is to make and document *observations*. These are defined by the standard as follows:

> *An observation is a statement of fact made during an audit that is substantiated by objective evidence.*

This is a subtly different goal from the identification of anomalies or the creation of action items, with an emphasis of risk, which are primary examination goals of other software review types. The goal of making observations is appropriate for audits, because of the required independence and objectivity of the *auditors*, and the translation of observations into action items by the *initiator*.

An important aspect of the audit process is discussion of observations between the auditors and the audited organization:

> *All observations shall be verified by discussing them with the audited organization before the closing audit meeting.*

An *Audit Report* must be issued by the lead auditor, and must contain the following information according to the standard:

a) *Purpose and scope of the audit*

b) *Audited organization, including location, liaison staff, and management*

c) *Identification of the software products audited*

d) *Applicable regulations, standards, guidelines, plans, and procedures used for evaluation*

e) *Evaluation criteria*

f) *Summary of auditor's organization*

g) *Summary of examination activities*

h) *Summary of the planned examination activities not performed*

i) *Observation list, classified as major or minor*

j) *A summary and interpretation of the audit findings including the key items of nonconformance*

k) *The type and timing of audit follow-up activities*

The classification of observations is specified by the standard as follows:

> *An observation should be classified as major if the non-conformity will likely have a significant effect on product quality, project cost, or project schedule.*

Additional information, including recommendations to the audited organization, can also be included in the *Audit Report*.

The decision-making process for an *audit* differs substantially from other types of software reviews because of the independence of the auditors from the audited organization. The *Audit Report* provides information to the *initiator*, who must decide on the action items, which must then be implemented by the *audited organization*.

Recommendations for Implementation

The level of detail provided by the standard for the different software review techniques facilitates its implementation. Nevertheless, the effort required for phase-in of formalized software reviews should not be underestimated. The greatest effort will be associated with *training* of personnel. Although the process might seem straightforward, its practical application can be challenging. An effective training program should include team exercises in conducting software reviews on sample materials. The standard itself recommends *formal facilitator training* for both *inspections* and *audits*, but some level of training is beneficial for all participants of all types of reviews.

A program for implementing software reviews should be conducted in stages. At first, one type of software review should be introduced for a limited purpose. For example, *Code Inspections* can be introduced first, because their purpose is easy to explain, and they will provide easily recognized benefits. Later, other types of software reviews can be introduced for different purposes. A program of introduction of different types of software reviews could consist of the following stages (as an example):

1. **Inspections** (or **Walk-throughs**) of software requirements specifications, software design descriptions, source code, and software user documentation to provide verification of primary work products.

2. **Audits**, for quality assurance purposes, to establish conformance to regulations, standards, guidelines, plans, and procedures.

3. **Management Reviews**, for evaluation of processes and plans by, or on behalf of, management for the purpose of monitoring progress, evaluating the effectiveness of management purposes, planning corrective action, and so on.

   Inspections, **Technical Reviews**, or **Walk-throughs** of secondary work products such as *software test documentation*.

Note

For very small software development organizations, *walk-throughs* are recommended instead of *inspections* simply because only two technical team members are required to conduct a walk-through, and because less training is required to implement walk-throughs. In all other cases, inspections are recommended, because they can provide even greater benefit.

Electronic (or paper) templates should be created for each type of *review report*. The reports can be maintained via a database application, or published via an intranet.

Summary of IEEE Std. 1028

Software reviews represent one of the most important software quality assurance techniques. Effective use of software reviews can decrease software project cost and schedule, and increase software product quality. Software review reports provide an audit trail for software quality activities.

The standard defines a process model for the most important types of software reviews, including *management reviews*, *technical reviews*, *inspections*, *walk-throughs*, and *audits*.

Management reviews are carried out by, or on behalf of, management personnel for the purpose of monitoring progress, evaluating management approaches, planning corrective actions, and so on.

Technical reviews, *inspections*, and *walk-throughs* are used to evaluate software products, by looking at software requirements specifications, software design descriptions, and other project documents, prior to testing. Inspections and walk-throughs are also suitable for evaluating the software source code prior to testing. Inspections are particularly effective, because they authorize the review team to require rework of the work product as needed to remove defects.

Audits represent a fundamental technique for software quality assurance. They can be used to evaluate conformance to regulations, standards, guidelines, plans, and procedures.

The standard provides a detailed process model for each of these techniques, and implementation of this standard will provide a substantive software process improvement with tangible benefits.

Quality Assurance

This section describes software *quality assurance* standards in the IEEE Software Engineering Standards collection.

The IEEE *element standard* on this topic is the following:

IEEE Std. 730-1998, IEEE Standard for Software Quality Assurance Plans

A standard is also provided at the *Guides and Supplements* layer of the *SESC Framework* model:

IEEE Std. 730.1-1995, IEEE Guide for Software Quality Assurance Planning

IEEE Std. 730.1 is not described in detail here.

Standards on closely related topics such as *software verification and validation*, and *software life cycle processes* are not described in this section. These are listed in the section "Relationship to Other Standards" later in the chapter.

Overview—IEEE Std. 730

IEEE Std. 730 specifies the minimum acceptable requirements for the information content and format of a *Software Quality Assurance Plan* (SQAP). Although this represents a work product standard, the work product being a plan, it implicitly specifies process requirements. This is particularly clear when the standard specifies minimum documents to be produced during the project, minimum reviews and audits to be conducted during the project, and so on.

Software *quality assurance* is defined by IEEE Std. 610.12 *(IEEE Standard Glossary of Software Engineering Terminology)* as follows:

> **quality assurance (QA):** *(1) A planned and systematic pattern of all actions necessary to provide adequate confidence that an item or product conforms to established technical requirements.*
>
> *(2) A set of activities designed to evaluate the process by which products are developed or manufactured.*

This can be compared to the definition of *verification and validation* by the same standard:

> **verification and validation (V&V):** *The process of determining whether the requirements for a system or component are complete and correct, the products of each development phase fulfill the requirements or conditions imposed by the previous phase, and the final system or component complies with specified requirements.*

From these definitions it is apparent that QA is a broader, more high-level topic than V&V, and indeed software verification and validation activities are stipulated by the SQAP. However, it should be mentioned that IEEE Std. 730 uses only the first definition from IEEE Std. 610.12, ignoring the process evaluation aspect of quality assurance.

IEEE Std. 730 is intended for *critical software*. The standard states:

> *This standard applies to the development and maintenance of critical software. For non-critical software, or for software already developed, a subset of this standard may be applied.*

Critical software is defined as follows:

> **critical software:** *Software whose failure would impact safety or cause large financial or social losses.*

No specific guidelines are provided for what subset of the standard to apply for non-critical software. For comparison, IEEE Std. 1012 *(IEEE Standard for Software Verification and Validation)* provides more detailed guidelines based on the *software integrity level*, which reflects the *criticality* of the software. *Critical software* in the sense of IEEE Std. 730 corresponds to software integrity levels 3 and 4 (correspond to *major* and *high criticality*, respectively) as per IEEE Std. 1012, or possibly only to level 4 *(high criticality)*. This correlation is not defined by the standards.

IEEE Std. 730 does not discuss the possibility that part of a software product might be critical, while other parts might be non-critical, as is often the case. A common practice is to trace the critical functions of the software to individual design elements, and to perform more comprehensive V&V activities on the more critical design elements and functionality. This is described in IEEE Std. 1012 *(IEEE Standard for Software Verification and Validation)*:

> The software integrity level (used by Std. 1012 to quantify software criticality) can be assigned to software requirements, functions, group of functions, or software components or subsystems.

The advantage of this approach is that limited time and resources for V&V can be focused on those parts of the software where the greatest benefit will result. This strategy can be applied to software quality assurance planning as well, as related to minimum requirements specified by IEEE Std. 730 on the following topics:

1. Documentation
2. Standards, practices, conventions, and metrics
3. Reviews and audits

This standard could be interpreted as specifying minimum requirements on these topics for those parts of the software that have been identified as critical. For example, reviews and audits could restrict their scope to the critical portions of the software. This presupposes that the software can be effectively partitioned.

The *minimum documentation requirements* (for *critical software)* specified by IEEE Std. 730 are as follows (associated IEEE standards describing those types of documents are also listed for convenience):

1. Software Requirements Specification (IEEE Std. 830)
2. Software Design Description (IEEE Std. 1016)
3. Software Verification and Validation Plan (IEEE Std. 1012)
4. Software Verification and Validation Report (IEEE Std. 1012)
5. User documentation (IEEE Std. 1063)
6. Software Configuration Management Plan (IEEE Std. 828)

The *Software Project Management Plan* (IEEE Std. 1058) is listed amongst the possible additional documents by IEEE Std. 730.

The *minimum set of standards, practices, conventions,* and *metrics (for critical software)* specified by IEEE Std. 730 are as follows:

1. Documentation standards
2. Logic structure standards
3. Coding standards
4. Commentary standards
5. Testing standards and practices (IEEE Std. 829)
6. Software quality metrics (IEEE Std. 1061)

The standard also specifies the *minimum review and audit requirements* (for *critical software)*, which are as follows:

1. Software Requirements Review
2. Preliminary Design Review
3. Critical Design Review
4. Software Verification and Validation Plan Review
5. Functional audit
6. Physical audit
7. In-process audits
8. Managerial reviews
9. Software Configuration Management Plan Review
10. Post-mortem review

A *User Documentation Review* is listed as a possible additional review by the standard. All of these reviews and audits can be conducted in compliance with IEEE Std. 1028 *(IEEE Standard for Software Reviews)*, as described in detail previously in the chapter. Figure 6.5 shows a possible mapping of the reviews and audits required by IEEE Std. 730 to the software review types defined by IEEE Std. 1028.

The astute reader will notice that these other standards have already been described, except for IEEE Std. 1012 and IEEE Std. 828. These standards are recommended for concurrent implementation with IEEE Std. 730, at the same maturity level, according to the *Pyramid of Applicability* model in Chapter 3. The reason why IEEE Std. 730 is presented prior to IEEE Std. 1012 and IEEE Std. 828 is very simple: It is a smaller, simpler standard. Furthermore, the *Software Verification and Validation Plan* and *Software Configuration Management Plan* can be provided as sections of the *Software Project Management Plan*, as defined in IEEE Std. 1058, and as already presented. IEEE Std. 730 might thus be implemented prior to achieving full compliance with IEEE Std. 1012 and IEEE Std. 828. In this regard, it is worth noting that IEEE Std. 730 was the first standard in the IEEE software standards set, and was thus originally intended for standalone implementation.

Benefits

The primary benefit of IEEE Std. 730 is improved software product quality, to be expected from its implementation.

This standard is the simplest standard defining aspects of the entire *software life cycle*. An implicit benefit of the standard is that it provides concise guidelines for planning and executing entire software projects.

Proper implementation of the processes required by this standard should result in reduced project cost and schedule, and should improve the manageability of the software project. This is largely because the structure and control mechanisms imposed on the software project by the quality assurance plan will enable identification and management of risks to be performed more effectively.

By specifying a *post-mortem review*, the standard encourages software process improvements, an additional benefit.

By creating a separate quality assurance plan document, as is implied by IEEE Std. 730, the organizational independence of the software quality assurance group is reinforced, and visibility to management is increased.

Relationship to Other Standards

IEEE Std. 730 draws on numerous lower-level standards, which can be used to create the documents or plans required by the standard, or to define processes to be followed according to the SQAP. Specific cross-references to other standards are given in the previous section "Overview—IEEE Std. 730" and the "Detailed Description" section that appears later in the chapter. Here is a list of the standards that IEEE Std. 730 draws on:

- IEEE Std. 828 (*IEEE Standard for Software Configuration Management Plans*)
- IEEE Std. 829 (*IEEE Standard for Software Test Documentation*)
- IEEE Std. 830 (*IEEE Recommended Practice for Software Requirements Specifications*)
- IEEE Std. 1012 (*IEEE Standard for Software Verification and Validation*)
- IEEE Std. 1016 (*IEEE Recommended Practice for Software Design Descriptions*)

- IEEE Std. 1028 (*IEEE Standard for Software Reviews*)
- IEEE Std. 1061 (*IEEE Standard for a Software Quality Metrics Methodology*)
- IEEE Std. 1062 (*IEEE Recommended Practice for Software Acquisition*)
- IEEE Std. 1063 (*IEEE Standard for Software User Documentation*)

Of these, IEEE Std. 1012 has a special relationship to IEEE Std. 730 because of some overlap in their topics. IEEE Std. 1012 provides more detailed guidelines for conducting the specific quality assurance activity of V&V.

The following standards relate to IEEE Std. 730 by describing information at the same or even higher levels:

- IEEE Std. 1074 (*IEEE Standard for Developing Software Life Cycle Processes*)
- IEEE/EIA Std. 12207.0 (*IEEE/EIA Standard for Industry Implementation of International Standard ISO/IEC 12207 Standard for Information Technology— Software life cycle processes*)
- IEEE/EIA Std. 12207.1 (*IEEE/EIA Standard for Industry Implementation of International Standard ISO/IEC 12207 Standard for Information Technology— Software life cycle processes—Life cycle data*)

IEEE/EIA Std. 12207.0 defines requirements for the *Quality Assurance Process* (Section 6.3 of that standard). IEEE/EIA Std. 12207.1 provides generic guidelines for plan contents (Section 5.2 of that standard) and specific guidelines for *Software Quality Assurance Plans* (Section 6.20) and *software quality assurance records* (Section 6.21). Annex A of IEEE Std. 730 provides guidelines for compliance with these two standards.

IEEE Std. 1074 provides a process for *creating software life cycle processes*. It includes specific guidelines for activities also covered by IEEE Std. 730, such as conducting reviews and audits, planning V&V and configuration management activities, requiring documentation such as an SRS, use of metrics, risk management, and so on. It is interesting to note that IEEE Std. 1074 avoids using the term *quality assurance*, perhaps to avoid apparent conflict with IEEE Std. 730. In any case, IEEE Std. 1074 has a broader range of applications, because it is oriented toward planning of all software life cycle processes, not just those relating to quality assurance. It is a larger and more complex standard, and thus more challenging to implement. It is described in a later section.

Audience

The introduction to IEEE Std. 730 categorizes those with an interest in the standard as follows:

There are three groups to whom this standard applies: the user, the developer, and the public.

a) *The user, who may be another element of the same organization developing the software, has a need for the product.*

b) *The developer needs an established standard against which to plan and be measured.*

c) *The public may be affected by the users' use of the product.*

Of course, the public cannot be expected to read the standard. The standard's audience categorization is more simplistic than that for IEEE Std. 830 *(IEEE Recommended Practice for Software Requirements Specifications)*, which distinguishes between the *customer* and *user* (see Section 5.2). With this distinction in terminology available, the *customer* and *developer* could be considered the target audience of the standard, but not the *user* or *public*, even though the latter two clearly have an interest in software product quality.

Responsibilities for individual organizational elements of the *developer* organization are inherently specific to the organizational structure. For example, this standard might be of interest to the following types of groups within an organization:

- **Management**   To plan, review, monitor, and take corrective action for the software quality assurance activities; to participate in the *managerial reviews* and *post-mortem review*.

- **Software Engineering**   To plan, implement, and report software development activities stipulated by the SQAP; to create the SRS and SDD; to participate in the *Software Requirements Review, Preliminary Design Review*, and *Critical Design Review, user documentation review* (if conducted) and *post-mortem review*; to provide information to the *functional audit, physical audit, in-process audits, and managerial reviews*.

- **Software Quality Assurance**   To plan, implement, and report software quality assurance activities; to create the SQAP; to conduct or initiate the *functional audit, physical audit*, and *in-process audits;* to observe the *SVVP Review, Software Requirements Review, Preliminary Design Review, Critical Design Review*, and *user documentation review* (if conducted); to provide information to the *managerial reviews*; to participate in the *post-mortem review*.

- **Software Testing**   To plan, implement, and report software testing activities stipulated by the SQAP; to provide information to the *functional audit, in-process audits*, and *managerial reviews*; to participate in the *post-mortem review*.

- **Software Verification and Validation**   To plan, implement, and report software verification and validation activities stipulated by the SQAP; to create the SVVP and SVVR; to participate in the *SVVP Review, Software Requirements Review, Preliminary Design Review, Critical Design Review, user documentation review* (if conducted), and *post-mortem review*; to provide information to the *functional audit, in-process audits*, and *managerial reviews*.

- **Software Configuration Management** To plan, implement, and report software configuration management activities stipulated by the SQAP; to create the SCMP; to participate in the *SCMP review* and *post-mortem review*; to provide information to the *physical audit* and *managerial reviews.*

- **Technical Writing** To create the *user documentation* stipulated by the SQAP; to provide information to the *functional audit, physical audit, in-process audits,* and *managerial reviews*; to participate in the *user documentation review* (if conducted) and *post-mortem review.*

The previous list is not meant to imply that each of these groups must exist within an organization, that these are the only possible groups interested in the SQAP, or even that the specific responsibilities must be as annotated. This is intended only as an example.

Project Phases Affected

This standard is applicable to all project phases. Software quality assurance activities should be conducted during the entire software life cycle. The *Software Quality Assurance Plan* should be created at the outset of the software project, prior to the *development process,* as per the terminology from IEEE Std. 1012 *(IEEE Standard for Software Verification and Validation).*

Detailed Description

The format recommended for a *Software Quality Assurance Plan* by IEEE Std. 730 is shown in Figure 6.11.

1. Purpose
2. Reference documents
3. Management
4. Documentation
5. Standards, practices, conventions, and metrics
6. Reviews and audits
7. Test
8. Problem reporting and corrective action
9. Tools, techniques, and methodologies
10. Code control
11. Media control
12. Supplier control
13. Records collection, maintenance, and retention
14. Training
15. Risk management

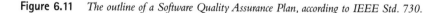

Figure 6.11   *The outline of a Software Quality Assurance Plan, according to IEEE Std. 730.*

Each of these sections must be provided, although they can be reorganized as long as a mapping table is provided. If a section is not applicable, it can be left blank, as specified by the standard:

> *If there is no information pertinent to a section, the following shall appear below the section heading, "This section is not applicable to this plan," together with the appropriate reasons for the exclusion.*

Such exclusion might be based on the non–criticality of the software, or because the software had been developed previously.

Sections 1 and 2 of the SQAP are self-explanatory. Subsequent sections will be described in more detail.

Section 3 of the SQAP (management) describes the organization, tasks, and responsibilities that influence or control software quality. Individual organizational elements must be described. The relative independence of SQA must be described:

> *Organizational dependence or independence of the elements responsible for SQA from those responsible for software development and use shall be clearly described or depicted.*

Tasks and their interrelationships, and the responsibilities of organizational elements for these tasks, must be defined.

Section 4 of the SQAP (documentation) specifies the documentation to be produced during the project. The associated reviews and audits listed in Section 6 of the SQAP must be referenced. The minimum documentation set has already been listed in the previous section "Overview—IEEE Std. 730." Of particular interest in this section are the requirements for the *Software Verification and Validation Plan* as per IEEE Std. 730:

> *The SVVP shall identify and describe the methods (for example, inspection, analysis, demonstration, or test) to be used to*
>
> a) *Verify that*
>
> > 1) *The requirements in the SRS have been approved by an appropriate authority;*
> >
> > 2) *The requirements in the SRS are implemented in the design expressed in the SDD; and*
> >
> > 3) *The design expressed in the SDD is implemented in the code.*
>
> b) *Validate that the code, when executed, complies with the requirements expressed in the SRS.*

This short description certainly cuts through the fog of confusion associated with the term *V&V*, and is one of the reasons why IEEE Std. 730 is an excellent standard. It summarizes what is truly essential in a V&V effort much more succinctly than IEEE Std. 1012 *(IEEE Standard for Software Verification and Validation)*, although the latter standard is excellent for its detailed and comprehensive approach. This information might be described in SPMP section 7.2 if a full SVVP is not developed in accordance with IEEE Std. 1012.

Similarly, the requirements for the *Software Configuration Management Plan* as per IEEE Std. 730 are of interest:

> *The SCMP shall document methods to be used for identifying software items, controlling and implementing changes, and recording and reporting change implementation status.*

This information might be documented in section 7.1 of the SPMP if a separate SCMP is not developed in accordance with IEEE Std. 828 *(IEEE Standard for Software Configuration Management Plans)*.

It is recommended that all documents listed in Section 4 of the SQAP be identified as *configuration items* and be subject to the software configuration management process, to be described in the SCMP.

Section 5 of the SQAP defines the standards, practices, conventions, and metrics to be applied. The minimum required set of these is listed in the "Overview—IEEE Std. 730" section. *Documentation standards* for documents specified in the SQAP are provided by various other IEEE standards, as described in the "Overview" section. IEEE Std. 829 *(IEEE Standard for Software Test Documentation)*, and IEEE Std. 1008 *(IEEE Standard for Software Unit Testing)* can be used to at least partially describe the *testing standards and practices*. IEEE Std. 1061 *(IEEE Standard for a Software Quality Metrics Methodology)*, and IEEE Std. 982.1 *(IEEE Standard Dictionary of Measures to Produce Reliable Software)* can be used to specify *quality metrics*.

Logic structure standards, *coding standards*, and *commentary standards* must be developed by each organization. These are usually grouped together as *programming standards*.

The standard lists *inspections* (and presumably intends *walk-throughs* as well) as a practice that can be included in Section 5 of the SQAP. These should be performed in accordance with IEEE Std. 1028 *(IEEE Standard for Software Reviews)*.

Section 6 of the SQAP defines the technical and managerial reviews and audits to be conducted. The minimum required reviews and audits are listed in the "Overview—IEEE Std. 730" section. The reviews and audits are most effectively implemented by following IEEE Std. 1028 *(IEEE Standard for Software Reviews)*. Figure 6.5 shows a possible mapping of the reviews and audits required by IEEE Std. 730 to the software review types defined by IEEE Std. 1028. Possible responsibilities of organizational elements for required reviews are described in the previous section "Audience." The organizational responsibilities for the reviews and audits can be specified in Section 3 of the SQAP, or in Section 6, with a forward reference from Section 3.

Note that the standard recommends listing *inspections* (and *walk-throughs*) under Section 5 of the SQAP instead.

Section 7 of the SQAP (test) describes any software testing not specified via the SVVP. For example, *beta testing* can be excluded from the scope of the SVVP, and could then be described in this section. Testing can be described via use of IEEE Std. 829 *(IEEE Standard for Software Test Documentation)*, but this approach might not be realistic for all types of testing. For example, the testing process, documentation, and evaluation of beta testing should be described explicitly in this section.

Section 8 of the SQAP (problem reporting and corrective action) describes the "practices and procedures to be followed for reporting, tracking, and resolving problems identified in both software items and the software development and maintenance process" and the "organizational responsibilities concerned with their implementation." Process problems can be identified via managerial and technical reviews and audits, and it is primarily a management responsibility to take corrective action regarding such process problems.

Problems with software items can be identified via *software reviews* (such as *inspections*) and be documented as *anomalies* via *review reports* (such as *inspection reports)*, as per IEEE Std. 1028 *(IEEE Standard for Software Reviews)*. Problems with software items can also be identified via *software testing* and can be documented via *Test Incident Reports*, as per IEEE Std. 829 *(IEEE Standard for Software Test Documentation)*. Problems can also come from external sources such as *complaints* from *users*. It is recommended that all problem reporting and corrective actions for software items be handled via the *software configuration management* process as described in the SCMP, as per IEEE Std. 858 *(IEEE Standard for Software Configuration Management Plans)*.

Section 9 of the SQAP describes the tools, techniques, and methodologies that will be used to support SQA. For example, a software metrics tool can be used to measure the complexity of the source code, and to evaluate software quality, as per IEEE Std. 1061 *(IEEE Standard for a Software Quality Metrics Methodology)*.

Note that Section 9 of the SQAP is not intended to describe development tools, techniques, and methodologies.

The tools and procedures for controlling different versions of the software are defined in Section 10 of the SQAP (code control). This refers both to the source code and executable code. It is recommended that you manage source code via a *version control* software tool. Such a tool is useful for archiving multiple versions of source files and for coordinating access to the source files by multiple programmers. Executable code is usually controlled via various release procedures. During software testing, executable code can be controlled via *Test Item Transmittal Reports*, as discussed previously. Transfer of executable software to manufacturing should be controlled with a standard release process. These activities can be defined in the SCMP, which is then simply referenced.

Section 11 of the SQAP (media control) defines the tools, facilities, and methods for identifying and protecting the media used to store software and documentation. These activities can be defined in the SCMP, which is then simply referenced.

Section 12 of the SQAP (supplier control) describes how to ensure that software provided by suppliers meets its requirements. This section might reference IEEE Std. 1062 *(IEEE Recommended Practice for Software Acquisition)*, which describes a process model for this purpose.

Section 13 of the SQAP (records collection, maintenance, and retention) specifies the documentation to be retained, the methods and facilities used for this purpose, and the retention period. This is an important issue for future *audits* (such as by regulatory agencies) and for accumulating information useful for planning software process improvements. Documents should be archived with all required approval signatures. Electronic document control systems can be used to facilitate this process. Access to the records must be appropriately safeguarded. It is quite common to find paper records missing from designated storage locations.

The training needed to implement the SQAP is specified in section 14. Because reviews and audits are so fundamental to the SQA process, training in *software reviews*, as defined by IEEE Std. 1028 *(IEEE Standard for Software Reviews)*, is particularly important. Training for tools, techniques, and methodologies, as specified in Section 9 of the SQAP, should also be considered.

Section 15 of the SQAP (risk management) specifies how risks will be identified and managed. Managerial and technical reviews, as listed in Section 6 of the SQAP, are intended to recommend a list of action items emphasizing risks. It is a management responsibility to act on these recommendations in a timely manner, according to IEEE Std. 1028 *(IEEE Standard for Software Reviews)*. Risk management can be described in Section 5.4 of the SPMP, as per IEEE Std. 1058 *(IEEE Standard for Software Project Management Plans)*, which can be referenced.

Recommendations for Implementation

It is recommended to use IEEE Std. 730 only as a guide (not attempting to achieve compliance with the standard) until the lower-level standards corresponding to Level 2 of the simple maturity model (the *Pyramid of Applicability)* have been implemented. The SPMP described in IEEE Std. 1058 *(IEEE Standard for Software Project Management Plans)* can be used at this level to document the plans for software quality assurance in Section 7.4 of that document.

After the necessary process maturity has been achieved to enable compliance with IEEE Std. 730, it is recommended that you create a separate SQAP. This is particularly important if an independent organizational element is responsible for software quality assurance. The SPMP can still be used at this level to specify plans for *software verification and validation* (Section 7.2 of the SPMP) and *software configuration management* (Section 7.1 of the SPMP).

Because reviews and audits play such a central role in the quality assurance activities, it is strongly recommended that you implement IEEE Std. 1028 *(IEEE Standard for Software Reviews)* prior to IEEE Std. 730. Training should be provided to all organizational elements for the specific types of software reviews that they are required to participate in.

It is recommended that you use the SQAP document format exactly as specified in IEEE Std. 730, to avoid the mapping table required by the standard otherwise.

For successful implementation of an effective software quality assurance program, the organizational structure must be carefully planned, and responsibilities appropriately assigned to individual organizational elements. This task is inherently specific to each organization, however, the independence of software quality assurance personnel is generally acknowledged as beneficial, if not mandatory. Possible responsibilities of different groups are listed in the previous "Audience" section.

Summary of IEEE Std. 730

Although IEEE Std. 730 is intended specifically for *critical software*, it is prudent to follow it for all software projects. It provides a standard format for specifying software quality assurance activities, and defines minimum requirements for documentation to be created and reviews and audits to be performed during a software project. These minimum requirements are appropriate for even small software projects.

Use of this standard should result in improved software product quality, and decreased project cost and schedule. The standard facilitates effective project management by imposing structure and control mechanisms on the development process. Risks can be identified and managed earlier and more effectively via these project controls. Information provided through the software quality assurance efforts for a specific project can be used to plan software process improvements; the *post-mortem review* is particularly helpful for this purpose.

Verification and Validation

This section describes software *verification and validation* (V&V) standards in the IEEE Software Engineering Standards collection.

The IEEE *element standard* on this topic is the following:

IEEE Std. 1012-1998, IEEE Standard for Software Verification and Validation

The following standards are also provided at the *Guides and Supplements* layer of the *SESC Framework* model:

IEEE Std. 1012a-1998, Supplement to IEEE Standard for Software Verification and Validation, Content Map to IEEE/EIA 12207.1-1997.

IEEE Std. 1059-1993, IEEE Guide for Software Verification and Validation Plans

These are not described in detail here.

Standards on closely related topics such as *software testing, software quality assurance,* and *software life cycle processes* are not described in this section. These are listed in the section "Relationship to Other Standards" later in the chapter.

Overview—IEEE Std. 1012

IEEE Std. 1012 describes software *verification and validation*. It defines these terms as follows (Annex I of the standard):

validation: *Confirmation by examination and provisions of objective evidence that the particular requirements for a specific intended use are fulfilled.*

verification: *Confirmation by examination and provisions of objective evidence that specified requirements have been fulfilled.*

Vague definitions like these have caused confusion in industry as to the difference in meaning of these two terms. IEEE Std. 610.12 *(IEEE Standard Glossary of Software Engineering Terminology)* provides the following alternative definitions:

validation: *The process of evaluating a system or component during or at the end of the development process to determine whether it satisfies specified requirements.*

verification: *The process of evaluating a system or component to determine whether the products of a given development phase satisfy the conditions imposed at the start of that phase.*

The definitions from IEEE Std. 610.12 are more specific and, hence, clearer. *Validation* involves system and acceptance testing during the test phase, whereas *verification* involves reviews and audits, software unit testing, and other techniques to evaluate intermediate work products such as the *software requirements specification, software design description,* and individual modules during earlier project phases.

IEEE Std. 1012 provides the following overview of software verification and validation, which further clarifies these terms:

The verification process provides supporting evidence that the software and its associated products

    1) Comply with requirements (for example, for correctness, completeness, consistency, accuracy) for all life cycle activities during each life cycle process (acquisition, supply, development, operation, and maintenance);

    2) Satisfy standards, practices, and conventions during life cycle processes; and

    3) Establish a basis for assessing the completion of each life cycle activity and for initiating other life cycle activities.

The validation process provides supporting evidence that the software satisfies system requirements allocated to software, and solves the right problem.

IEEE Std. 1012 describes the processes to be used for these purposes in detail, and specifies format and content for both the *Software Verification and Validation Plan* (SVVP) and the *Software Verification and Validation Report* (SVVR).

An excellent overview of software verification and validation, including differentiation of the two terms, is also provided by IEEE Std. 730 *(IEEE Standard for Software Quality Assurance Plans)*, as minimum requirements for *critical software*:

The SVVP shall identify and describe the methods (for example, inspection, analysis, demonstration, or test) to be used to

    a) Verify that

        1) The requirements in the SRS have been approved by an appropriate authority;

        2) The requirements in the SRS are implemented in the design expressed in the SDD; and

        3) The design expressed in the SDD is implemented in the code.

    b) Validate that the code, when executed, complies with the requirements expressed in the SRS.

The previous versions of IEEE Std. 1012 (IEEE Std. 1012-1986) was a work product standard, describing the format and information content of the SVVP, and only implicitly defining the V&V processes. The standard has been rewritten to place primary emphasis on defining the V&V processes, while still specifying the format of the SVVP and SVVR. The *processes* defined by the standard are as follows:

1. Management process
2. Acquisition process
3. Supply process

4. Development process

5. Operation process

6. Maintenance process

Each of these processes is described in terms of *activities*, but only the *development process* is composed of multiple activities. The activities of the development process correspond to the software life cycle phases described in Chapter 4. These are as follows:

1. Concept activity

2. Requirements activity

3. Design activity

4. Implementation activity

5. Test activity

6. Installation and checkout activity

For each of the activities in each of the processes, the standard defines minimum V&V tasks as a function of the *software integrity level*. The minimum V&V tasks are discussed in the "Detailed Description" section later in the chapter. The *software integrity level* is used to quantify the *criticality* of the software, and to guide the intensity and rigor to be applied to the V&V tasks. This is defined by the standard with reference to ISO/IEC 15026 as follows:

> **software integrity level:** *The integrity level of a software item.*

This begs the following definition, also from ISO/IEC 15026:

> **integrity level:** *A denotation of a range of values of a property of an item necessary to maintain system risks within acceptable limits. For items that perform mitigating functions, the property is the reliability with which the item must perform the mitigating functions. For items whose failure can lead to a threat, the property is the limit on the frequency of that failure.*

The software integrity level is a value assigned to maintain software *risks* within acceptable values. The latter term is defined as follows, following IEC 60300-3-9:

> **risk:** *The combination of the frequency, or probability, and the consequence of a specified hazardous event.*

This definition is, in turn, based on the concept of a *hazard*, for which the following definition is provided, also from IEC 60300-3-9:

> **hazard:** A source of potential harm or a situation with a potential for harm in terms of human injury, damage to health, property, or the environment, or some combination of these.

Ultimately, then, software verification and validation is planned as a function of software hazards. The determination of the level of rigor and intensity of the software V&V efforts can be made separately for different parts of the software. IEEE Std. 1012 states:

> *The software integrity level can be assigned to software requirements, functions, group of functions, or software components or subsystems.*

For example, *unit testing* is required by the standard only for software integrity levels 2 and higher, and independent V&V unit testing is only required for levels 3 and 4. By identifying the software integrity levels of individual software modules, only the more critical software modules need to be unit tested. This allows substantial savings in project cost and schedule, while allowing limited time and resources for V&V to be focused on those parts of the software where the greatest benefit can be expected.

Benefits

The most important benefit of IEEE Std. 1012 is to increase software product quality. Software V&V activities are intended to ensure that the software meets its requirements, the very definition of software quality. The standard itself states:

> *(V&V) demonstrates whether the software requirements and system requirements (that is, those allocated to software) are correct, complete, accurate, consistent, and testable.*

Verification activities performed during early project phases will reduce project cost and schedule, because anomalies will be detected earlier than by testing alone. A risk-based approach to planning software verification and validation activities, taken by IEEE Std. 1012, further enables optimizing the project schedule and resource usage. If the standard has been properly implemented within an organization, it will decrease project cost and schedule, particularly for the overall software life cycle.

By providing a technical program for evaluating software work products during the entire software life cycle, IEEE Std. 1012 supports software project management efforts.

These additional benefits are stated by the standard:

1. *Facilitate early detection and correction of software errors;*
2. *Enhance management insight into process and product risk; and*
3. *Support the software life cycle processes to ensure compliance with program performance, schedule, and budget requirements.*

Use of IEEE Std. 1012 also facilitates compliance with higher-level quality standards and regulations. IEEE Std. 1012 has been harmonized with international standards and other IEEE standards for this purpose. For example, IEEE Std. 1012 is listed as a reference in FDA guidelines for medical device software.

Relationship to Other Standards

IEEE Std. 1012 draws on lower-level standards to specify the requirements for work products or to specify the process or techniques for specific V&V activities:

- IEEE Std. 829 (*IEEE Standard for Software Test Documentation*)
- IEEE Std. 830 (*IEEE Recommended Practice for Software Requirements Specifications*)
- IEEE Std. 982.1 (*IEEE Standard Dictionary of Measures to Produce Reliable Software*)
- IEEE Std. 1016 (*IEEE Recommended Practice for Software Design Descriptions*)
- IEEE Std. 1028 (*IEEE Standard for Software Reviews*)
- IEEE Std. 1061 (*IEEE Standard for a Software Quality Metrics Methodology*)
- IEEE Std. 1063 (*IEEE Standard for Software User Documentation*)

The topic of V&V metrics is discussed in Annex E of IEEE Std. 1012, referencing IEEE Std. 982.1 and IEEE Std. 1061. This annex provides a list of metrics recommended for V&V purposes.

The following standards relate to IEEE Std. 1012 by describing information at the same or even higher level:

- IEEE Std. 730 (*IEEE Standard for Software Quality Assurance Plans*)
- IEEE Std. 1074 (*IEEE Standard for Developing Software Life Cycle Processes*)
- IEEE Std. 1228 (*IEEE Standard for Software Safety Plans*)
- IEEE/EIA Std. 12207.0 (*IEEE/EIA Standard for Industry Implementation of International Standard ISO/IEC 12207 Standard for Information Technology, Software life cycle processes*)
- IEEE/EIA Std. 12207.1 (*IEEE/EIA Standard for Industry Implementation of International Standard ISO/IEC 12207 Standard for Information Technology, Software life cycle processes, Life cycle data*)

IEEE Std. 730 defines a framework inside of which V&V activities are to be conducted. It requires creation of the SVVP and SVVR, and defines minimum requirements for V&V, as quoted in the "Overview—IEEE Std. 1012" section.

Mappings from IEEE/EIA Std. 12207.0 to IEEE Std. 1012, from IEEE Std. 1012 to IEEE/EIA Std. 12207.0, and from IEEE Std. 1074 to IEEE Std. 1012 are provided in Annex B of IEEE Std. 1012. The mapping from IEEE/EIA Std. 12207.1 to IEEE Std. 1012 is presented by IEEE Std. 1012a.

Although not listed as a reference by IEEE Std. 1012, IEEE Std. 1228 is nevertheless relevant, because it specifies a plan for the overall process to ensure software safety. This directly relates to the determination of the software integrity level, as required by IEEE Std. 1012 for determining the minimum required V&V activities. IEEE Std. 1228 also specifies the following V&V requirements, that

a) *All system safety requirements have been satisfied by the life cycle phases*

b) *No additional hazards have been introduced by the work done during the life cycle activity*

Audience

IEEE Std. 1016 states:

The audience for this standard is software suppliers, acquirers, developers, maintainers, V&V practitioners, operators, and managers in both the supplier and acquirer organizations.

Other quality personnel, such as might be involved in reviews and audits of V&V activities, should also be considered a target audience for this standard. These might be the supplier, acquirer, independent third-party organizations engaged by either the acquirer or supplier, or regulatory agencies.

Project Phases Affected

Software V&V activities should be performed during the entire software life cycle, during all project phases. The standard makes the following important point:

V&V processes are most effective when conducted in parallel with software development processes; otherwise, V&V objectives might not be realized.

The unfortunate tendency in industry to develop software and then to initiate software V&V activities afterward is contrary to the intentions of this standard. Quality cannot be tested into a finished software product.

The specific V&V tasks for different project phases is summarized in the following section.

Detailed Description

Software integrity levels are used to plan software V&V activities, according to IEEE Std. 1012. They are used to quantify software criticality, in order to maintain risks within acceptable limits. They *might* be assigned to individual requirements or software modules. The standard defines four software integrity levels, as shown in Figure 6.12.

Criticality	Description	Level
High	Selected function affects critical performance of the system.	4
Major	Selected function affects important system performance.	3
Moderate	Selected function affects system performance, but workaround strategies can be implemented to compensate for loss of performance.	2
Low	Selected function has noticeable effect on system performance but only creates inconvenience to the user if the function does not perform in accordance with requirements.	1

Figure 6.12 *Software integrity levels, taken from IEEE Std. 1012.*

A level 0 is only mentioned in Annex B of the standard:

> *A software integrity level 0 (zero) may be assigned if there are no consequences associated with a software error that may occur in the system. For software integrity level 0, no V&V tasks are implemented.*

A risk-based example of a software integrity level scheme is given in Annex B of the standard. (This is informative only, and is not a part of the standard required for compliance.) It defines *consequences* as shown in Figure 6.13.

Consequence	Description
Catastrophic	Loss of human life, complete mission failure, loss of system security and safety, or extensive financial or social loss.
Critical	Major and permanent injury, partial loss of mission, major system damage, or major financial or social loss.
Marginal	Severe injury or illness, degradation of secondary mission, or some financial or social loss.
Negligible	Minor injury or illness, minor impact on system performance, or operator inconvenience.

Figure 6.13 *Sample definitions of error consequences, taken from IEEE Std. 1012 Annex B.*

Possible error consequences are combined with an estimate of the *likelihood of occurrence* to calculate the *software integrity level*, as shown in Figure 6.14.

Error Consequence	Likelihood of occurrence of an operating state that contributes to the error			
	Reasonable	Probable	Occasional	Infrequent
Catastrophic	4	4	4 or 3	3
Critical	4	4 or 3	3	2 or 1
Marginal	3	3 or 2	2 or 1	1
Negligible	2	2 or 1	1	1

Figure 6.14   *Sample assignment of software integrity levels, taken from IEEE Std. 1012 Annex B.*

Not all software integrity level schemes take into account the likelihood of occurrence. For example, FDA guidelines for medical device software *(Guidance for FDA Reviewers and Industry, Guidance for the Content of Premarket Submissions for Software Contained in Medical Devices)* state:

> In general, risk is considered the product of the severity of injury and the probability of its occurrence. However, software failures are systematic in nature and therefore their probability of occurrence can not be determined using traditional statistical methods. As such, risk estimation for software products should be based on the severity of the hazard resulting from failure, assuming that the failure will occur.

This FDA guidance goes on to define the following *levels of concern* used to rate software criticality:

> **Major**   The level of concern is major if operation of the software associated with device function directly affects the patient and/or operator so that failures or latent flaws could result in death or serious injury to the patient and/or operator, or if it indirectly affects the patient and/or operation (for example, through the action of care provider) such that incorrect or delayed information could result in death or serious injury of the patient and/or operator.

> **Moderate**   The level of concern is moderate if the operation of the software associated with device function directly affects the patient and/or operator so that failures or latent design flaws could result in non-serious injury to the patient and/or operator, or if it indirectly affects the patient and/or operator (for example, through the action of a care provider) where incorrect or delayed information could result in non-serious injury of the patient and/or operator.

> **Minor**   The level of concern is minor if failures or latent design flaws would not be expected to result in any injury to the patient and/or operator.

The FDA levels of concerns would need to be mapped to the IEEE software integrity levels to apply IEEE Std. 1012 for medical devices. However, such mapping is outside the scope of this book.

The integrity level determines the minimum required V&V tasks. Table 2 of IEEE Std. 1012 shows the minimum V&V tasks assigned to each software integrity level (with no V&V tasks required for software integrity level 0).

The V&V effort is described in terms of a three-tiered hierarchy by IEEE Std. 1012: V&V processes, V&V activities, and V&V tasks. Minimum required V&V tasks are specified as a function of the software integrity level. V&V processes as defined by the standard can be mapped to whatever Software Life Cycle Model is selected, to become part of the software life cycle processes used. Figure 1 of IEEE Std. 1012 shows an example of software V&V using a waterfall model. The V&V processes, activities, and tasks, and the software integrity levels for which they are required, are shown in Figure 6.15.

1. Purpose
2. Reference documents
3. Definitions
4. V&V Overview
    4.1. Organization
    4.2. Master Schedule
    4.3. Software Integrity Level Scheme
    4.4. Resources Summary
    4.5. Responsibilities
    4.6. Tools, Techniques, and Methods
5. V&V Processes
    5.1. Process: Management
        5.1.1.Activity: Management of V&V
    5.2. Process: Acquisition
        5.2.1 Activity: Acquisition Support V&V
    5.3. Process: Supply
        5.3.1 Activity: Planning V&V
    5.4. Process: Development
        5.4.1. Activity: Concept V&V
        5.4.2. Activity: Requirements V&V
        5.4.3. Activity: Design V&V
        5.4.4. Activity: Implementation V&V
        5.4.5. Activity: Test V&V
        5.4.6. Activity: Installation and Checkout V&V
    5.5. Process: Operation
        5.5.1 Activity: Operation V&V
    5.6. Process: Maintenance
        5.6.1. Activity: Maintenance V&V
6. V&V Reporting Requirements
7. V&V Administrative Requirements
    7.1. Anomaly Resolution and Reporting
    7.2. Task Iteration Policy
    7.3. Deviation Policy
    7.4. Control Procedures
    7.5. Standards, Practices, and Conventions
8. V&V Documentation Requirements

Figure 6.15   *V&V processes, activities, and tasks, according to IEEE Std. 1012-1998.*

Caution should be urged regarding using Table 1 and 2 in IEEE Std. 1012-1998, because there are numerous minor errors in these tables that can lead to confusion, such as the following:

1. Formatting errors for *Required Inputs* and *Required Outputs* in Table 1. These are difficult to decipher because only whitespace is used to separate items, and in some cases the whitespace is used incorrectly. For example, for required outputs of *Baseline Change Assessment* and *Management Review of V&V*, surely separate outputs of *Updated SVVP* and *Task Report(s)* are intended.

2. Inconsistencies in terminology in Table 1. For example, in Table 1, *Hazard Analysis* tasks are listed with *Hazard Analysis Report* as a required input, but *Task Report(s) Hazard Analysis* are also listed as a required output, even though these surely refer to the same items.

3. Easily confused names in Table 1. For example, under *System V&V Test Plan Generation and Verification*, references to the *System Test Plan* refers to a separate developer's plan, distinct from the *System V&V Test Plan*. For easier reading, it would be helpful to call the former the *Developer's System Test Plan*.

4. Lack of harmonization with terminology from other standards. For example, the term *Component Testing* is called *Unit Testing* by IEEE Std. 1008, which specializes on that topic.

5. Inconsistent ordering in Table 2. For example, *Risk Analysis* precedes *Retirement Assessment*, and *Acceptance V&V test procedure generation and verification* is listed separately rather than as item d) under *V&V test procedure generation and verification*.

6. Assignment of *Management Process* tasks to other V&V processes in Table 2. Management tasks, such as *SVVP Generation*, is shown delegated to other V&V processes in Table 2, which is inconsistent with Table 1 and the body of the standard. Conceptually, the *Management Process* runs concurrently with other V&V processes, but remains a distinct process (similarly, other processes can also run concurrently).

7. Misleading V&V test requirements in Table 2. For integrity levels 1 and 2, Table 2 requires that V&V test documentation be generated, but Table 1 requires only that the developer's test documentation be verified (Table 1 should be trusted in this case.)

8. Other inconsistencies between the tables. For example, *Operation procedures evaluation* is specified as a *Concept Activity* task in Table 2, but not in Table 1, or the main body of the standard. (Table 2 appears to be in error here.)

Hopefully, more effective V&V techniques will be used for the next release of the standard!

Reviews and audits specified in IEEE Std. 1012 are most effectively performed in accordance to IEEE Std. 1028 *(IEEE Standard for Software Reviews)*. A recommended mapping of specific reviews and audits required by IEEE Std. 1012 to types of software reviews as defined by IEEE Std. 1028 is provided in Figure 6.5.

IEEE Std. 1012 specifies the required content of a *Software Verification and Validation Plan* (SVVP) and provides a sample SVVP outline. An SVVP is required by IEEE Std. 730 *(IEEE Standard for Software Quality Assurance Plans)* for *critical software*, and is also specified by IEEE Std. 1058 *(IEEE Standard for Software Project Management Plans)* as a required section of an SPMP. The sample SVVP outline from IEEE Std. 1012 is shown in Figure 6.16.

	Implementation	1. Traceability Analysis	X	X	X	
		2. Source Code and Source Code Documentation Evaluation	X	X	X	X
		3. Interface Analysis	X	X	X	
		4. Criticality Analysis	X	X	X	
		5. V&V Test Case Generation and Verification				
		a) Component	X	X	X	
		b) Integration	X	X	X	X
		c) System	X	X	X	X
		d) Acceptance	X	X	X	
		6. V&V Test Procedure Generation and Verification				
		a) Component	X	X	X	
		b) Integration	X	X	X	X
		c) System,	X	X	X	X
		d) Acceptance	X	X	X	
		7. Component V&V Test Execution and Verification	X	X	X	
		8. Hazard Analysis	X	X		
		9. Risk Analysis	X	X		
	Test	1. Traceability Analysis	X	X	X	
		2. Acceptance V&V Test Execution and Verification	X	X	X	
		3. Integration V&V Test Execution and Verification	X	X	X	X
		4. System V&V Test Execution and Verification	X	X	X	X
		5. Acceptance V&V Test Execution and Verification	X	X	X	
		6. Hazard Analysis	X	X		
		7. Risk Analysis	X	X		
	Installation and Checkout	1. Installation Checkout	X	X		
		2. Hazard Analysis	X	X		
		3. Risk Analysis	X	X		
		4. V&V Final Report Generation	X	X	X	
Operation	Operation	1. Evaluation of New Constraints	X	X	X	
		2. Proposed Change Assessment	X	X	X	
		3. Operation Procedures Evaluation	X	X		
		4. Hazard Analysis	X	X		
		5. Risk Analysis	X	X		
Maintenance	Maintenance	1. SVVP Revision	X	X	X	X
		2. Proposed Change Assessment	X	X	X	
		3. Anomaly Evaluation	X	X	X	
		4. Criticality Analysis	X	X	X	
		5. Migration Assessment	X	X		
		6. Retirement Assessment	X	X		
		7. Hazard Analysis	X	X		
		8. Risk Analysis	X	X		
		9. Task Iteration	X	X	X	X

Figure 6.16 *The sample Software V&V Plan outline, taken from IEEE Std. 1012-1998.*

Some of the sections of the SVVP are self-explanatory. However, sections 4 through 8 are worth examining in more detail.

Important high-level information regarding the V&V efforts is included in section 4 of the SVVP (V&V Overview). The organizational structure used for the V&V efforts, including the degree of independence required, is described. The schedule, resources, and responsibilities of V&V tasks are described. The very critical software integrity level scheme is defined, and the assignment of software integrity levels to individual components is specified, determining the scope of the required V&V efforts.

Section 5 of the SVVP (V&V Processes) describes the processes, activities, and tasks to be performed in V&V. The minimum set of required tasks is determined by the *software integrity level*, as specified in Section 4.3; optional tasks can also be included. For each task, the SVVP should define the methods and procedures, inputs, outputs, schedule, resources, risks and assumptions, and roles and responsibilities.

Section 6 (V&V Reporting Requirements) of the SVVP specifies the various types of V&V reports to be produced during the V&V effort These include *task reports*, *activity summary reports*, *anomaly reports*, and the *V&V Final Report*. The set of all the reports generated by the V&V effort is referred to as the *Software Verification and Validation Report* (SVVR), as described in more detail later.

Anomaly resolution and reporting, task iteration policy, deviation policy, control procedures, standards, practices, and conventions are all specified in section 7 of the SVVP (V&V Administrative Requirements).

Section 8 of the SVVP (V&V Documentation Requirements) specifies the V&V test documentation to be produced in accordance with the plan. V&V reports are specified in Section 6 of the SVVP instead. The test documentation should be produced in accordance with IEEE Std. 829 *(IEEE Standard for Software Test Documentation)*. Test documents should be produced at different levels: component level, integration level, system level, or acceptance level. Minimum requirements for which levels of testing are required is determined according to the software integrity level, as shown in Figure 6.16. However, for integrity levels 1 and 2, instead of producing independent V&V test documentation, it suffices to verify the developer's test documentation (according to Table 1 of the standard).

IEEE Std. 730 *(IEEE Standard for Software Quality Assurance Plans)* requires that a *Software Verification and Validation Report* (SVVR) be created. IEEE Std. 1012 defines the SVVR as follows:

> *V&V reporting occurs throughout the software life cycle. The SVVP shall specify the content, format, and timing of all V&V reports. The V&V reports shall constitute the Software Verification and Validation Report (SVVR). The V&V reports shall consist of*

required V&V reports (i.e., V&V Task Reports, V&V Activity Summary Reports, V&V Anomaly Reports, and V&V Final Report). The V&V reports may also include optional reports.

Section 7.6 of the standard provides specific guidelines for specific types of V&V reports. Only the required content, not the format, of these reports is specified in the standard, as follows:

1. **V&V Task Report:** Must include V&V task results and status.

2. **V&V Activity Summary Report:** Must include a description of V&V tasks performed, a summary of task results, a summary of anomalies and resolution, an assessment of software quality, identification and assessment of technical and management risks, and recommendations.

3. **V&V Anomaly Report:** Must contain a description and location in document or code, the impact, the cause of the anomaly, and descriptions of the error scenario, the anomaly criticality level, and recommendations.

4. **V&V Final Report:** Must contain a summary of all life cycle V&V activities, a summary of task results, a summary of anomalies and resolutions, an assessment of overall software quality, lessons learned and best practices, and recommendations.

In some cases, other standards might define specific format and information content of V&V reports. For example, IEEE Std. 829 *(IEEE Standard for Software Test Documentation)* specifies *Test Incident Reports,* which are a type of *V&V Anomaly Report,* and *Test Summary Reports,* which are a type of *V&V Task Summary Report.*

Recommendations for Implementation

Compliance with this standard presupposes a certain level of software process maturity on the part of the organization. Documents such as *Software Requirements Specifications* and *Software Design Descriptions,* and processes such as for software testing and reviews, are presupposed. Prior to the maturity level required for compliance with this standard, it is recommended that you use the standard as a guide, to implement some subset of the V&V tasks.

Appropriate organizational planning, staffing, and training is required to implement an effective V&V program. Management commitment to the implementation of a V&V program is an essential prerequisite to its success. Independence (technical, managerial, and financial) of V&V is an important issue, which is inherently specific to the organization and industry. This is discussed in Annex C of the standard, which is intended to be informative only. Independent V&V can be specified by regulations or external standards for particular industries, and this issue should be carefully researched.

To implement this standard, it is necessary to be able to determine the *software integrity level* of the software. It might be necessary to map an external criticality scheme to the software integrity levels used by IEEE Std. 1012 to specify required V&V tasks. For example, the approach recommended by FDA for software risk estimation (see the section "Detailed Description") would need to be mapped to the IEEE Std. 1012 software integrity levels to apply this standard.

The decision process by which the software integrity level is to be determined can be performed according to IEEE Std. 1228. For medical device software, for example, FDA guidelines specify a five-question decision-making process to determine the *level of concern* of the software *(Guidance for FDA Reviewers and Industry, Guidance for the Content of Premarket Submissions for Software Contained in Medical Devices)*.

Summary of IEEE Std. 1012

IEEE Std. 1012 provides detailed guidelines for performing software *verification and validation* tasks as a function of software criticality, as quantified via *software integrity levels*. It specifies format and information content of the *Software Verification and Validation Plan* and *Software Verification and Validation Report*, as required by IEEE Std. 730 *(IEEE Standard for Software Quality Assurance Plans)*.

V&V is the most important part of a software quality system. No software quality system can be established without V&V. Implementation of this standard will improve software product quality, will decrease software life cycle costs, will enhance software project management, and will facilitate compliance with quality standards and regulations.

Configuration Management

This section describes *software configuration management* (SCM) standards in the IEEE Software Engineering Standards collection.

The IEEE *element standard* on this topic is the following:

> IEEE Std. 828-1998, IEEE Standard for Software Configuration Management Plans

A standard is also provided at the *Guides and Supplements* layer of the *SESC Framework* model:

> IEEE Std. 1042-1987 (R1993), IEEE Guide to Software Configuration Management

Tools and techniques as related to source code control and software builds are not described in this section (and, in fact, are not a primary topic of the IEEE standards on software configuration management).

Overview—IEEE Std. 610.12

The purpose of SCM is to manage changes to *configuration items*. This is defined as follows by IEEE Std. 610.12:

> **Configuration item (CI):** *An aggregation of hardware, software, or both, that is designated for configuration management and treated as a single entity in the configuration management process.*

A CI can be any deliverable produced during the software development process. Documents such as the SRS and SDD, source code, or executable code can all be identified as CIs.

Placing a CI under formal change control is referred to as *baselining*.

When a CI is baselined, further changes to the CI require approval according to the SCM process.

The SCM process consists of the following four types of activities:

1. Configuration identification
2. Configuration control
3. Status accounting
4. Configuration audits and reviews

Configuration control is performed by a *Configuration Control Board* (CCB), also referred to as a *Change Control Board*. This is defined by IEEE Std. 610.12 as follows:

> **Configuration control board (CCB):** *A group of people responsible for evaluating and approving or disapproving proposed changes to configuration items, and for ensuring the implementation of approved changes.*

Multiple CCBs can be established for a software project, corresponding to different CIs. A hierarchy of CCBs can be established for complex projects.

The SCM process model allows for a systematic approach to controlling changes to the configuration items. By designating a CCB, the decision-making process is established at the outset of the project. Decisions can thus be made more quickly, and with less ambiguity.

Use of a version control system for managing source code files is often confused with the broader topic of software configuration management. Such version control systems are important, for coordinating access to the source files in a team environment, and for archiving the revision history of the source files in a straightforward manner. However, version control systems do not generally address the most critical aspect of configuration control, namely the approval or disapproval of changes.

IEEE Std. 828 also specifies the format and information content of a *Software Configuration Management Plan* (SCMP). This is simply a document containing all planning information for SCM for a software project.

Benefits

Software configuration management might be the key to containing project cost and schedule in your organization. Often, software projects fail to complete on schedule and within budget because the project scope is changed without adequate controls. Most commonly, requests for changes to software requirements are made well past the requirements phase. Change requests can come from multiple sources, each appearing to have a legitimate interest in the project, but perhaps none having a sufficient understanding of the impact of those changes. Adoption of the IEEE software configuration management standards will establish an effective process model for controlling changes to the software. A well-defined decision process will speed up your projects, and proper documentation of changes, and associated reviews and audits, will improve the quality of your software products.

Relationship to Other Standards

The software configuration management standards are relatively independent of the other IEEE software engineering standards.

IEEE Std. 1058 *(IEEE Standard for Software Project Management Plans)* defines a section of the SPMP for software configuration management. A simple SCMP might thus be written as a section of the SPMP. Alternatively, a separate SCMP might be referenced by the SPMP.

IEEE Std. 730 *(IEEE Standard for Software Quality Assurance Plans)* specifies a SCMP as part of the minimum documentation requirements for development of critical software. It also specifies that a *Software Configuration Management Plan Review* (SCMPR) be conducted when developing critical software.

IEEE Std. 1074 *(IEEE Standard for Developing Software Life Cycle Processes)* provides guidelines for planning software configuration management activities for the SLC (in Annex section A.5.2 of the standard).

IEEE Std. 1028 *(IEEE Standard for Software Reviews)* can be used to perform configuration audits and reviews.

Audience

Software management personnel and lead technical personnel are the primary audience for the software configuration management standards. They are the primary group responsible for creating and updating the configuration items during the software life cycle.

Project Phases Affected

Software configuration management should be performed throughout the software life cycle. The SCMP should be developed at the outset of a software project, in conjunction with the SPMP.

Software configuration management should continue to be performed past the software development process, during the operation and maintenance phases.

Detailed Description

IEEE Std. 828 specifies SCM activities to be performed during the software life cycle. These activities are as follows:

- **Configuration Identification:** Identifying of CIs, assigning unique identifiers to CIs, and "acquiring" CIs. The last refers to the physical storage and retrieval mechanisms for CIs.
- **Configuration Control:** Requesting, evaluating, approving or disapproving, and implementing changes to CIs.
- **Configuration Status Accounting:** Recording and reporting the status of CIs.
- **Configuration Audits and Reviews**: Auditing and reviewing of SCM.
- **Interface Control:** Coordinating changes to the CIs included in the SCMP to items outside the scope of the SCMP.
- **Subcontractor/Vendor Control:** Incorporating CIs developed outside the project environment into the project.

The *configuration control* activity requires the following four steps:

1. **Requesting Changes:** Requests for a change to a baselined CI must be documented. Information should include the CI identification and version, requestor, date, urgency, the reason, and a description of the change.
2. **Evaluating Changes:** Each change request must be analyzed for impact. This can require technical personnel.

3. **Approving or Disapproving Changes:** The CCB(s) for the affected CI must approve or disapprove the change request. If necessary, the CCB can request additional analysis prior to making a decision, or may defer a decision for business reasons.

4. **Implementing the Change:** If the change is approved, it must be implemented and verified. The completion of this activity must be documented, including a reference to the change request, the CI identification and version, verification responsible party and date, release or installation responsible party and date, and the new CI version.

Configuration audits examine the actual CIs to determine whether they meet their requirements. Configuration reviews provide information to management to help determine a baseline. A minimum requirement is to conduct a configuration audit for all CIs prior to release.

IEEE Std. 828 specifies the following sections for a SCMP:

- **Introduction.** Describes the plan's purpose and scope. Includes definitions and references.

- **SCM Management.** Describes the responsibilities for SCM activities during the project.

- **SCM Activities.** Describes the SCM activities to be performed during the project. The minimum activities are defined previously.

- **SCM Schedules.** Shows how SCM activities are to be synchronized with other software development process activities.

- **SCM Resources.** Specifies tools, hardware, and personnel required for SCM during the project.

- **SCM Plan Maintenance.** Describes how the SCMP will be updated.

A different organization of the SCMP can be used, but a mapping to these required sections must then be provided in the introduction.

For the interface control activities, for each external item, you must specify the nature of the interface, the affected organizations, how the item is to be controlled, and how the item is to be approved and released into a baseline.

The subcontractor/vendor control activities include both software developed by a subcontractor, and finished software provided by a vendor. The following information must be specified in the SCMP for any CIs provided by subcontractor or vendor:

1. SCM terms of a subcontractor's agreement
2. Monitoring of subcontractor compliance

3. Configuration audits and reviews of subcontractor CIs

4. Verification, acceptance, and integration of subcontractor or vendor CIs

5. Handling of security and ownership issues, such as copyright and royalties

6. Change processing, including that of the subcontractor

See also IEEE Std. 1062 *(IEEE Recommended Practice for Software Acquisition)* as it relates to acquisition of software from subcontractors and vendors.

Recommendations for Implementation

When first introducing software configuration management, it might suffice to specify the plan for these activities in the SPMP. If the size of configuration management activities warrants it, a separate SCMP can be created.

It is recommended to specify default configuration items for your organization. These should include the following:

- Plans, because these affect the scope of the project. These can include the SPMP, SQAP, test plans, and even the SCMP itself.

- Documents such as the SRS and SDD. Although any type of document can be designated to be a configuration item, software review reports, test incident reports, and other V&V deliverables are not recommended for this purpose because they never undergo an update. They only reflect the status of a software work product.

- The software itself, including both the source code and executable code. It might be sufficient to view the entirety of the source code and executable code as a single configuration item. In this case, the CCB decides whether the software should be modified in response to a change request. Typically, executable code is not included as a CI because it can always be re-created from the source code.

It is also recommended to specify default CCBs for your organization, to provide guidelines for individual projects. A CCB should be specified for each default configuration item. The CCB for the SRS might differ from the CCB for the SDD, because software design changes are usually approved by a more restricted group than software requirements changes. Software management, lead technical personnel, SQA, systems engineering, and others can be specified. The details are necessarily dependent on the structure of your organization.

It is recommended that software project deliverables be *baselined* when first approved during the project phase in which they were created. Any subsequent requests for changes to those deliverables then will require approval or disapproval by the corresponding CCB. Approval for the change should be obtained prior to implementing any changes, although analysis by technical personnel might be required before a final disposition can be reached.

Configuration audits and reviews should be performed according the software review process models defined in IEEE Std. 1028 *(IEEE Standard for Software Reviews)*. Configuration reviews, and possibly configuration audits, can be combined with technical reviews for the project deliverables, such as the *Software Requirements Review* (SRR) conducted for the SRS as per IEEE Std. 730 *(IEEE Standard for Software Quality Assurance Plans)*.

It is common in an engineering department to have an *Engineering Change Order* (ECO) or similar process for releasing software designs to production. The ECO process can also be phrased in terms of a CCB, and so the question might arise as to the difference between the SCM and ECO processes. The easiest explanation is that an ECO process is usually restricted to approving a completed design, at the end of the development process, whereas the SCM process is intended to approve or disapprove software change requests during the software development process, prior to implementing and documenting such changes. The SCM process must be reconciled with any such ECO process in your organization.

Summary—IEEE Std. 610.12

Software configuration management is often confused with use of a version control software tool. These tools are important for controlling access to source code files, but fail to capture the essence of software configuration management.

Software configuration management identifies the items created during a software project for which changes must be controlled, and provides a process model for controlling those changes. The decisions of approving or disapproving changes are handled by CCBs specified in advance in the SCMP. Configuration status accounting and configuration audits and reviews provide confidence in the proper implementation of changes. The well-defined decision-making process and documentation of changes are the biggest benefits of configuration management. Implementation of SCM should result in decreased project cost and schedule and increased software quality.

CHAPTER 7

Practical Lessons

Software technology developments continue at a rapid pace. Operating systems, programming languages, tools, design methods, and even computing paradigms seem to change continually. Software engineering principles, however, do not change at the same pace. Although standards have evolved to be more comprehensive and more sophisticated in their presentation, good software engineering principles today are fundamentally similar to those of a decade or even two decades ago.

Software development practices have changed dramatically, moving from programs measured in thousands of lines to ones measured in millions of lines. Unstructured or overly rigid approaches, which might have worked for small projects in the past, simply do not scale effectively to large modern software project needs.

For example, an electrical engineer working alone on a small control application might be able to succeed in getting the software to function correctly with little documentation, no peer reviews, and no systematic configuration management practices. For a larger project, these omissions could spell disaster.

On the other end of the spectrum, application of rigid waterfall models—in which no design is allowed until requirements are fully specified, and no coding is allowed until all design is done, and no testing is performed until all coding is complete—might work for very small projects. This model works if the scope of each project phase is sufficiently small and low in risk so that there is a reasonable probability that it will not need to be revisited due to issues arising during a later phase. In larger projects this assumption is not valid, and it might be expected that requirements can only be fully understood after some design and coding have been completed. Process flexibility is thus a key.

Software engineering standards have been developed largely to solve the practical problem of developing software more efficiently and with higher quality. Good software engineering practices are becoming increasingly essential for managing increasingly large and complex software projects.

This book is not about latest or best software practices. However, this chapter provides some thoughts on reconciling some well-respected industry practices with the use of the IEEE Software Engineering Standards.

Standard Operating Procedures

Organizations write software SOPs for a good reason: to define the processes associated with software acquisition, supply, development, operation, and maintenance, as well as supporting and organizational processes. SOPs should tailor the processes to the organization and specify interfaces to non-software processes as needed.

I have seen problems related to developing SOPs in a number of organizations over the years. These problems invariably stem from trying to develop completely custom process models, terminology, and document standards. The following are some of the most common issues:

- Excessive time investment. Many person-years can be invested in writing custom procedures. This can interfere with important software projects.
- Bad procedures. Custom procedures are often inconsistent, ambiguous, unverifiable, and not harmonized with standards and regulations of concern to the organization.
- Differences of opinion. Development of custom procedures invariably results in debates regarding processes, documentation, tools, techniques, and many peripheral issues. Personnel whose opinions are not mirrored in the procedures may view the procedures as unworkable and may fail to follow them systematically.

In my experience, an excellent solution is to harmonize software SOPs with the IEEE standards collection, referencing individual element standards for which compliance is required. This approach addresses the problems listed above. The time to develop SOPs is minimized, the IEEE standards provide a mature set of standards, and the authority of recognized standards encourages individuals to comply.

SOPs may tailor use of the standard, by

- Mapping between terminology used by the standard and terminology used by the organization
- Specifying sections of the standards for which compliance is to be optional
- Augmenting the standard with additional mandatory requirements
- Providing guidance on the use of the standard, via examples or describing optional means of achieving compliance

It is very helpful in writing SOPs to adopt the convention used in the IEEE software engineering standards collection regarding the words *shall, should,* and *may:*

- *Shall* specifies mandatory compliance.
- *Should* expresses a recommendation.
- *May* describes alternative or optional methods for achieving compliance.

The biggest problem in the use of SOPs is failure to follow them. Failure to comply with standards is worse than not having the standards. It is important to define SOPs that are realistic for the organization, and for which compliance is feasible. After suitable SOPs have been established, it is a critical management responsibility to ensure that they are followed.

Project Management

A common mistake in project management is to assume that only a project schedule should be created. For non-trivial software projects, a *Software Project Management Plan* should be written, as per IEEE Std 1058 (*IEEE Standard for Software Project Management Plans*). Such a plan helps document many other important issues relating to project management, including responsibilities, risks, and so on.

Improper software life cycle planning is another common problem, particularly inappropriate use of iterative SLCMs. Software project managers who feel more comfortable with an unstructured approach sometimes mask this as an iterative approach. The following are tell-tale indicators that something is wrong:

- Software requirements are finalized very late in the project.
- Software design documentation is completed well after the implementation is complete.
- Configuration management begins only as the software project is completed.

These types of problems are extremely common! Chapter 4 provides a detailed discussion of software life cycle planning, and the applicable IEEE standards IEEE/EIA 12207.0 and IEEE Std. 1074.

Requirements Analysis

Failure to develop good software requirements specifications is perhaps the single biggest cause of software project failures, in my experience. The most basic problem is not to write down requirements at all.

A more subtle problem comes from not applying configuration management on the SRS until the project completes. This means that changes to the requirements are allowed to occur during the course of a project without any control mechanisms, and effective approval of the requirements occurs only at the end. Continual changes in requirements are perhaps the most common reason why software projects fail to complete on schedule. Configuration management does not prevent changes in requirements, but helps to define the process by which those changes are requested, reviewed, approved, and implemented.

Recall the attributes of a good SRS according to IEEE Std 830: It should be *correct, unambiguous, complete, consistent, verifiable, modifiable,* and *traceable.* I have seen many amusing specific requirements that fall short of these goals. I have seen the following two a number of times:

- *"The software shall be reliable."* This requirement is ambiguous and unverifiable. A quantitative reliability measure should be specified for the software, or the requirement should be omitted.

- *"The software response shall be instantaneous."* This requirement is also ambiguous and unverifiable. A quantitative measure is needed to specify software timing. Perhaps the author would be satisfied with a software response time of less than 50 milliseconds, for example.

Errors of omission cause the SRS to be incomplete. Frequently, software interfaces are not fully specified. IEEE Std. 830 requires that user interfaces, hardware interfaces, software interfaces, and communications interfaces all be specified, including all inputs and outputs from the software, including the contents and format of messages, and so on. External interface specifications may be referenced, of course. Many software engineers believe this level of detail should be reserved for design documentation (the SDD). However, full specification of interfaces should be completed during requirements analysis. This allows the design of multiple software and hardware systems to proceed independently, and for test planning to proceed independently of design.

The opposite problem can also occur: Many SRSs contain too much information, namely design information. The SRS should not be used to describe the design of the software, only its externally visible characteristics. Sometimes it is expedient or even unavoidable to describe the required outputs of software according to a computational model, such as an algorithm or state diagram. Such models should not be construed as design of the software, but only as a means of specifying required outputs.

In order for an SRS to be traceable, the individual specific requirements (Section 3 of the SRS) should be clearly identified with unique identifiers. I have found that lettering the individual specific requirements is a simple solution to this problem. Frequently, introductory sentences or paragraphs are required to improve readability of the SRS, but these are not themselves testable requirements. A lettered list (A, B, C, and so on) in each subsection of Section 3 of the SRS clearly marks the specific requirements, and allows them to be referenced in other documents, such as the SDD, test case specifications, and others.

One last common pitfall I have observed in documenting requirements is that sometimes multiple SRSs are created when a single one would do. This can be counterproductive for several reasons:

- Introductory and overview sections (sections 1 and 2 of the SRS) are duplicated, or inappropriately omitted.
- If a hierarchical approach is taken in organizing multiple SRSs, it is unclear what specific requirements (section 3 of the SRS) should be contained in the top-level SRS.
- Lower-level SRSs often correspond roughly to some design entities, confusing the distinction between requirements and design. Requirements should not be specified on a design entity level.

If possible given limitations imposed by word processors, a single SRS should be written for each software product. If multiple contributors are involved, their sections can be easily merged into a single document by a technical editor.

Design

There are more legitimate differences of opinion regarding SDDs than SRSs, even though creating a good SRS is usually more difficult. IEEE Std. 1016 requires description of *design entities*, but not everyone agrees on what these should refer to. Part of the reason is that there are many different design methods in use, and the answer depends on the method used.

For *procedural* designs, the lowest-level design entities are the procedures and global data structures. The decomposition descriptions may involve software libraries to help organize the many procedures. The dependency view primarily describes the control flow, via the calling relation (*procedure A calls procedure B,*) as well global data flow, according to the read and write relations (*procedure X reads data item Y, procedure X writes data item Y*). Procedure interfaces should be described in terms of the procedure parameters, return values, inputs and outputs of global data, and exceptions. The details view should describe the control flow of the procedures, which may be done via flow-charts or pseudo-code.

Procedural design is no longer considered a best practice for most applications. The overhead provided by flow-charts or pseudo-code for each procedure is too inefficient for large, modern software applications. Also, such low-level descriptions are so close to the source code itself that they quickly become out of date. Programmers then invariably trust the source code more than the SDD. I recommend only describing the control flow for individual procedures when complex and non-standard algorithms are used, the procedure is safety-critical, or the procedure must be implemented in assembly language.

Modular design identifies modules (consisting of procedures, data structures, types, and so on) as design entities. The decomposition view describes the hierarchy of modules, and the dependency view describes the relationships between modules, including both control flow and data flow. Module interfaces should describe the procedure interfaces of those procedures contained in the module that are intended to be called by external modules. Similarly, data structures, types, and constants intended for use by external modules should be described. The details view should describe the internals of the module, including private procedures, data structures, types, and constants (those not intended to be used by external modules).

One problem is that the term "module" is not completely standardized. In some SDDs I have seen the decomposition described only down to very large software subsystems consisting of hundreds of thousands of lines of source code. This is too coarse a granularity, and is not a good practice. The modules should correspond one-to-one with source files, and programmers will voluntarily limit these to a manageable size. If the lowest-level modules described in the SDD cannot be reasonably implemented via individual source files, more detail should be added to the SDD.

Object-oriented design (OOD) describes classes and objects as design entities. The decomposition view will still be similar to the modular design method, since a hierarchy of modules is usually still advantageous to organize the software. The dependency view should describe the relationships between classes and objects. UML notation or other OOD notation may be used for this, for example, class diagrams and object diagrams. The interface view simply represents the public class interfaces, and the details view should describe the private methods, fields, and so forth of the classes.

Whatever the design method, if a multi-processing or multi-threading application is being developed, the processes and threads, and the operating system primitives such as semaphores used to synchronize them, represent design entities that should be described in the SDD. Particularly in Windows applications, I have observed that these design entities are not described at all.

SDDs should be useful during software maintenance, and should be written with this in mind. They should avoid redundancy with the source code and comments embedded in the source code. Most importantly, they should describe the software architecture (via the decomposition and dependency views). They should describe interfaces of design entities, including everything a designer, programmer, or tester needs to know to correctly use the entity.

Unlike SRSs, it is entirely reasonable to create a hierarchy of SDDs for a single software product, and this is a common practice.

To summarize, I have seen the following common pitfalls in writing SDDs:

- Too much detail—SDD is redundant with source code, and becomes obsolete.
- Too little detail—SDD decomposes software into very large software subsystems only.
- Missing multi-processing/multi-threading descriptions—SDD fails to describe processes, threads, semaphores, and so on.
- Interfaces not fully specified—SDD fails to describe everything one needs to know to use each design entity.

These issues should be considered during design reviews, as a reality-check on the SDDs.

Configuration Management

Many organizations mistakenly believe that use of a source code change control tool exhausts the topic of software configuration management. There are a number of such tools, and their use should be considered mandatory, even for single-programmer projects. These tools allow controlling changes to individual source files, including branching and labeling of changes. Some of these tools allow automatic merging of source code, but this cannot be guaranteed to work correctly in all cases. I strongly recommend that programmers review and test any source files merged via an automatic tool.

Software changes usually affect multiple source files, and it is only by convention that *Software Change Descriptions* (SCDs) affecting multiple files are documented.

SCDs may be documented via text files, email, a database, or commercial software applications for change tracking. I have found creation of SCDs to be an extremely effective technique, and strongly recommend it. Key guidelines for this are

- A *change tracking number* should be assigned and documented in the SCD.
- Each SCD should be functionally atomic. (Unrelated changes should be described in separate SCDs.)
- Each SCD should be complete. (Partial changes that don't create a functional software build should not be allowed.)
- Each SCD should be well documented. A cross-reference to any test incident reports or other reason for creating the change should be included. An overall description of the change should also be included, as well as a list of all affected source files.

Software version identifiers are a closely related topic. Often there are external requirements for labeling software releases, but the need for unique identification of software builds during the development process, in particular during testing, should not be overlooked. At a minimum, each build delivered as a test item must have a unique software version number. An excellent scheme for realizing this is to use the *change tracking number* (as mentioned in the previous section) as part of the software version identifier.

One set of problems is triggered by good intentions—creating special software version identifier conventions to indicate that the software is not yet released. After final testing, the software must be modified to change such an identifier, but then the software should again be tested. One issue is, How much testing? An exhaustive regression would be unwarranted, but some level of testing should be done to verify that the new build is functional. A more troubling issue occurs when this post-final testing reveals a software defect. How should the software version be referenced in a test incident report? I have seen organizations destroy all evidence of such flawed builds in order to avoid associated documentation and version numbering dilemmas. I recommend that the software version identifier *not* specify the release status, at least during the final testing activity. Unique version identifiers for each build should be assigned, and the final successful build should be released without further modification.

Many organizations have a document control department that facilitates approval, archival, and release of software as well as documents. An *Engineering Change Order* (ECO) is issued to place items under configuration management. I recommend that the software configuration management process be directly coupled to any such overall configuration management process. I recommend issuing *Checkpoint ECOs* at least at the end of each software project phase, to control all outputs of that software phase.

Typically, document control departments operate only on completed documents, and do not address the issue of *Software Change Requests (SCRs)*. Thus, software procedures or plans must specify how SCRs are to be documented, approved, and tracked. Once a change is completed, an ECO may be issued to transfer the updated configuration items to document control. A CCB should be specified for each configuration item.

What does this all mean? Here is an example. The entire source code may be viewed as one configuration item. It is released to document control at the end of the implementation phase, placing it under active configuration management. During the test phase, test incident reports are created; these represent software change requests. A designated group should review the test incident reports and decide whether a software change should be made. If this group approves a change, a programmer should be assigned to implement the change. A number of changes can be made before another software build is created. The new build represents a new test item. Different organizations might make different decisions on whether an ECO is required for each software build delivered as a test item.

My experience has been that many engineers resist configuration management during the software development process, and consider it to be unnecessary overhead. At the same time, my experience has been that lack of configuration management results in many problems. Ironically, one major resulting problem is schedule slippage. This is due to a lack of a well-defined process for deciding on changes. I have seen a number of projects founder because decisions on changes took too long, or were reversed multiple times, or were not clearly communicated.

Software configuration management is a critical supporting process.

Training

Many organizations fail to provide necessary training, for example, in the use of the organization's SOPs. It is not uncommon to find personnel who are unfamiliar with, or even unaware of the existence of, their organization's SOPs. This represents a critical quality system breakdown, and must be addressed via training.

Organizations should facilitate training of software engineers in new technology, but usually not mandate it. Some programmers find it helpful to take a class in order to learn a new programming language, whereas others might be able to learn it effectively by studying a reference book.

Training should be practical. It should provide the necessary information, with enough time allocated for this purpose, but not so much time as to bore the participants. In the case of SOPs, the author may be a good choice as a trainer, assuming he/she is not a "droner." Professional trainers may be brought in to provide customized training (for example, for SOPs), or generic external training may be provided (for example, for interpersonal skills, new programming languages, and so on)

An issue in many organizations is failure to maintain adequate training records. This is a management responsibility. Failure to maintain training records impedes training planning, and can result in some personnel not being trained. Failure to maintain training records can result in regulatory or other compliance problems. Use of training records software can help, but in many cases use of spreadsheets can be sufficient.

Outsourcing

Outsourcing of software development projects is an increasingly common practice. Outsourcing is different from the use of temporary personnel, because the client organization controls the software development process in the latter case. For outsourcing, the supplier typically provides personnel, facilities, and other resources, as well as the organizational expertise on how to develop software. The supplier defines the software development process, although this can be constrained by terms of a project agreement.

Outsourcing has advantages, if the supplier is able to deliver the following:

- Resources. The client does not need to hire, train, and manage the technical personnel needed to execute the project, and does not need to supply the computer and facilities infrastructure for software development.
- A mature process. The client might be lacking in software development know-how, and might not want to invest in this.
- Technological expertise. The supplier might be much more of an expert at certain software technologies that are pertinent to the project, perhaps Java programming.

There are also risks associated with consulting, and it is not always the right decision. Some things to watch out for include

- Unclear requirements. Especially for a fixed-price project, it is essential that the software requirements are clearly specified and agreed on by both parties.
- Lack of management oversight. If project status reporting, intermediate milestones, and client reviews of deliverables are not properly implemented, the client will not be able to assess progress or manage risks effectively.
- Ineffective acceptance testing. If the client does not perform adequate acceptance testing of the software, the obligations of the supplier according to the contract may be fulfilled even if the software will fail to meet the needs of its users.

IEEE Std. 1062 *(IEEE Recommended Practice for Software Acquisition)* specifies a 9-step process model suitable for outsourcing. Two key steps are for the acquirer to specify software requirements up front (Step #3), and to perform acceptance testing of the software at the end (Step #8). Creating a good SRS and having an effective acceptance testing process are two key steps in reducing the risks associated with outsourcing.

Step #6, *Evaluating Proposals and Selecting the Supplier,* is often not given sufficient attention. Consideration should be given to the development process standards, documentation standards, and V&V practices of competing suppliers. If only cost, schedule, and application expertise are considered for evaluating proposals, software quality can suffer. Process, documentation, and V&V standards should be considered when creating a contract between the two parties.

Compliance with specific IEEE standards is a straightforward and excellent mechanism for specifying the process to be followed by the supplier, and for specifying project deliverables such as an SRS, SDD, or test documentation.

Summary

Software engineering standards must be flexible enough to allow for, even to facilitate, technological change, both in the software development process and the software products created. At the same time, software engineering standards must provide a stable firmament for software development projects. Basic principles of software engineering for achieving software quality should not be ignored with the advent of new technology. New operating systems, new programming languages, new design methods, and even new computing paradigms do not obviate the need for applying sound software engineering techniques. The best way to produce high-quality software is to take advantage of technology advances while following a proper process.

APPENDIX A

List of IEEE Software Engineering Standards

This appendix contains a list of the IEEE Software Engineering Standards in the 1999 edition. These are grouped according to the four volumes published by IEEE.

Volume 1: Customer and Terminology Standards

These standards describe the interaction between the customer and supplier of a software engineering project. Included are a description of the agreement for software development, operation, and maintenance, detailed aspects of the customer/supplier relationship, and a glossary of software engineering terms.

IEEE Std. 610.12-1990, IEEE Standard Glossary of Software Engineering Terminology

IEEE Std. 1062, 1998 Edition, IEEE Recommended Practice for Software Acquisition

IEEE Std. 1220-1998, IEEE Standard for Application and Management of the Systems Engineering Process

IEEE Std. 1228-1994, IEEE Standard for Software Safety Plans

IEEE Std. 1233, 1998 Edition, IEEE Guide for Developing System Requirements

IEEE Std. 1362-1998, IEEE Guide-System Definition-Concept of Operations Document

IEEE Std. 12207.0-1996, IEEE/EIA Standard for Industry Implementation of International Standard ISO/IEC 12207:1995 (ISO/IEC 12207), Standard for Information Technology-Software life cycle processes

IEEE Std. 12207.1-1997, IEEE/EIA Guide-Industry Implementation of International Standard ISO/IEC 12207:1995 (ISO/IEC 12207), Standard for Information Technology-Software life cycle processes-Life cycle data

IEEE Std. 12207.2-1997, IEEE/EIA Industry Implementation of International Standard ISO/IEC 12207:1995 (ISO/IEC 12207), Standard for Information Technology-Software life cycle processes-Implementation considerations

Volume 2: Process Standards

These standards describe primary processes including acquisition, supply, development, maintenance, operations, and measurements.

IEEE Std. 730-1998, IEEE Standard for Software Quality Assurance Plans

IEEE Std. 730.1-1995, IEEE Guide for Software Quality Assurance Planning

IEEE Std. 828-1998, IEEE Standard for Software Configuration Management Plans

IEEE Std. 1008-1987 (R1993), IEEE Standard for Software Unit Testing

IEEE Std. 1012-1998, IEEE Standard for Software Verification and Validation

IEEE Std. 1012a-1998, Supplement to IEEE Standard for Software Verification and Validation-Content Map to IEEE/EIA 12207.1-1997

IEEE Std. 1028-1997, IEEE Standard for Software Reviews

IEEE Std. 1042-1987 (R1993), IEEE Guide to Software Configuration Management

IEEE Std. 1045-1992, IEEE Standard for Software Productivity Metrics

IEEE Std. 1058-1998, IEEE Standard for Software Management Plans

IEEE Std. 1059-1993, IEEE Guide for Software Verification and Validation Plans

IEEE Std. 1074-1997, IEEE Standard for Developing Software Life Cycle Processes

IEEE Std. 1219-1998, IEEE Standard for Software Maintenance

IEEE Std. 1490-1998, IEEE Guide to the Project Management Body of Knowledge

Volume 3: Product Standards

These standards explain the requirements for classes of software products[md]characteristics, measurements, evaluations, and specifications.

IEEE Std. 982.1-1988, IEEE Standard Dictionary of Measures to Produce Reliable Software

IEEE Std. 982.2-1988, IEEE Guide for the Use of IEEE Standard Dictionary of Measures to Produce Reliable Software

IEEE Std. 1061-1998, IEEE Standard for a Software Quality Metrics Methodology

IEEE Std. 1063-1987 (R1993), IEEE Standard for Software User Documentation

IEEE Std. 1465-1998, IEEE Standard Adoption of ISO/IEC 12119:1994(E), Information Technology-Software packages-Quality requirements and testing

Volume 4: Resource and Technique Standards

These standards recommend proper documentation for a well-managed software program and its related processes.

IEEE Std. 829-1998, IEEE Standard for Software Test Documentation

IEEE Std. 830-1998, IEEE Recommended Practice for Software Requirements Specifications

IEEE Std. 1016-1998, IEEE Recommended Practice for Software Design Descriptions

IEEE Std. 1044-1993, IEEE Standard Classification for Software Anomalies

IEEE Std. 1044.1-1995, IEEE Guide to Classification for Software Anomalies

IEEE Std. 1320.1-1998, IEEE Standard for Functional Modeling Language-Syntax and Semantics for IDEFO

IEEE Std. 1320.2-1998, IEEE Standard for Conceptual Modeling Language-Syntax and Semantics for IDEF1X97(IDEFobject)

IEEE Std. 1348-1995, IEEE Recommended Practice for the Adoption of Computer-Aided Software Engineering (CASE) Tools

IEEE Std. 1420.1-1995, IEEE Standard for Information Technology-Software Reuse-Data Model for Reuse Library Interoperability: Basic Interoperability Data Model (BIDM)

IEEE Std. 1420.1a-1996, IEEE Guide for Information Technology-Software Reuse-Data Model for Reuse Library Interoperability: Asset Certification Framework

IEEE Std. 1430-1996, IEEE Guide for Information Technology-Software Reuse-Concept of Operations for Interoperating Reuse Libraries

IEEE Std. 1462-1998, IEEE Standard Adoption of ISO/IEC 14102:1995-Guidelines for the Evaluation and Selection of CASE Tools

APPENDIX B

A List of Additional Standards

The standards listed here are not included in the 1999 edition of the IEEE Software Engineering Standards Collection, but are available separately from the IEEE-SA catalog at http://standards.ieee.org/. Some of these are draft standards only, whereas others have been approved. Some brief comments are provided for each one.

ANSI/ISO/ASQ Q9000-3-1997, Quality Management and Quality Assurance Standards, Part 3: Guidelines for the Application of ANSI/ISO/ASQC Q9001-1994 to the Development, Supply, Installation, and Maintenance of Computer Software
Print Only: 32 pages [SH94727-NYF]
Not available to resellers or distributors.

This document is the bridge between software engineering and quality management. It provides a detailed cross-reference of the clauses of ISO 9001 and ISO/IEC 12207.

J-STD-016-1995 EIA/IEEE, Interim Standard for Information Technology Software Life Cycle Processes, Software Development Acquirer-Supplier Agreement (Issued for Trial Use)
Print: 232 pages [SH94377-NYF]
PDF: [0-7381-0427-2] [SS94377-NYF]

The demilitarized version of Mil-Std-498. Although its trial period has expired for IEEE use, EIA still lists it as an active "Interim" standard.

1517-1999 IEEE, Standard for Information Technology, Software Life Cycle Processes, Reuse Processes
Print: 52 pages [0-7381-1735-8] [SH94751-NYF]
PDF: [0-7381-1736-6] [SS94751-NYF]

This standard adds additional processes to 12207 to deal with institutionalized software reuse.

P1540, D7.0, Draft Standard for Software Life Cycle Processes, Risk Management
Print: 24 pages [DS5789-NYF]

This is still under development. It will add a risk management process to 12207.

14143.1-2000 IEEE, Standard for Adoption of ISO/IEC 14143-1:1998 Information Technology, Software Measurement, Functional Size Measurement, Part 1: Definition of concepts
Print: 20 pages [0-7381-2165-7] [SH94840-NYF]
PDF: [0-7381-2166-5] [SS94840-NYF]

This adopts the SC7 standard that defines "Functional Size Measurement."

1420.1b-1999 IEEE, Trial-Use Supplement to IEEE Standard for Information Technology, Software Reuse, Data Model for Reuse Library Interoperability: Intellectual Property Rights Framework
Print: 24 pages [0-7381-1765-X] [SH94766-NYF]

This supplement adds a place for intellectual property information in the data model provided by 1420.1.

P1471, D5.2 Draft Recommended Practice for Architectural Description
Print: 30 pages [DS5716-NYF]

This standard is expected to be approved soon. It provides a data model and a lexicon for describing architectures. Particular architecture description techniques or instances of architectural description might conform to this standard.

Index

implementation, 110–111
input documents, 106
integration, 103
interface, 103
logging, 109–110
process measures, 111
project phases affected, 107
quality, 188
relationship to other standards,
  105–106
scenarios
  SRSs, 100
  test case specifications comparison, 111
software, 6, 9, 41, 52, 103, 106
SRSs, 92–93
summary, 111
system testing, 103
system-level, 42
test case specifications, 111
test documents, 101, 107–109
test incident reports, 110–111
testing levels, 102–103
test logs, 110
test summary reports, 111
units, 103
use cases
  SRSs, 100
  test case specifications comparison, 111
TIR (Test Incident Report), 36
**TITR (Test Item Transmittal
  Report), 36**
TL (Test Log), 36
tools, 19
Tools (SESC alternative model), 30
TP (Test Plan), 36
**TPS (Test Procedure Specification),
  37**
tracking, 11, 141
training
  personnel, 21, 169
  SOPs, 211–212
  SQAPs, 181
**training process (organizational life
  cycle process), 54**
training tools, SOPs, 19
treaceable SRS, 207
troubleshooting
  project management, 205
  SDDs, 209

SOPs, 204–205
SRS, 207
TSR (Test Summary Report), 37

U

U.S. Quality System Regualtion, 10
UML notation, 208
unit testing, 45
units (software), 45, 103–104, 113. *See
  also* **modules**
  compilation, 104
  design entities, 113
  examples, 104
  IEEE Std. 829, 103–104
  testing, 103–104
unproductive cynicism, 18
use cases
  SRSs, 100
  test case specifications comparison,
  111
user documentation. *See also* documentation
**User documentation (IEEE Std.
  1063), 172**
**User Documentation Review,
  173–174**
**User Representative (Management
  Reviews), 156**
users, 93

V

**V&V (Verification and Validation),
  34, 182**
  advantages, 186–187
  defining processes, 184
  development processes, 185
  efforts, 194
  implementing, 195–196
  initiating, 188
  standards, 182–190, 192, 194–196
  test documentation, 194
V&V Activities, 34, 43–44, 191
V&V Final Report, 194–195
V&V Outputs, 34
V&V processes, 191
V&V tasks, 191
  integrity levels, 44
  required, 191
  software, integrity levels, 39

validating
  critical applications, 45
  documentation, 84
  retrospective validations, 100
validation, 8, 183
Validation and Verification (IEEE
  Std. 1012), 43-44
validation process (supporting life
  cycle process), 53
vendor control activity (SCM), 199
verification, 183, 186
verification and validation. See V&V
Verification & Validation (IEEE Std.
  1012), 62
Verification and Validation (IEEE
  Std. 1012-1998), 183-196
Verification and Validation Content
  Map (IEEE Std. 1012a-1998), 183
Verification and Validation Plans
  (IEEE Std. 1059-1993), 183
verification process (supporting life
  cycle process), 53
verifying software, 11
version identifiers (software), 210
versions, controlling, 197
views, design (IEEE Std. 1016),
  117-119
visual inspections, 148
volume (sales), increasing, 7

work product, identifying defects, 67
Work Product (organizational models), 34
work product standards, 81, 83
  lack of directly applicable software
    standards, 82
  Software Design Description, 81-82
  SRS, 81-82
work products
  controlled, 43
  data flow, 66, 73, 75
  reviewing, 68
  specifying subsets, 41
writing Software Requirements
  Specification, 41

W-Z

Walk-Throughs, 42, 148, 164-166, 170
warnings (IEEE Std. 1063), 88
waterfall model (SLCMs), 51-57,
  62-70
  modified, 61, 65, 75
    milestone build, 61, 77
    study project, 76
    waterfall/spiral hybrid, 75
  phases, 63-65
    overlap, 51-54, 57, 64-65, 70
    one phase overlap, 65
    review meetings, 63
  pure, 65
  rapid prototyping, 68, 70
  Sashimi, 65
Web sites, FDA Center for Devices
  and Radiological Health, 14